Teen Titans spotlight: Wonder Girl

J. Torres Writer

Sanford Greene Penciller

Nathan Massengill Inker

Guy Major Colorist

Pat Brosseau / Phil Balsman / Steve Wands Letterers

Sanford Greene and **Nathan Massengill**
Original series covers

Dan DiDio Senior VP-Executive Editor
Nachie Castro Editor-original series
Sean Mackiewicz Editor-collected edition
Robbin Brosterman Senior Art Director
Paul Levitz President & Publisher
Georg Brewer VP-Design & DC Direct Creative
Richard Bruning Senior VP-Creative Director
Patrick Caldon Executive VP-Finance & Operations
Chris Caramalis VP-Finance
John Cunningham VP-Marketing
Terri Cunningham VP-Managing Editor
Alison Gill VP-Manufacturing
David Hyde VP-Publicity
Hank Kanalz VP-General Manager, WildStorm
Jim Lee Editorial Director-WildStorm
Paula Lowitt Senior VP-Business & Legal Affairs
MaryEllen McLaughlin VP-Advertising & Custom Publishing
John Nee Senior VP-Business Development
Gregory Noveck Senior VP-Creative Affairs
Sue Pohja VP-Book Trade Sales
Steve Rotterdam Senior VP- Sales & Marketing
Cheryl Rubin Senior VP-Brand Management
Jeff Trojan VP-Business Development, DC Direct
Bob Wayne VP-Sales

Cover by Sanford Greene and Nathan Massengill.

TEEN TITANS SPOTLIGHT: WONDER GIRL

DC Comics, 1700 Broadway, New York, NY 10019
A Warner Bros. Entertainment Company
Printed in Canada. First Printing.

ISBN: 978-1-4012-1830-0

Teen Titans spotlight:

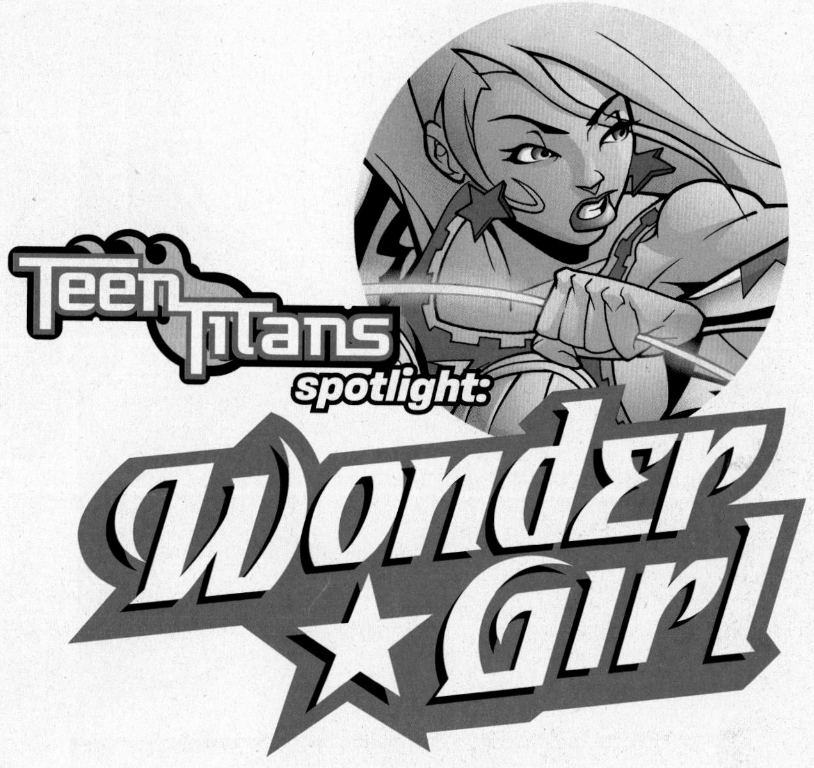

Wonder Girl

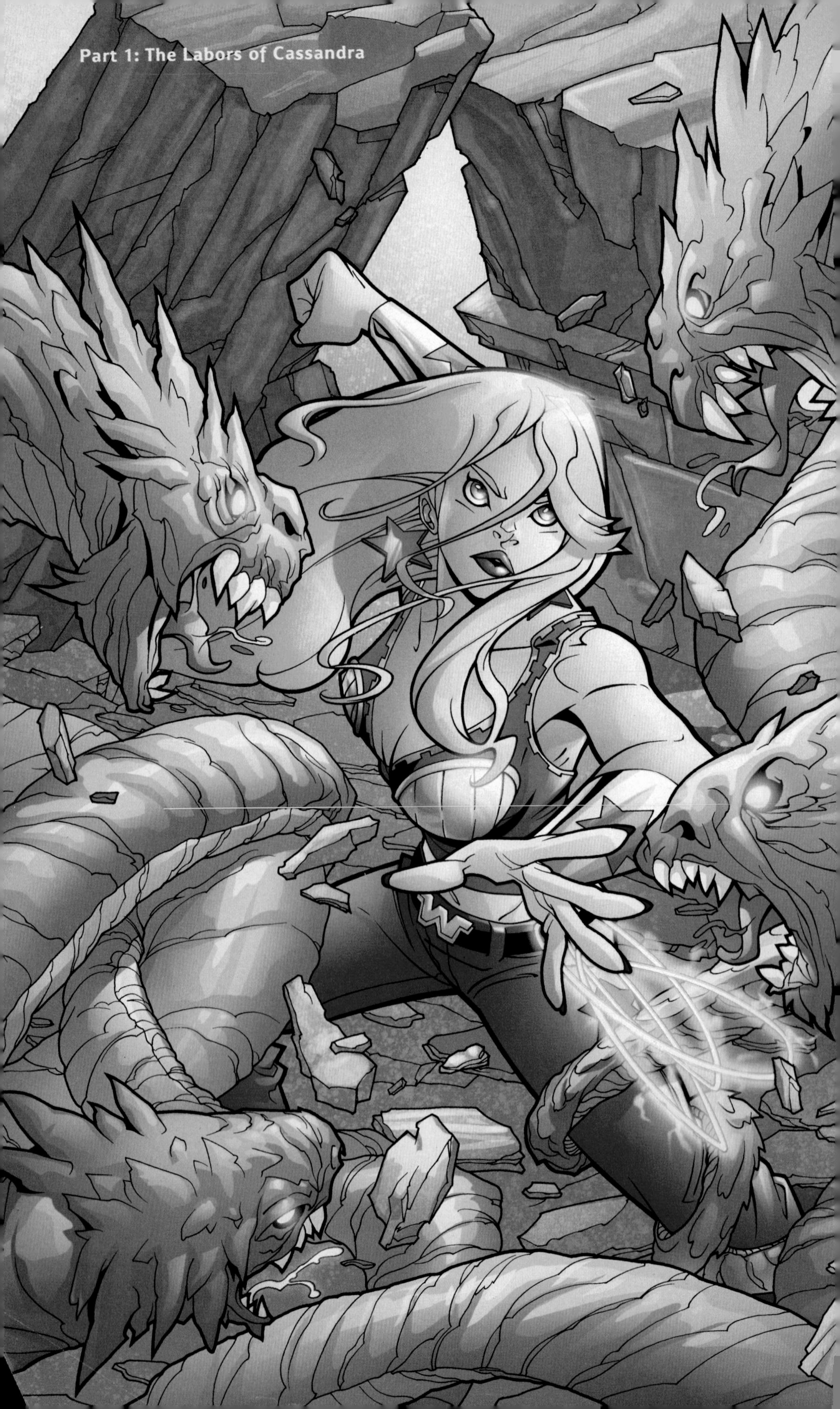

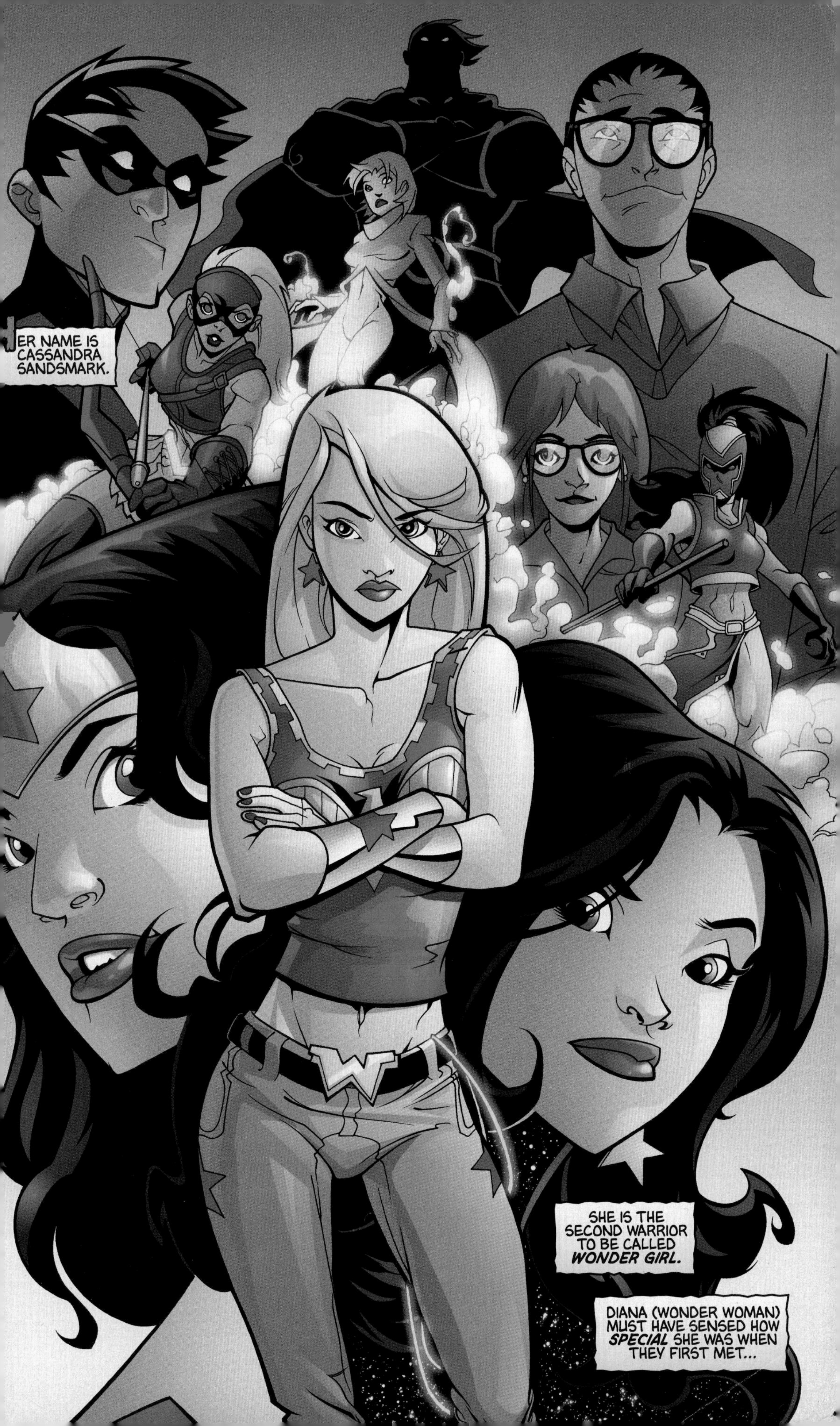
ER NAME IS CASSANDRA SANDSMARK.
SHE IS THE SECOND WARRIOR TO BE CALLED *WONDER GIRL.*
DIANA (WONDER WOMAN) MUST HAVE SENSED HOW *SPECIAL* SHE WAS WHEN THEY FIRST MET...

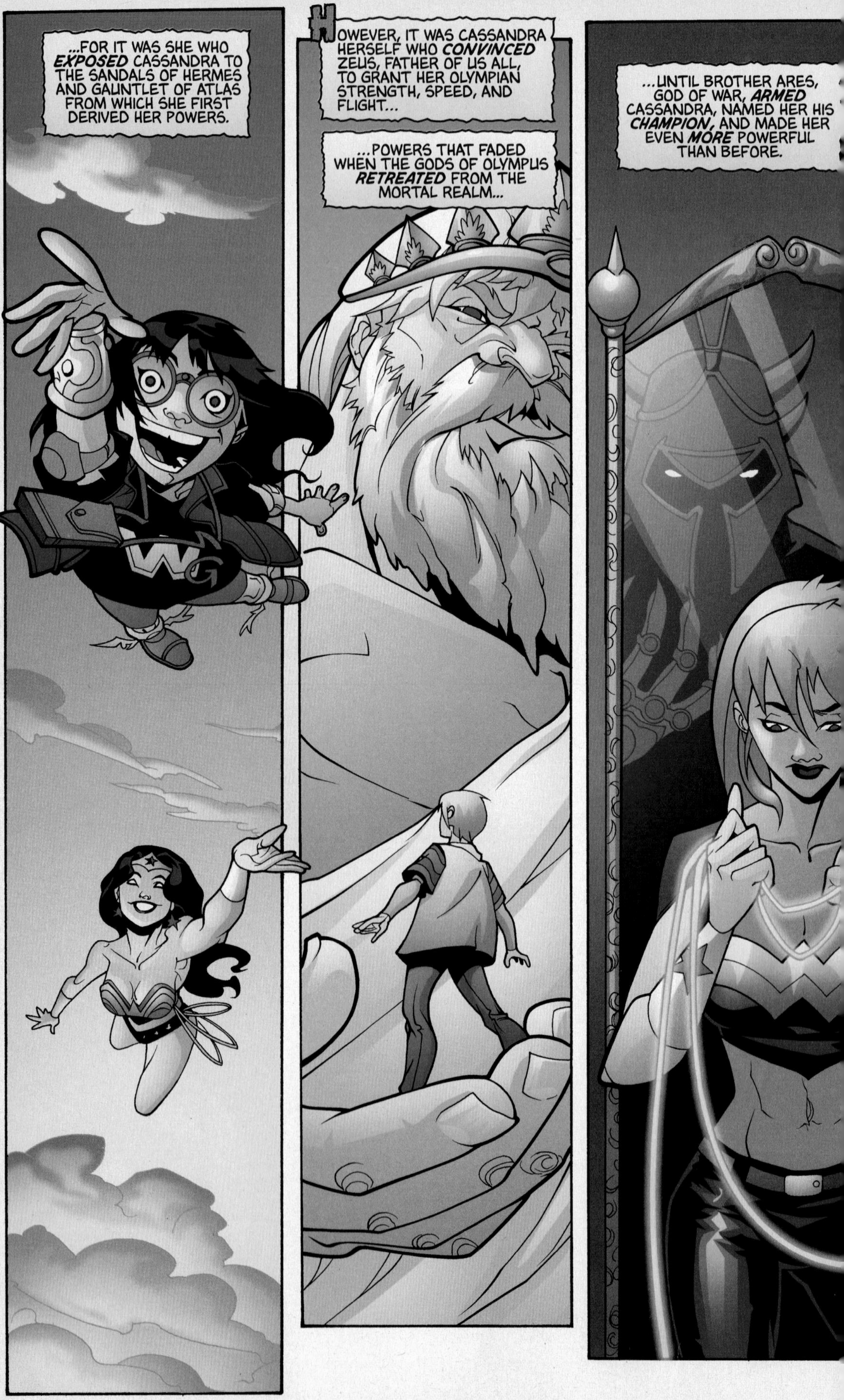
...FOR IT WAS SHE WHO EXPOSED CASSANDRA TO THE SANDALS OF HERMES AND GAUNTLET OF ATLAS FROM WHICH SHE FIRST DERIVED HER POWERS.
HOWEVER, IT WAS CASSANDRA HERSELF WHO CONVINCED ZEUS, FATHER OF US ALL, TO GRANT HER OLYMPIAN STRENGTH, SPEED, AND FLIGHT...
...POWERS THAT FADED WHEN THE GODS OF OLYMPUS RETREATED FROM THE MORTAL REALM...
...UNTIL BROTHER ARES, GOD OF WAR, ARMED CASSANDRA, NAMED HER HIS CHAMPION, AND MADE HER EVEN MORE POWERFUL THAN BEFORE.

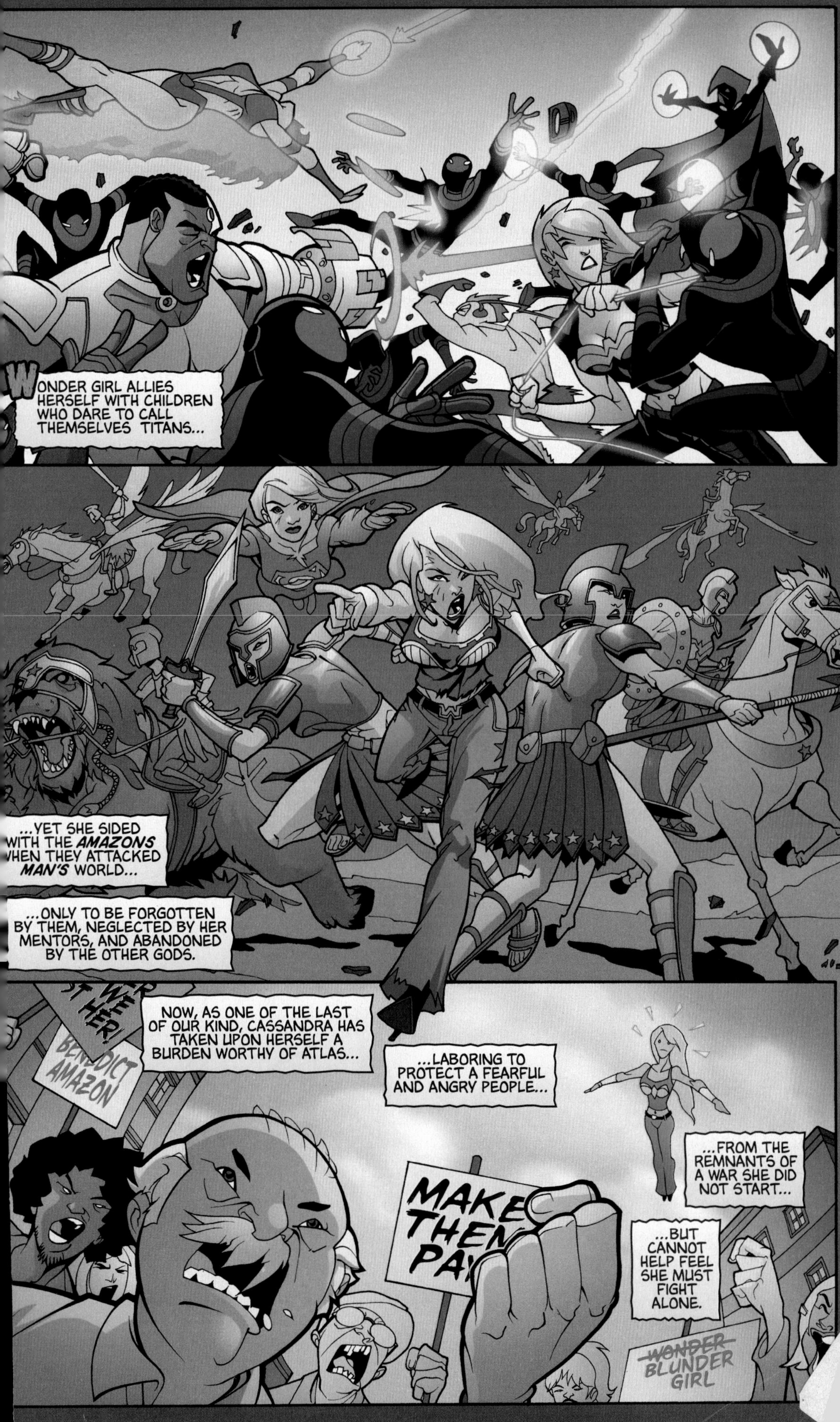
WONDER GIRL ALLIES HERSELF WITH CHILDREN WHO DARE TO CALL THEMSELVES TITANS...
...YET SHE SIDED WITH THE AMAZONS WHEN THEY ATTACKED MAN'S WORLD...
...ONLY TO BE FORGOTTEN BY THEM, NEGLECTED BY HER MENTORS, AND ABANDONED BY THE OTHER GODS.
BENEDICT AMAZON
NOW, AS ONE OF THE LAST OF OUR KIND, CASSANDRA HAS TAKEN UPON HERSELF A BURDEN WORTHY OF ATLAS...
...LABORING TO PROTECT A FEARFUL AND ANGRY PEOPLE...
...FROM THE REMNANTS OF A WAR SHE DID NOT START...
...BUT CANNOT HELP FEEL SHE MUST FIGHT ALONE.
WONDER BLUNDER GIRL

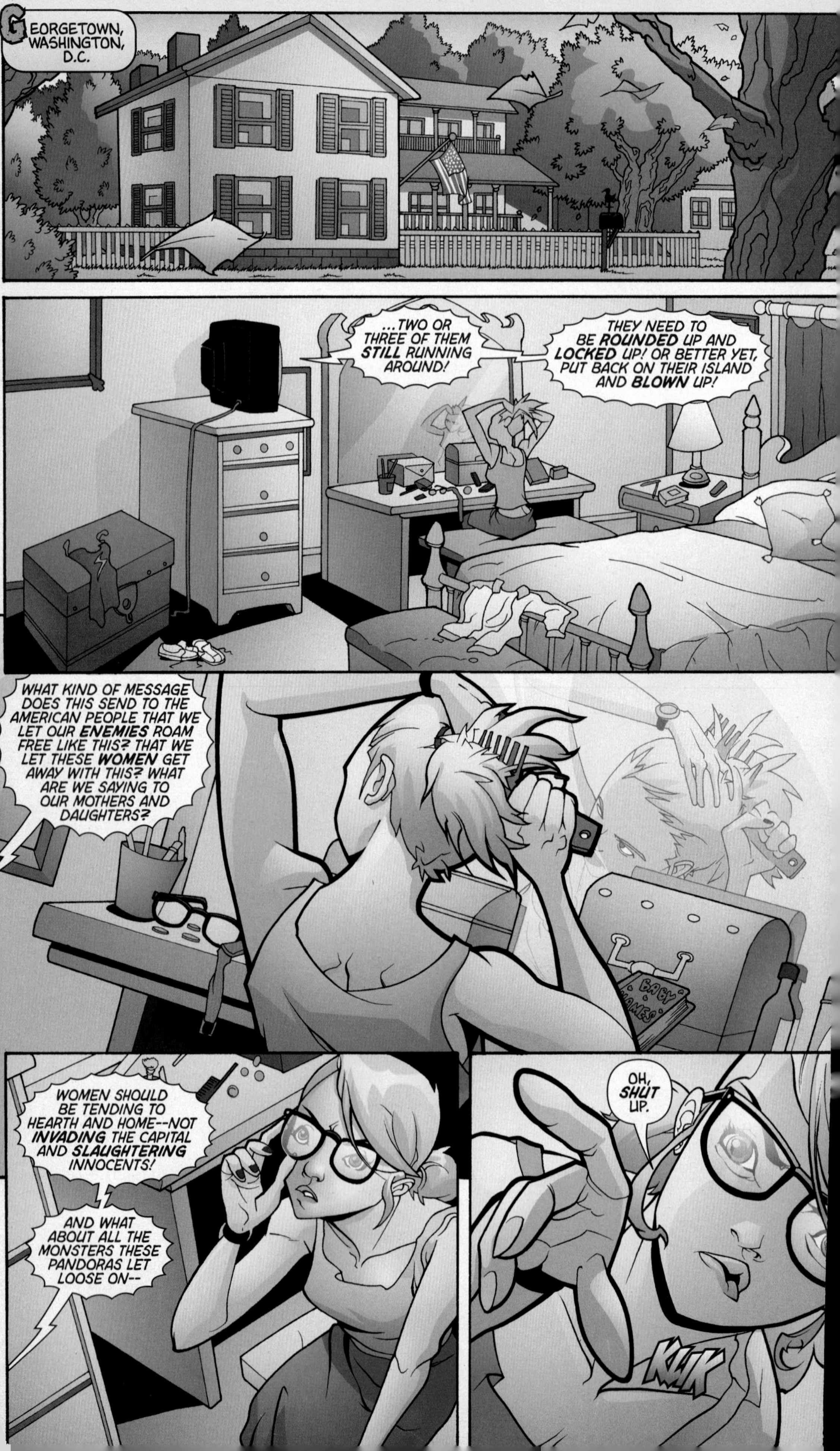
GEORGETOWN, WASHINGTON, D.C.
...TWO OR THREE OF THEM STILL RUNNING AROUND!
THEY NEED TO BE ROUNDED UP AND LOCKED UP! OR BETTER YET, PUT BACK ON THEIR ISLAND AND BLOWN UP!
WHAT KIND OF MESSAGE DOES THIS SEND TO THE AMERICAN PEOPLE THAT WE LET OUR ENEMIES ROAM FREE LIKE THIS? THAT WE LET THESE WOMEN GET AWAY WITH THIS? WHAT ARE WE SAYING TO OUR MOTHERS AND DAUGHTERS?
BABY NAMES
WOMEN SHOULD BE TENDING TO HEARTH AND HOME--NOT INVADING THE CAPITAL AND SLAUGHTERING INNOCENTS!
AND WHAT ABOUT ALL THE MONSTERS THESE PANDORAS LET LOOSE ON--
OH, SHUT UP.
KLIK

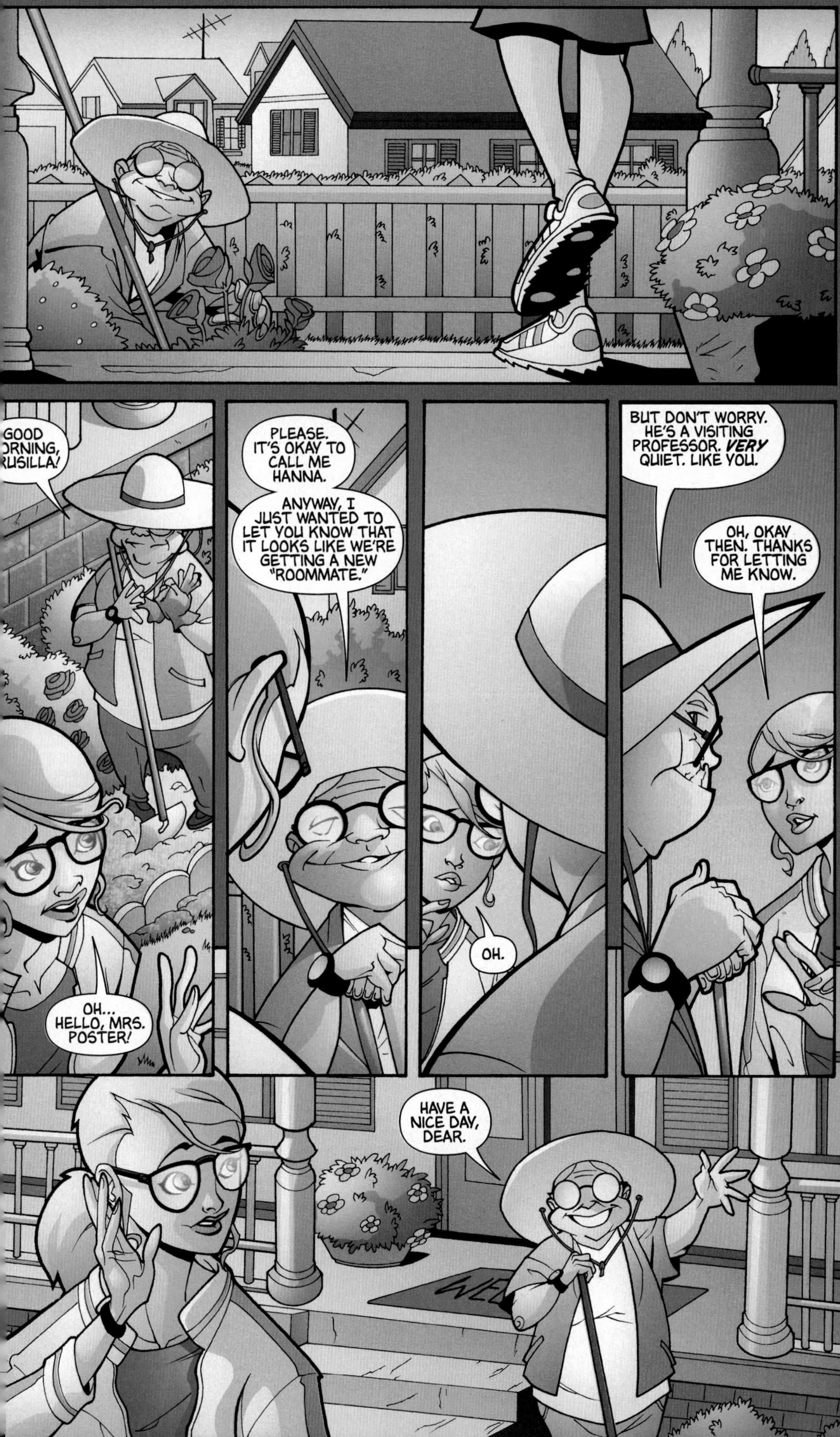
GOOD
ORNING,
RUSILLA!
OH...
HELLO, MRS.
POSTER!
PLEASE.
IT'S OKAY TO
CALL ME
HANNA.
ANYWAY, I
JUST WANTED TO
LET YOU KNOW THAT
IT LOOKS LIKE WE'RE
GETTING A NEW
"ROOMMATE."
OH.
BUT DON'T WORRY.
HE'S A VISITING
PROFESSOR. VERY
QUIET. LIKE YOU.
OH, OKAY
THEN. THANKS
FOR LETTING
ME KNOW.
HAVE A
NICE DAY,
DEAR.

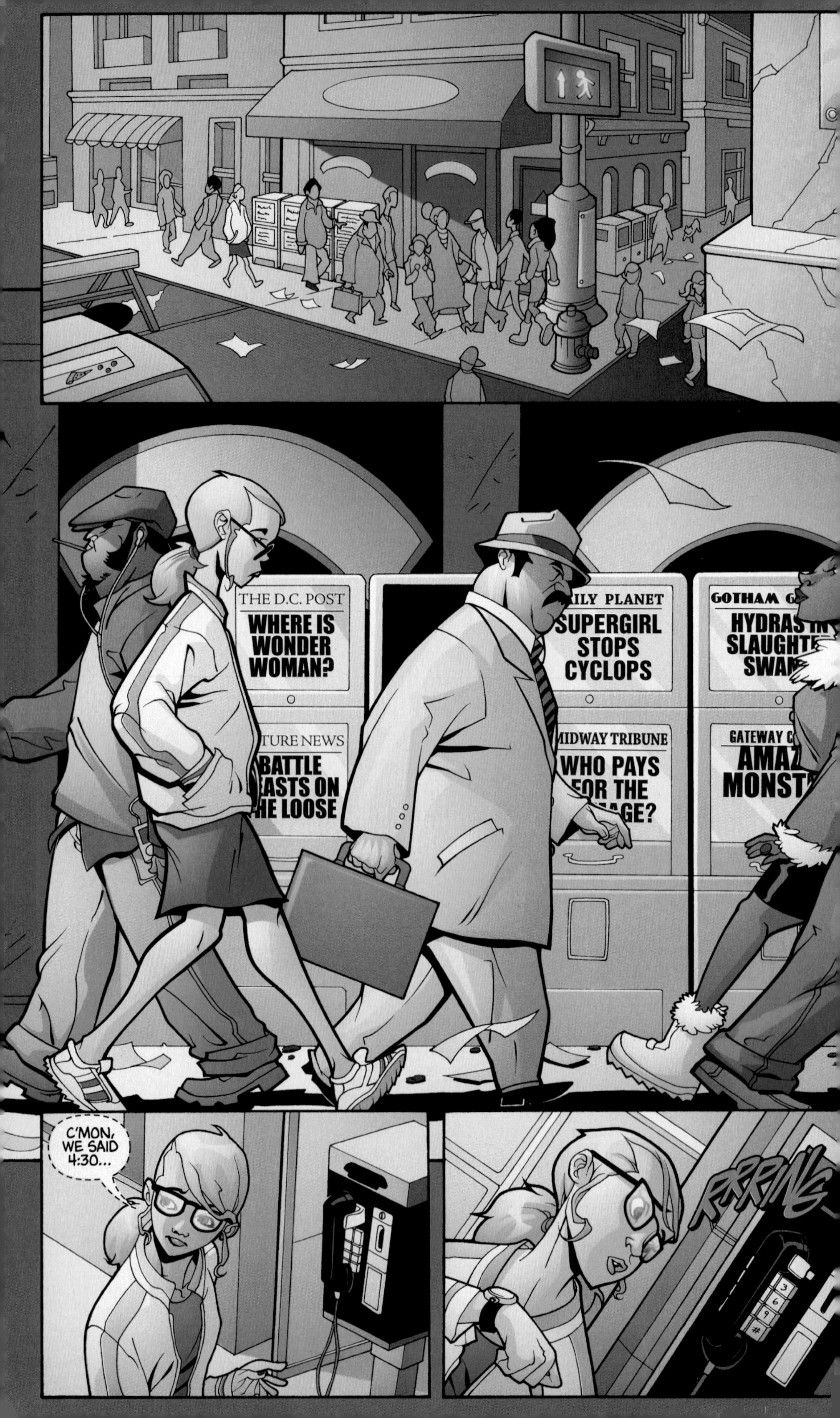
THE D.C. POST
WHERE IS WONDER WOMAN?
SUPERGIRL STOPS CYCLOPS
MIDWAY TRIBUNE
WHO PAYS FOR THE
BATTLE
C'MON, WE SAID 4:30...
RRRING

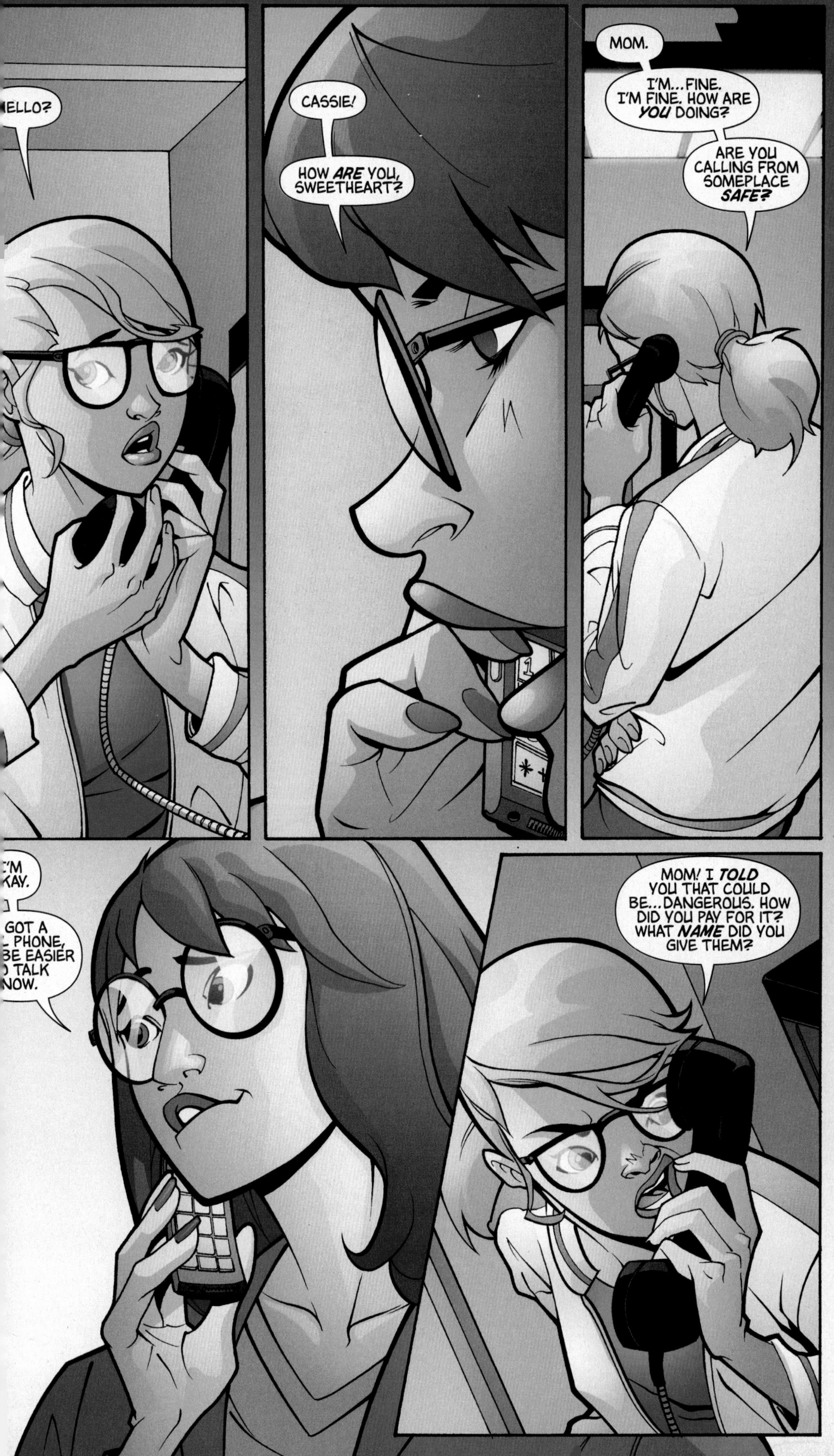

ELLO?
CASSIE!
HOW ARE YOU, SWEETHEART?
MOM.
I'M... FINE. I'M FINE. HOW ARE YOU DOING?
ARE YOU CALLING FROM SOMEPLACE SAFE?
'M KAY.
GOT A PHONE, BE EASIER TALK NOW.
MOM! I TOLD YOU THAT COULD BE... DANGEROUS. HOW DID YOU PAY FOR IT? WHAT NAME DID YOU GIVE THEM?

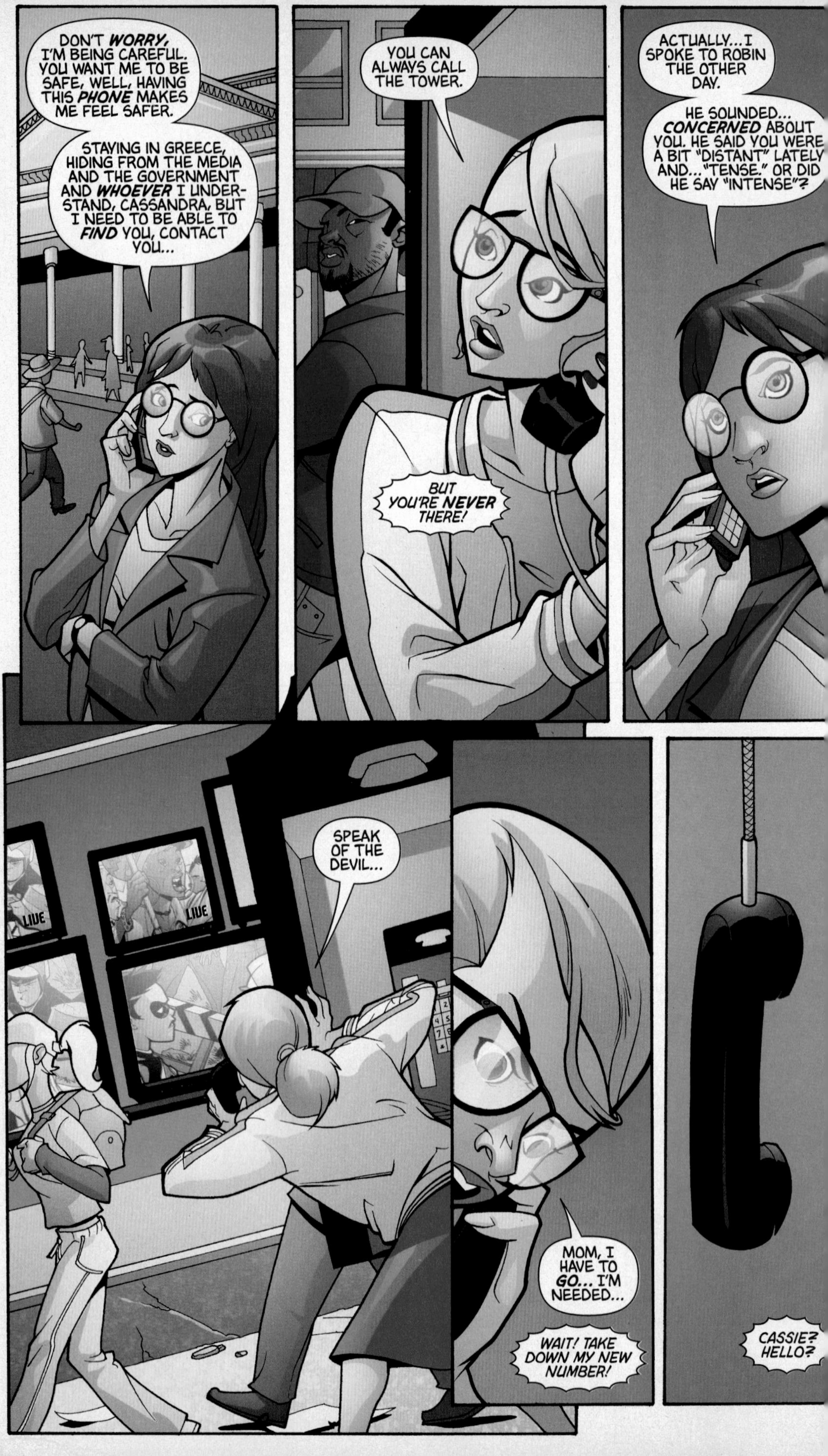
DON'T WORRY, I'M BEING CAREFUL. YOU WANT ME TO BE SAFE, WELL, HAVING THIS PHONE MAKES ME FEEL SAFER.
STAYING IN GREECE, HIDING FROM THE MEDIA AND THE GOVERNMENT AND WHOEVER I UNDERSTAND, CASSANDRA, BUT I NEED TO BE ABLE TO FIND YOU, CONTACT YOU...
YOU CAN ALWAYS CALL THE TOWER.
BUT YOU'RE NEVER THERE!
ACTUALLY...I SPOKE TO ROBIN THE OTHER DAY.
HE SOUNDED... CONCERNED ABOUT YOU. HE SAID YOU WERE A BIT "DISTANT" LATELY AND..."TENSE." OR DID HE SAY "INTENSE"?
LIVE
LIVE
SPEAK OF THE DEVIL...
MOM, I HAVE TO GO... I'M NEEDED...
WAIT! TAKE DOWN MY NEW NUMBER!
CASSIE? HELLO?

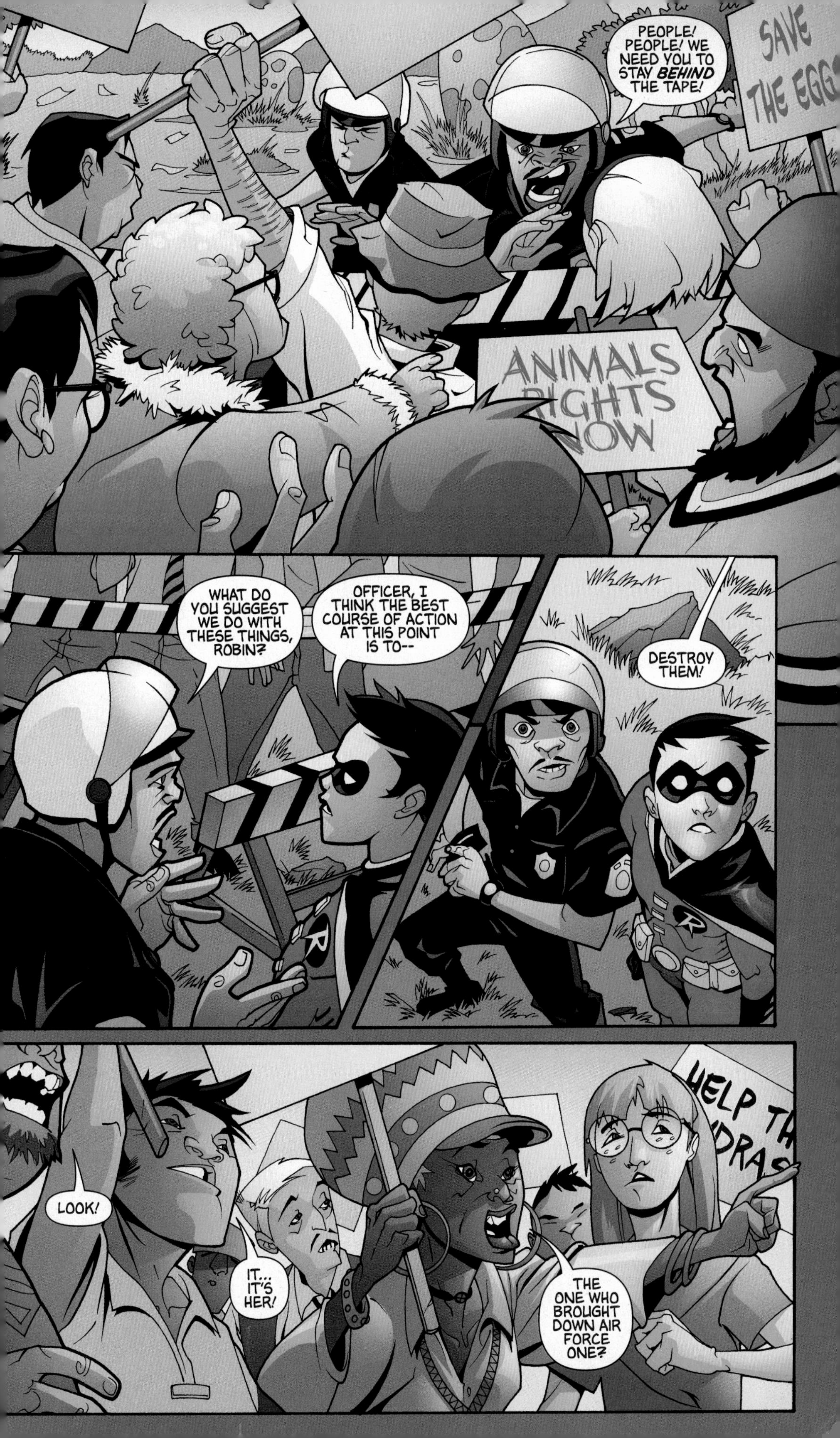
PEOPLE! PEOPLE! WE NEED YOU TO STAY *BEHIND* THE TAPE!
SAVE THE EGG
ANIMALS RIGHTS NOW
WHAT DO YOU SUGGEST WE DO WITH THESE THINGS, ROBIN?
OFFICER, I THINK THE BEST COURSE OF ACTION AT THIS POINT IS TO--
DESTROY THEM!
HELP TH
LOOK!
IT... IT'S HER!
THE ONE WHO BROUGHT DOWN AIR FORCE ONE?

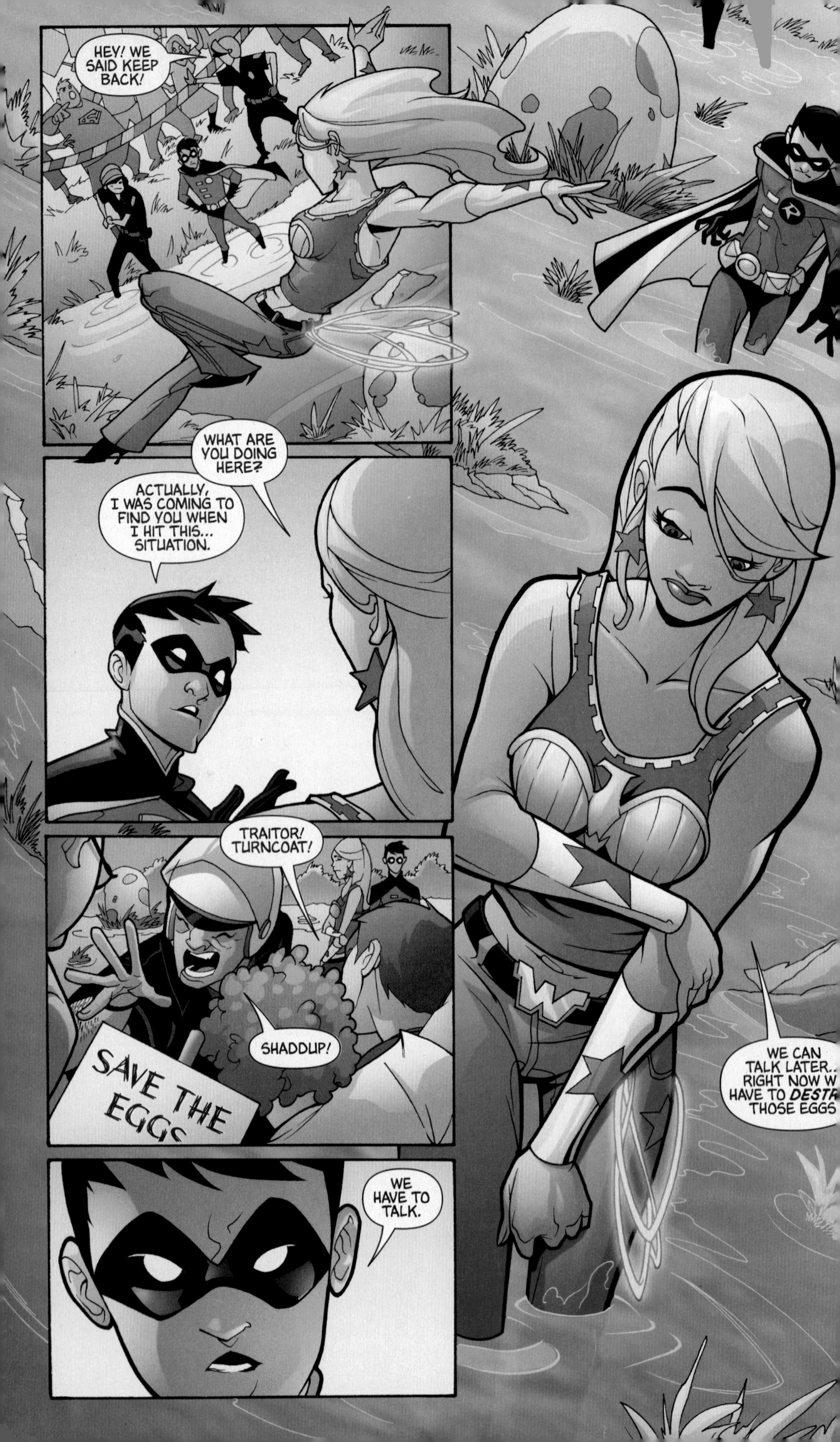
HEY! WE SAID KEEP BACK!
WHAT ARE YOU DOING HERE?
ACTUALLY, I WAS COMING TO FIND YOU WHEN I HIT THIS... SITUATION.
WE CAN TALK LATER... RIGHT NOW W HAVE TO DESTR THOSE EGGS
TRAITOR! TURNCOAT!
SHADDUP!
SAVE THE EGGS
WE HAVE TO TALK.

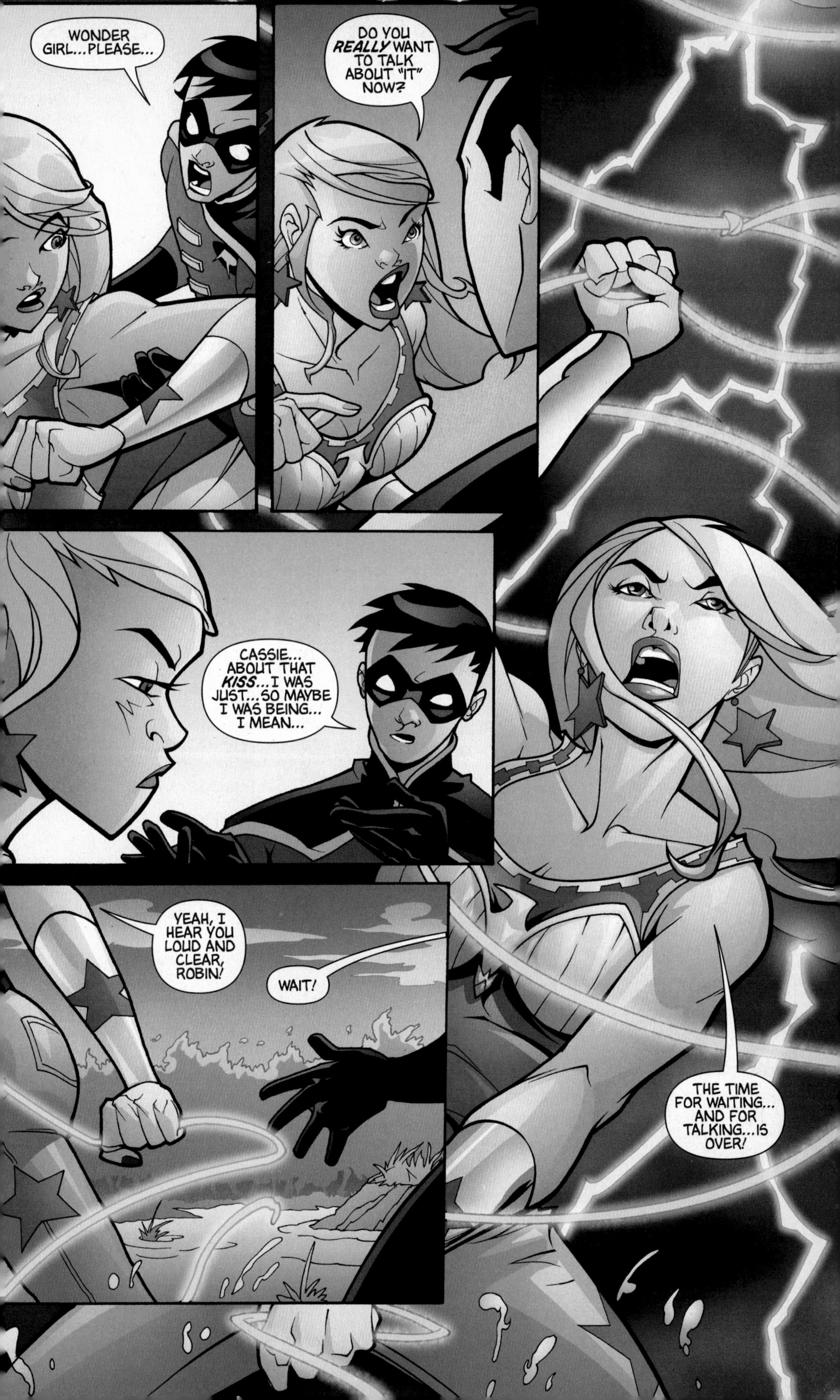
WONDER GIRL...PLEASE...
DO YOU *REALLY* WANT TO TALK ABOUT "IT" NOW?
CASSIE... ABOUT THAT *KISS*...I WAS JUST...SO MAYBE I WAS BEING... I MEAN...
YEAH, I HEAR YOU LOUD AND CLEAR, ROBIN!
WAIT!
THE TIME FOR WAITING... AND FOR TALKING...IS OVER!

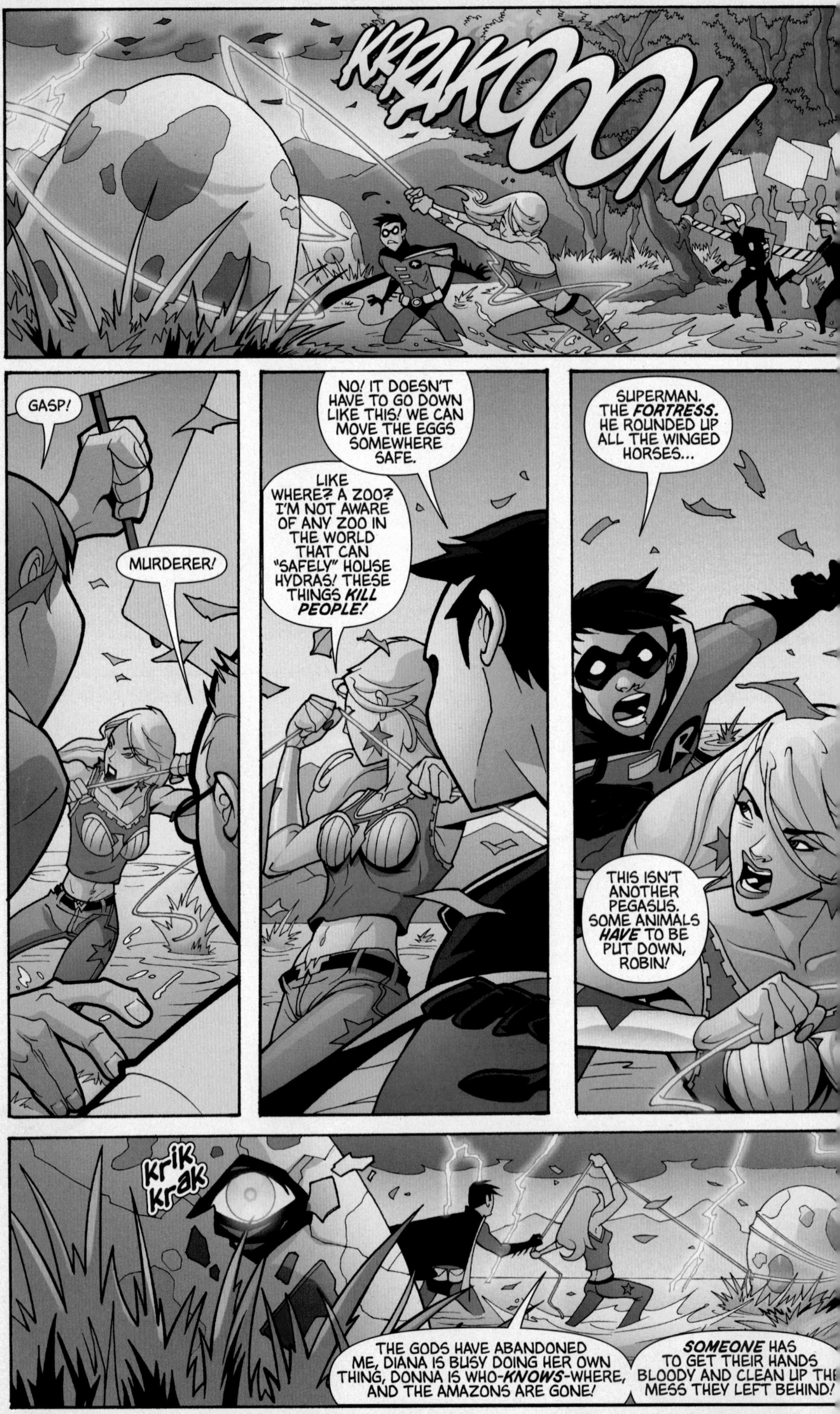
KRRAKOOOM
GASP!
MURDERER!
NO! IT DOESN'T HAVE TO GO DOWN LIKE THIS! WE CAN MOVE THE EGGS SOMEWHERE SAFE.
LIKE WHERE? A ZOO? I'M NOT AWARE OF ANY ZOO IN THE WORLD THAT CAN "SAFELY" HOUSE HYDRAS! THESE THINGS KILL PEOPLE!
SUPERMAN. THE FORTRESS. HE ROUNDED UP ALL THE WINGED HORSES...
THIS ISN'T ANOTHER PEGASUS. SOME ANIMALS HAVE TO BE PUT DOWN, ROBIN!
krik krak
THE GODS HAVE ABANDONED ME, DIANA IS BUSY DOING HER OWN THING, DONNA IS WHO-KNOWS-WHERE, AND THE AMAZONS ARE GONE!
SOMEONE HAS TO GET THEIR HANDS BLOODY AND CLEAN UP THE MESS THEY LEFT BEHIND!

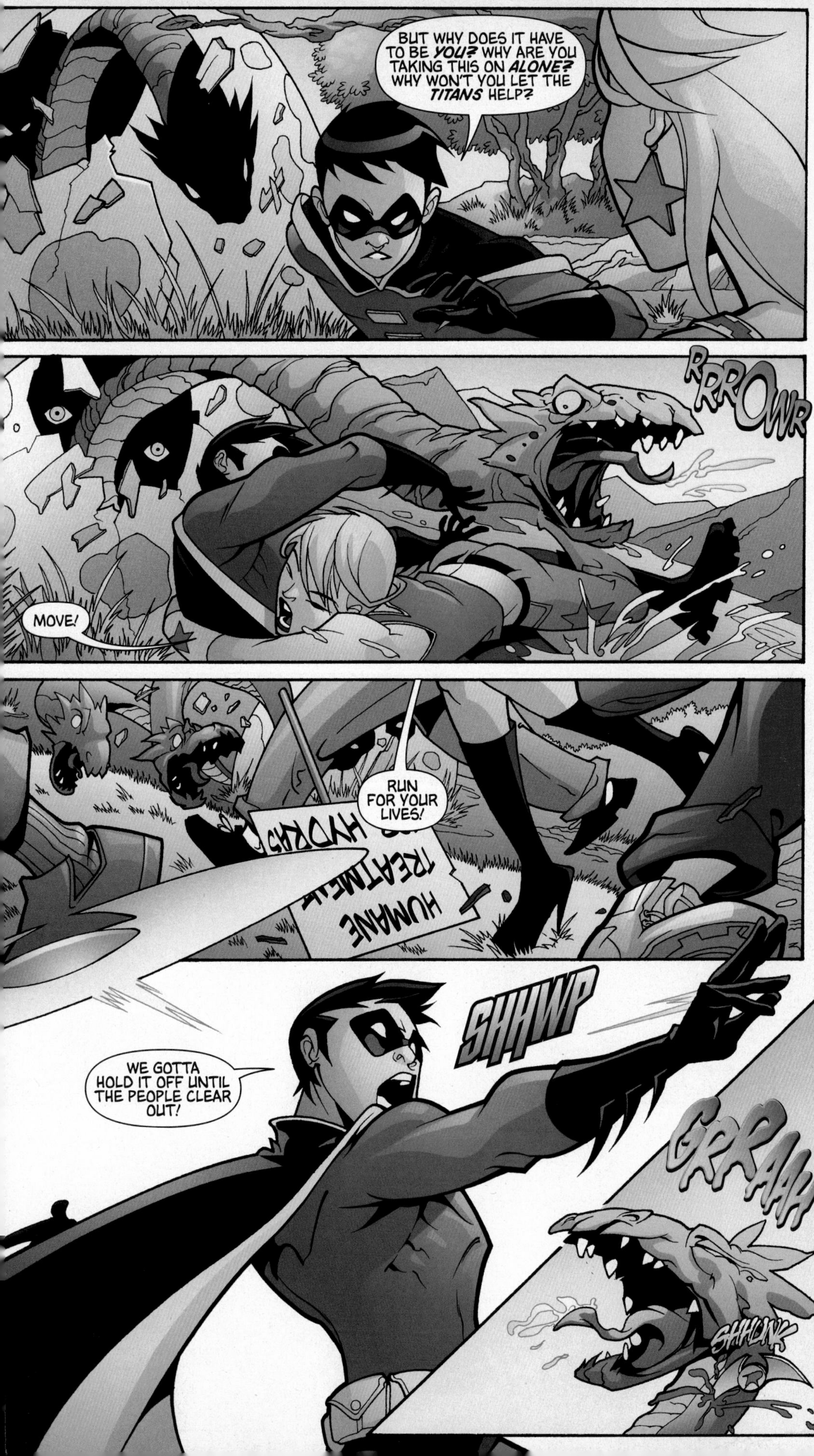
BUT WHY DOES IT HAVE TO BE *YOU?* WHY ARE YOU TAKING THIS ON *ALONE?* WHY WON'T YOU LET THE *TITANS* HELP?
RRROWR
MOVE!
RUN FOR YOUR LIVES!
HUMANE
SHHWP
WE GOTTA HOLD IT OFF UNTIL THE PEOPLE CLEAR OUT!
GRRAAH
SHHLINK

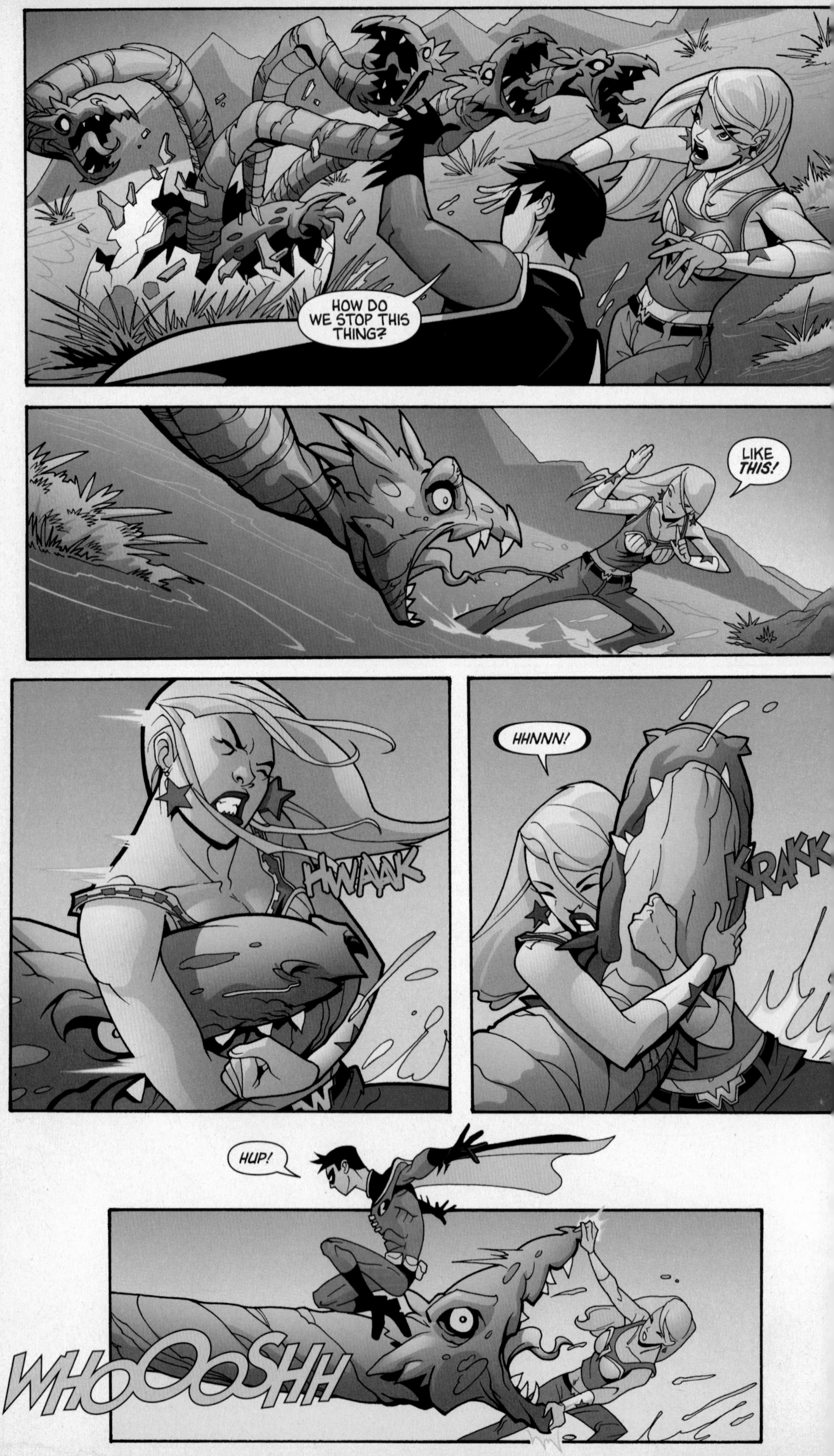

HOW DO WE STOP THIS THING?
LIKE *THIS!*
HWAAK
HHNNN!
KRAKK
HUP!
WHOOOOSHH

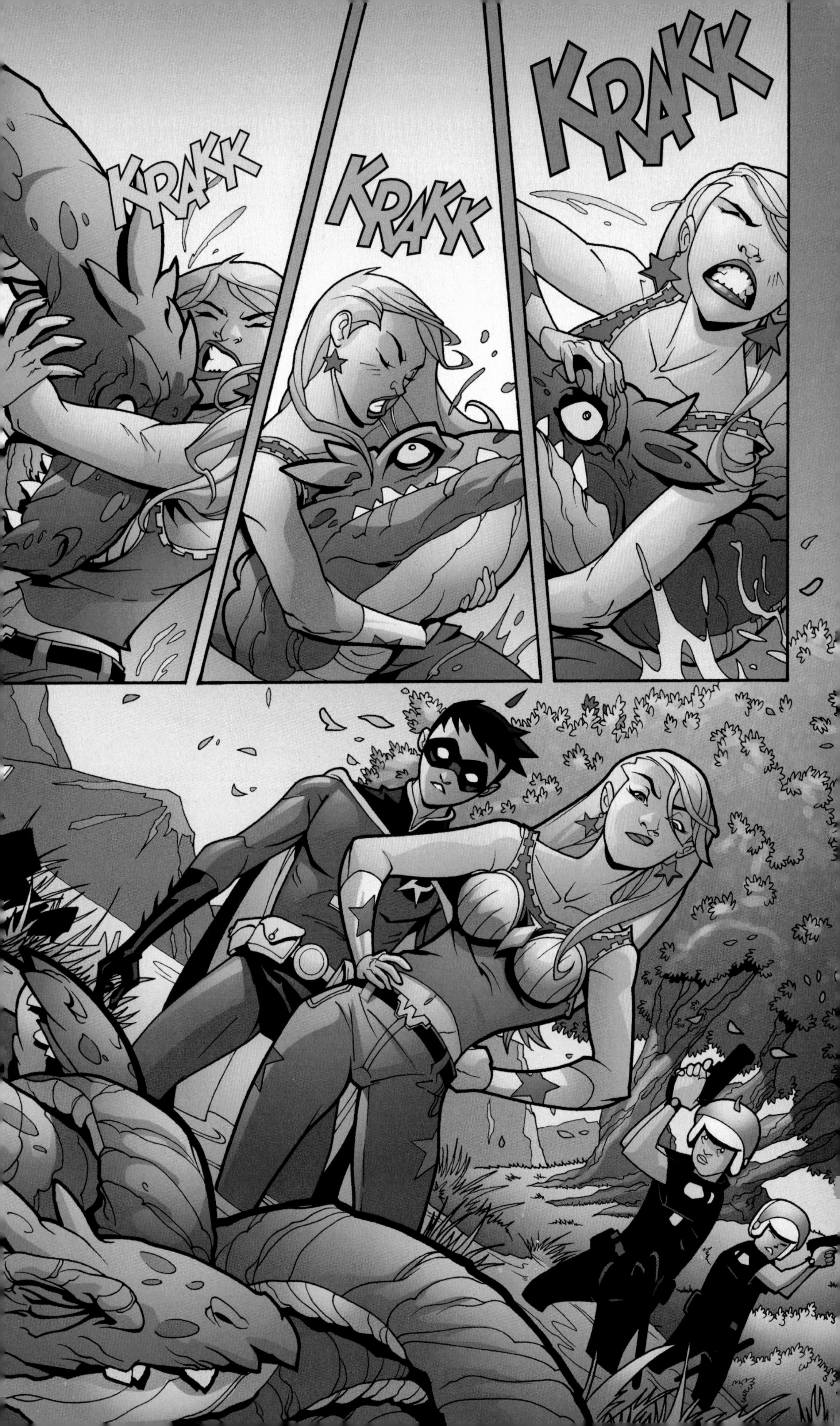
KRAKK
KRAKK
KRAKK

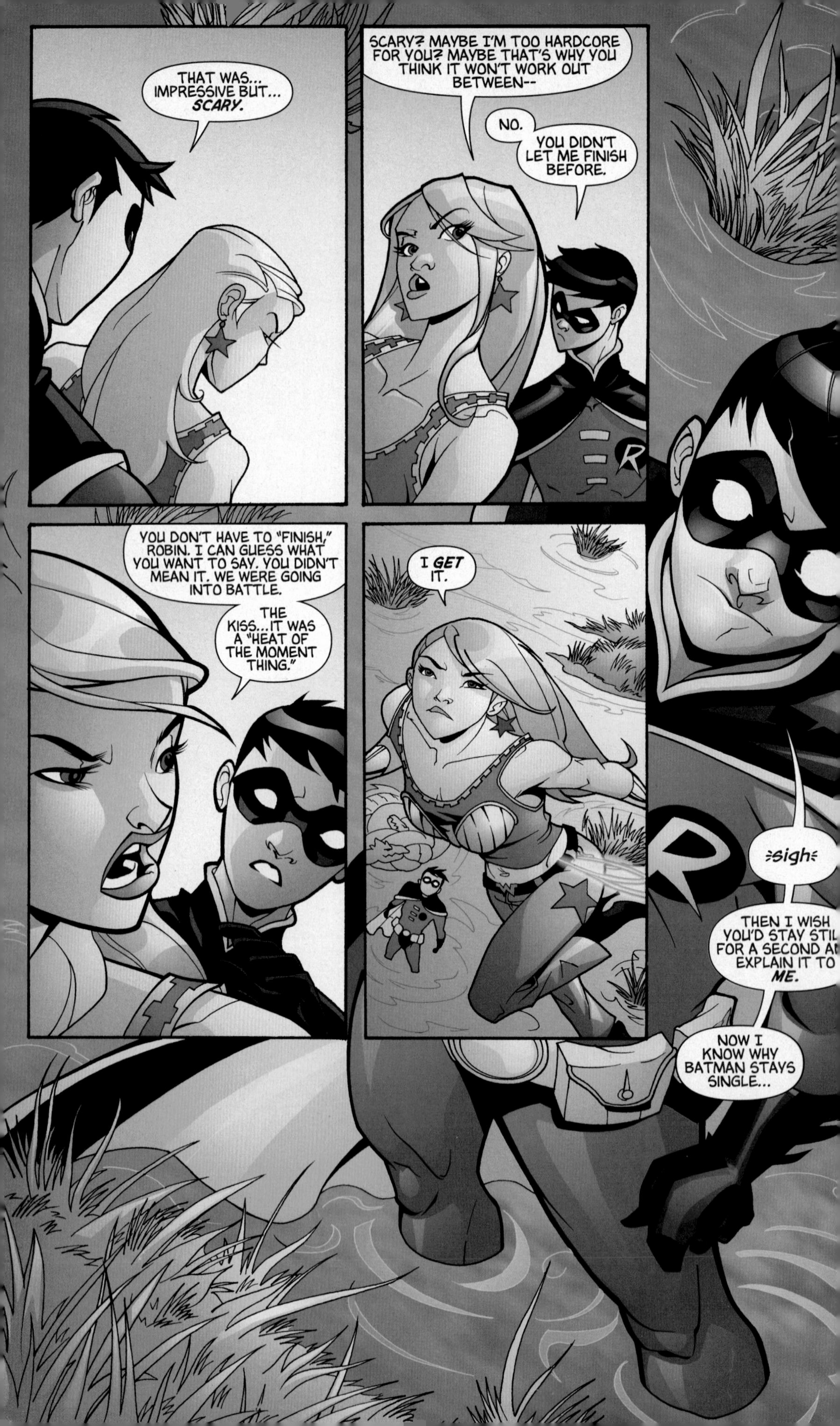
THAT WAS... IMPRESSIVE BUT... *SCARY.*
SCARY? MAYBE I'M TOO HARDCORE FOR YOU? MAYBE THAT'S WHY YOU THINK IT WON'T WORK OUT BETWEEN--
NO.
YOU DIDN'T LET ME FINISH BEFORE.
YOU DON'T HAVE TO "FINISH," ROBIN. I CAN GUESS WHAT YOU WANT TO SAY. YOU DIDN'T MEAN IT. WE WERE GOING INTO BATTLE.
THE KISS...IT WAS A "HEAT OF THE MOMENT THING."
I *GET* IT.
sigh
THEN I WISH YOU'D STAY STIL FOR A SECOND A EXPLAIN IT TO *ME.*
NOW I KNOW WHY BATMAN STAYS SINGLE...

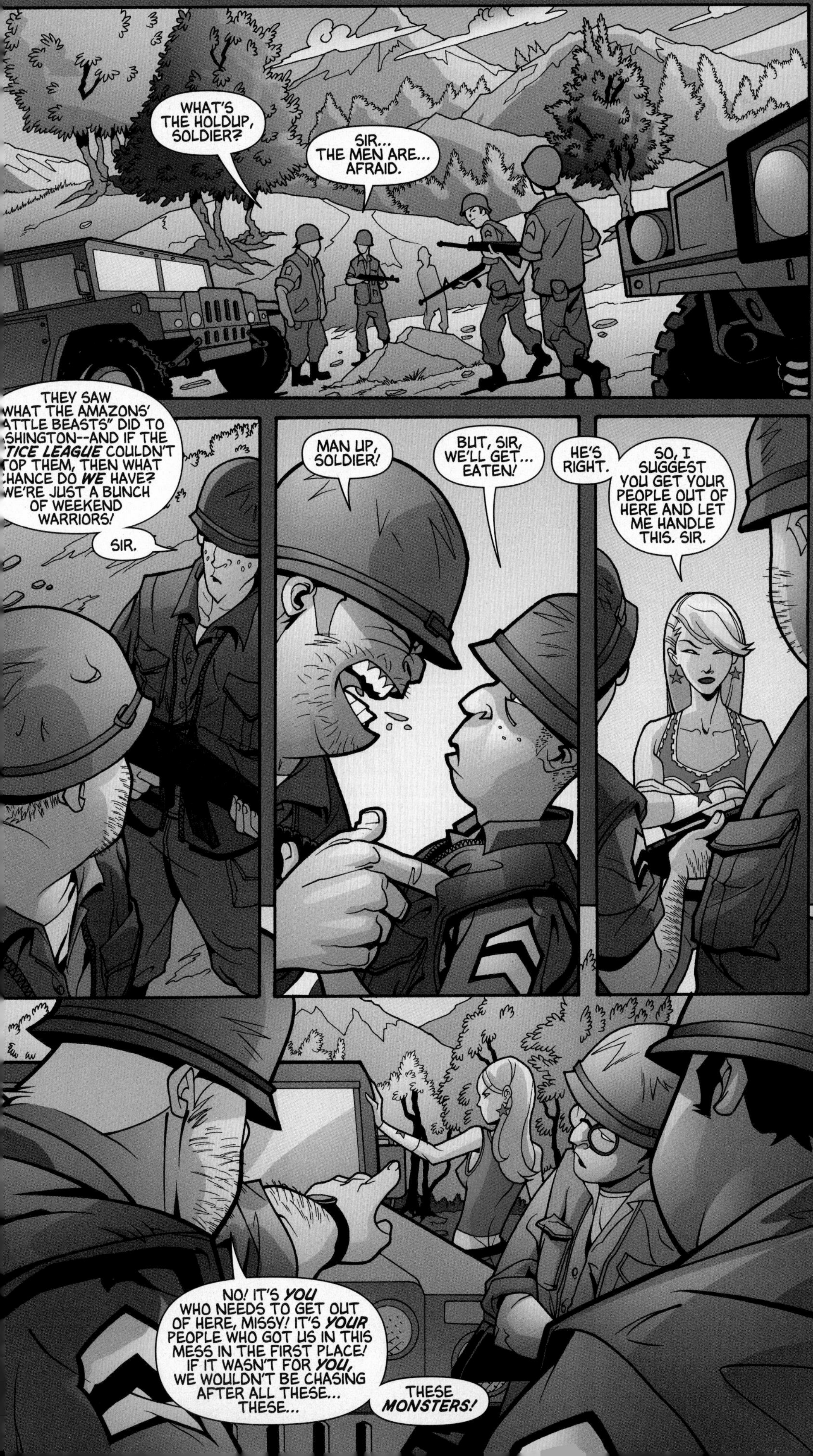
WHAT'S THE HOLDUP, SOLDIER?
SIR... THE MEN ARE... AFRAID.
THEY SAW WHAT THE AMAZONS' "ATTLE BEASTS" DID TO SHINGTON--AND IF THE TICE LEAGUE COULDN'T TOP THEM, THEN WHAT CHANCE DO WE HAVE? WE'RE JUST A BUNCH OF WEEKEND WARRIORS!
SIR.
MAN UP, SOLDIER!
BUT, SIR, WE'LL GET... EATEN!
HE'S RIGHT.
SO, I SUGGEST YOU GET YOUR PEOPLE OUT OF HERE AND LET ME HANDLE THIS. SIR.
NO! IT'S YOU WHO NEEDS TO GET OUT OF HERE, MISSY! IT'S YOUR PEOPLE WHO GOT US IN THIS MESS IN THE FIRST PLACE! IF IT WASN'T FOR YOU, WE WOULDN'T BE CHASING AFTER ALL THESE... THESE...
THESE MONSTERS!

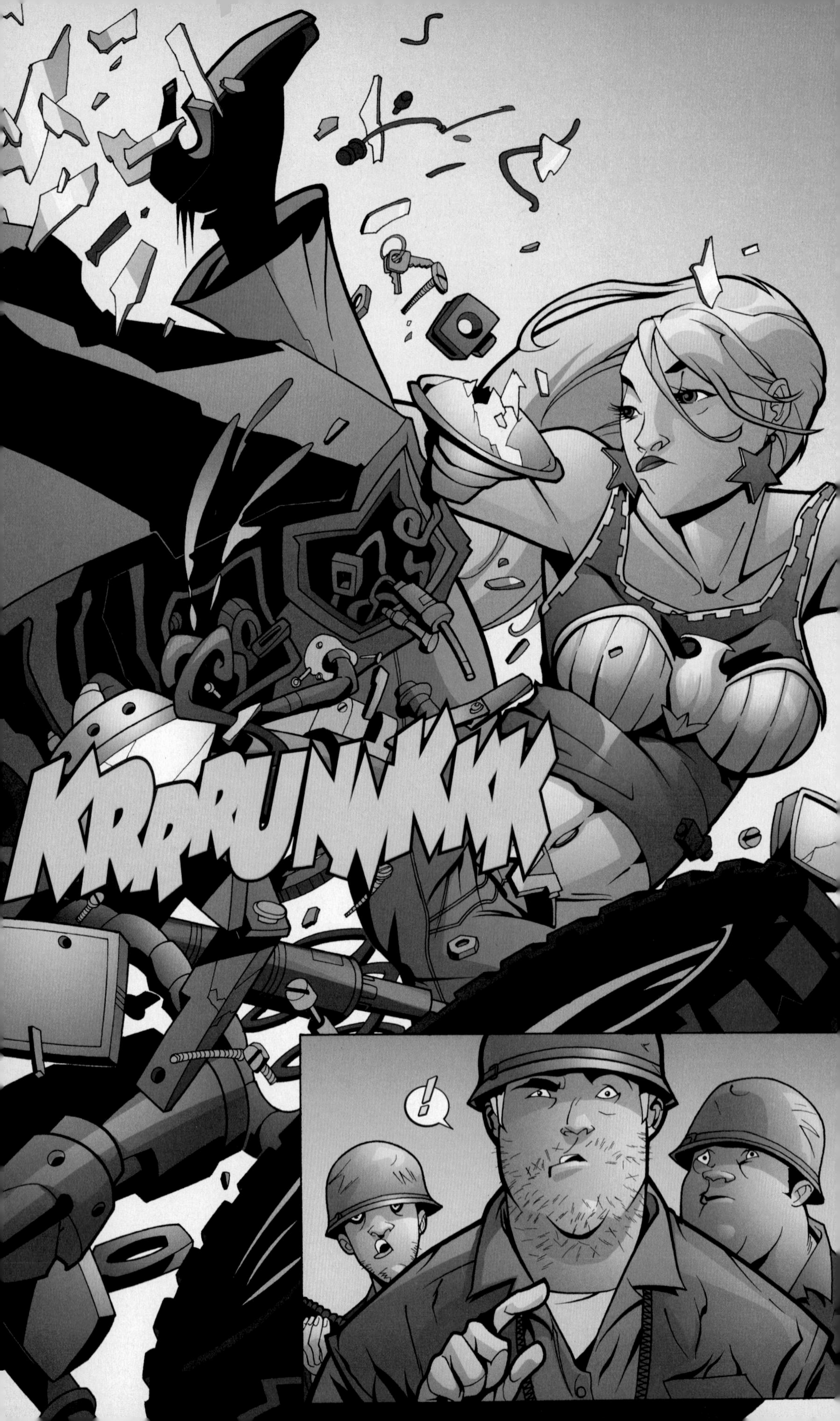
KRRRUNNNK
!

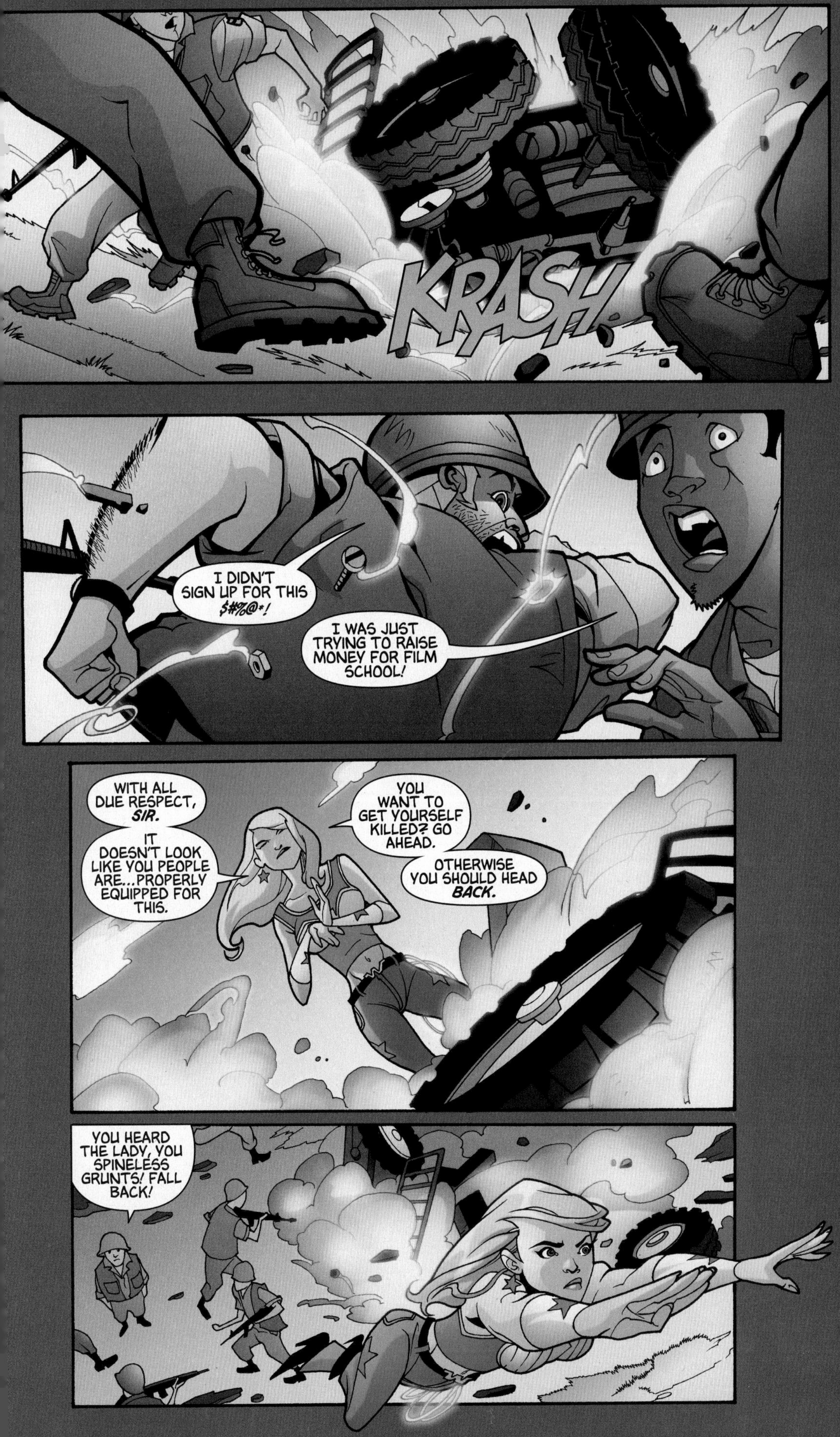
KRASH
I DIDN'T SIGN UP FOR THIS $#%@*!
I WAS JUST TRYING TO RAISE MONEY FOR FILM SCHOOL!
WITH ALL DUE RESPECT, SIR.
IT DOESN'T LOOK LIKE YOU PEOPLE ARE...PROPERLY EQUIPPED FOR THIS.
YOU WANT TO GET YOURSELF KILLED? GO AHEAD.
OTHERWISE YOU SHOULD HEAD BACK.
YOU HEARD THE LADY, YOU SPINELESS GRUNTS! FALL BACK!

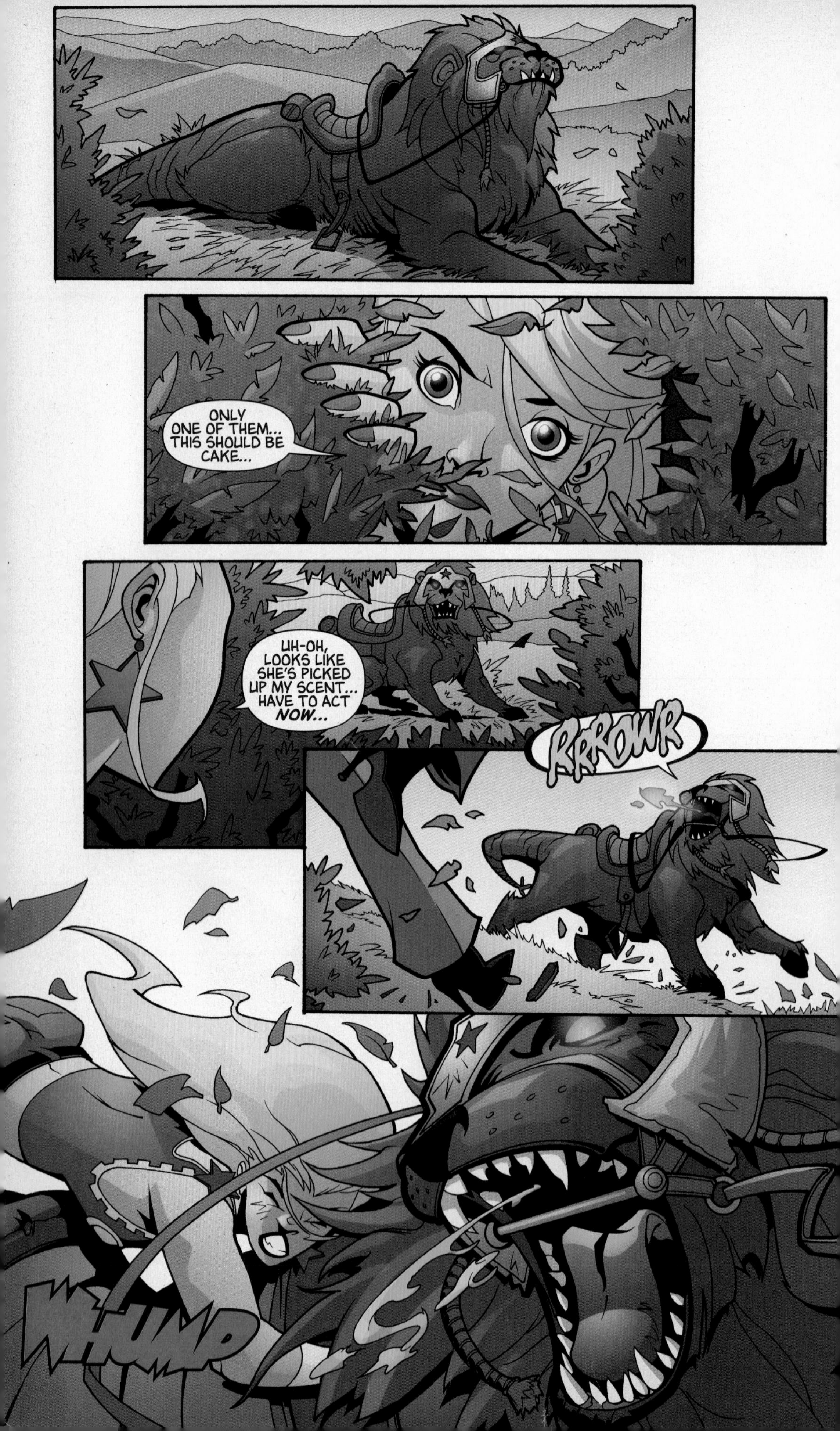
ONLY ONE OF THEM... THIS SHOULD BE CAKE...
UH-OH, LOOKS LIKE SHE'S PICKED UP MY SCENT... HAVE TO ACT *NOW*...
RRROWR
WHUMP

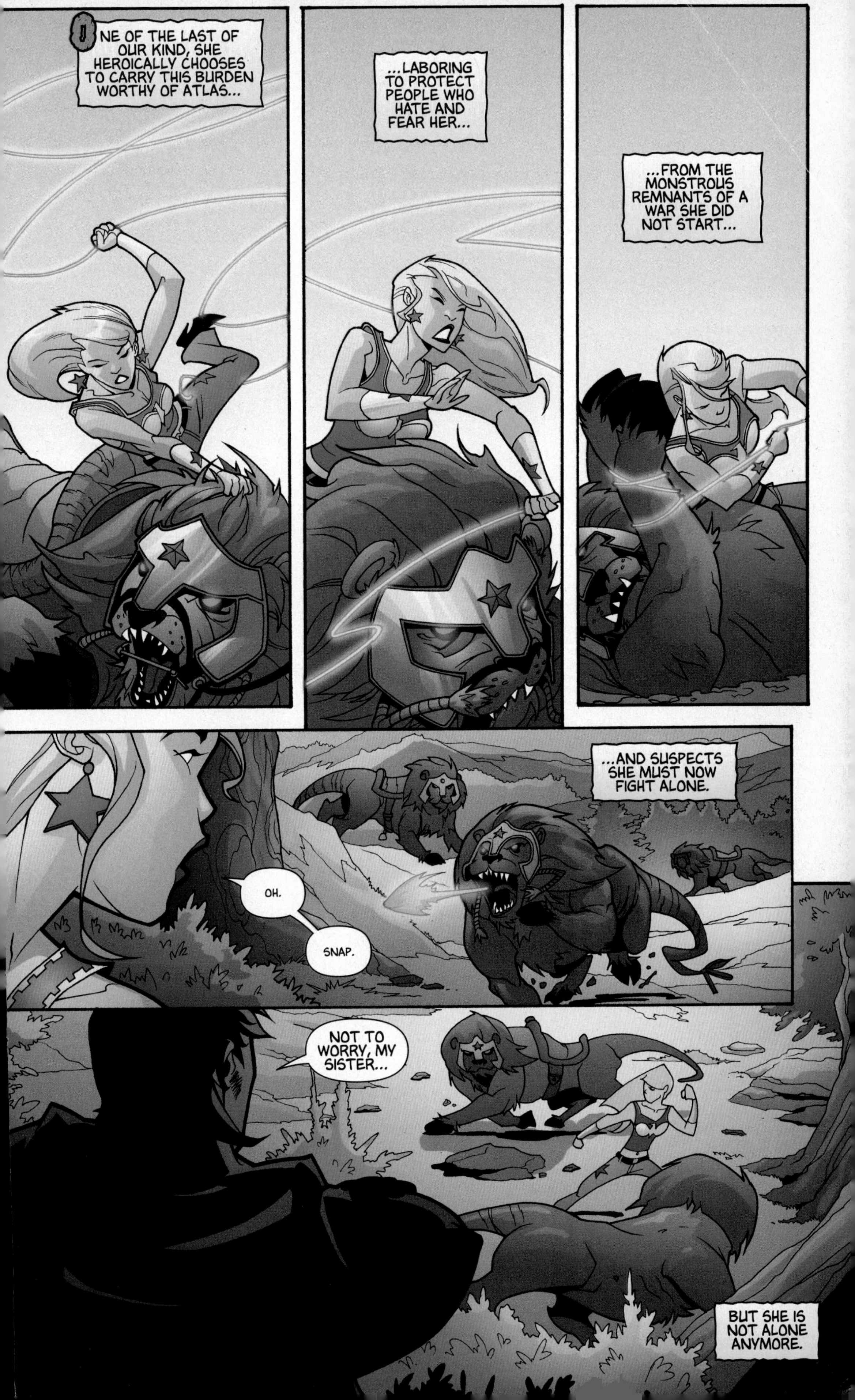
ONE OF THE LAST OF OUR KIND, SHE HEROICALLY CHOOSES TO CARRY THIS BURDEN WORTHY OF ATLAS...
...LABORING TO PROTECT PEOPLE WHO HATE AND FEAR HER...
...FROM THE MONSTROUS REMNANTS OF A WAR SHE DID NOT START...
...AND SUSPECTS SHE MUST NOW FIGHT ALONE.
OH.
SNAP.
NOT TO WORRY, MY SISTER...
BUT SHE IS NOT ALONE ANYMORE.

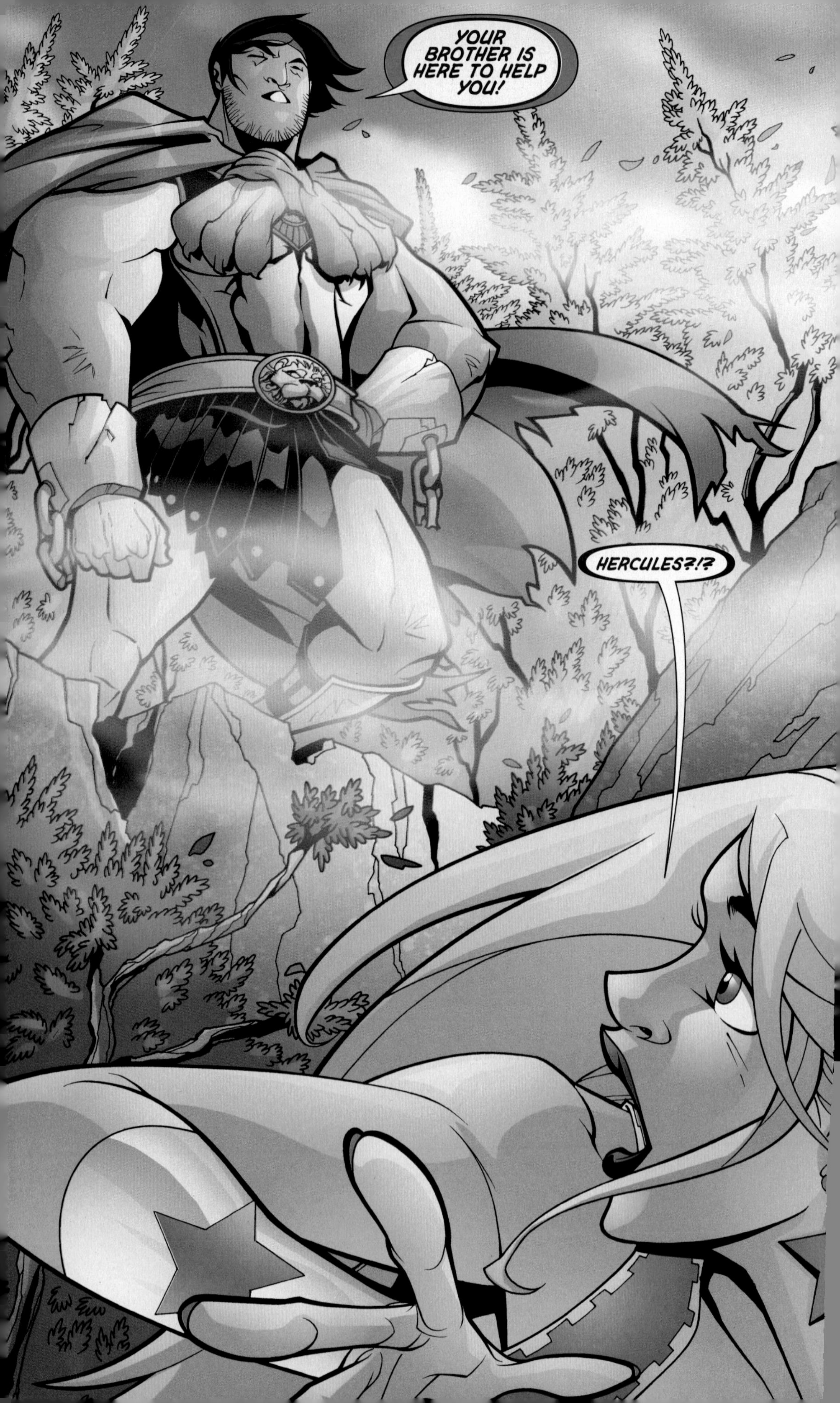
YOUR BROTHER IS HERE TO HELP YOU!
HERCULES?!?

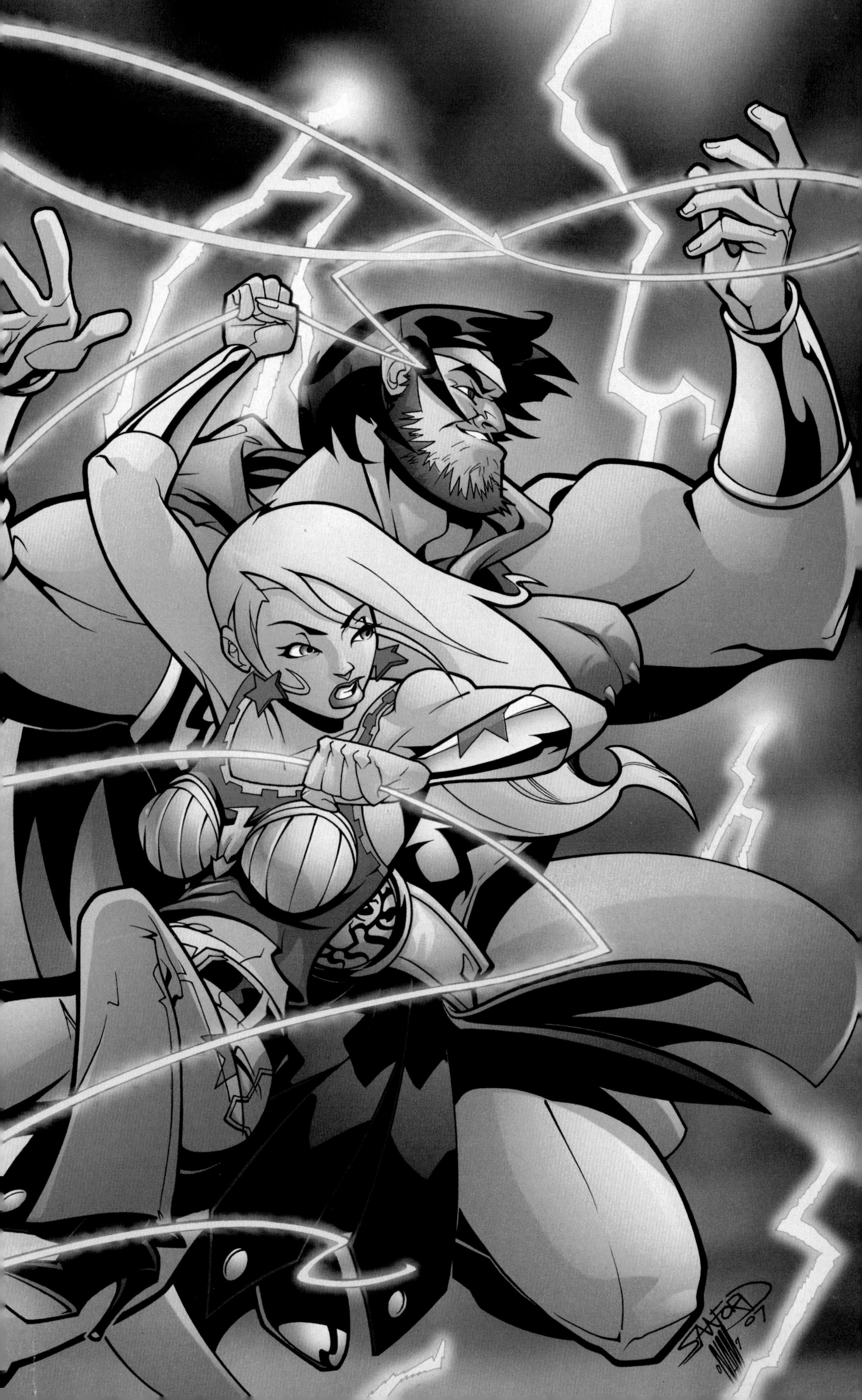

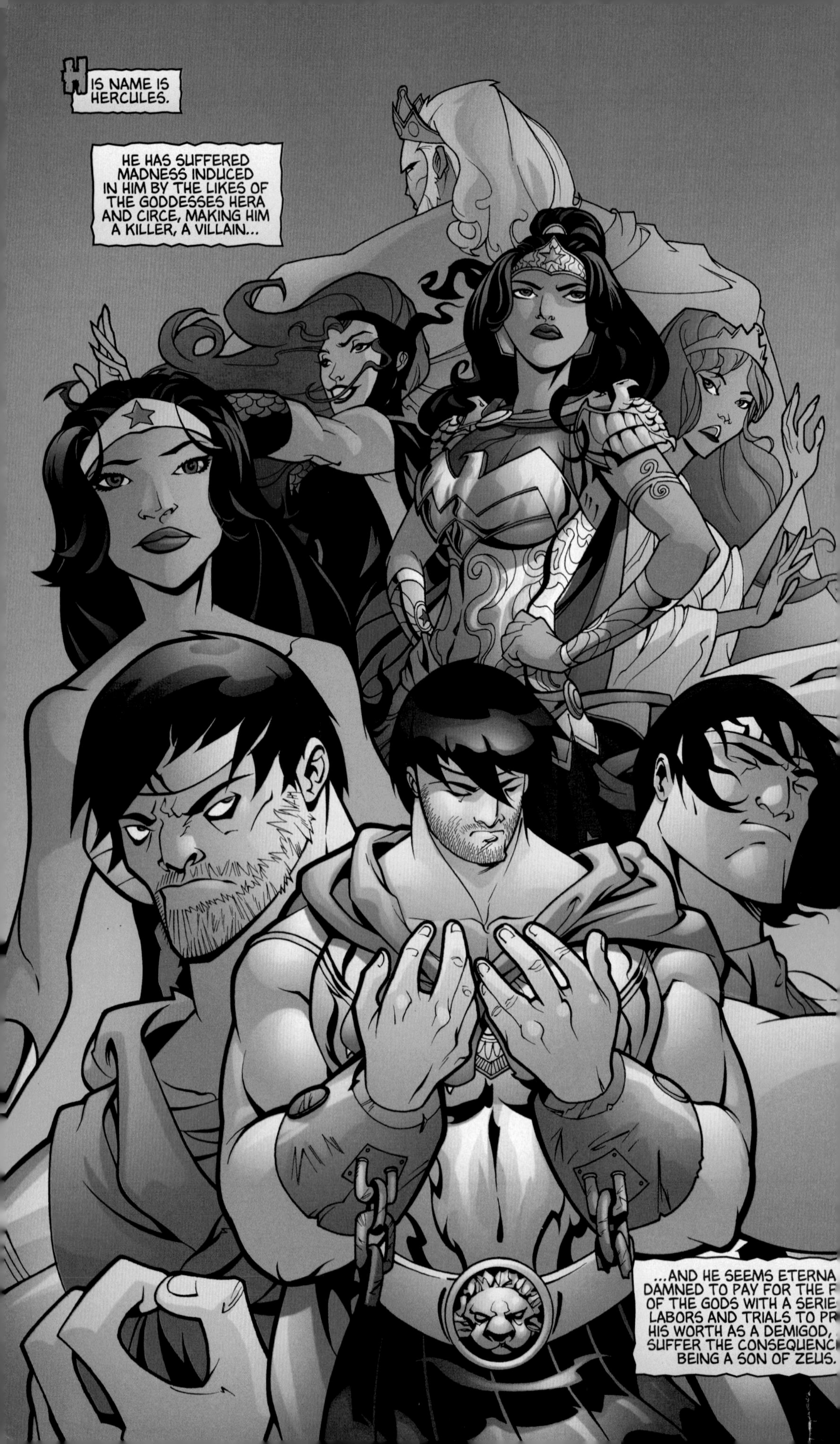
HIS NAME IS HERCULES.
HE HAS SUFFERED MADNESS INDUCED IN HIM BY THE LIKES OF THE GODDESSES HERA AND CIRCE, MAKING HIM A KILLER, A VILLAIN...
...AND HE SEEMS ETERNA DAMNED TO PAY FOR THE F OF THE GODS WITH A SERIE LABORS AND TRIALS TO PR HIS WORTH AS A DEMIGOD, SUFFER THE CONSEQUENC BEING A SON OF ZEUS.

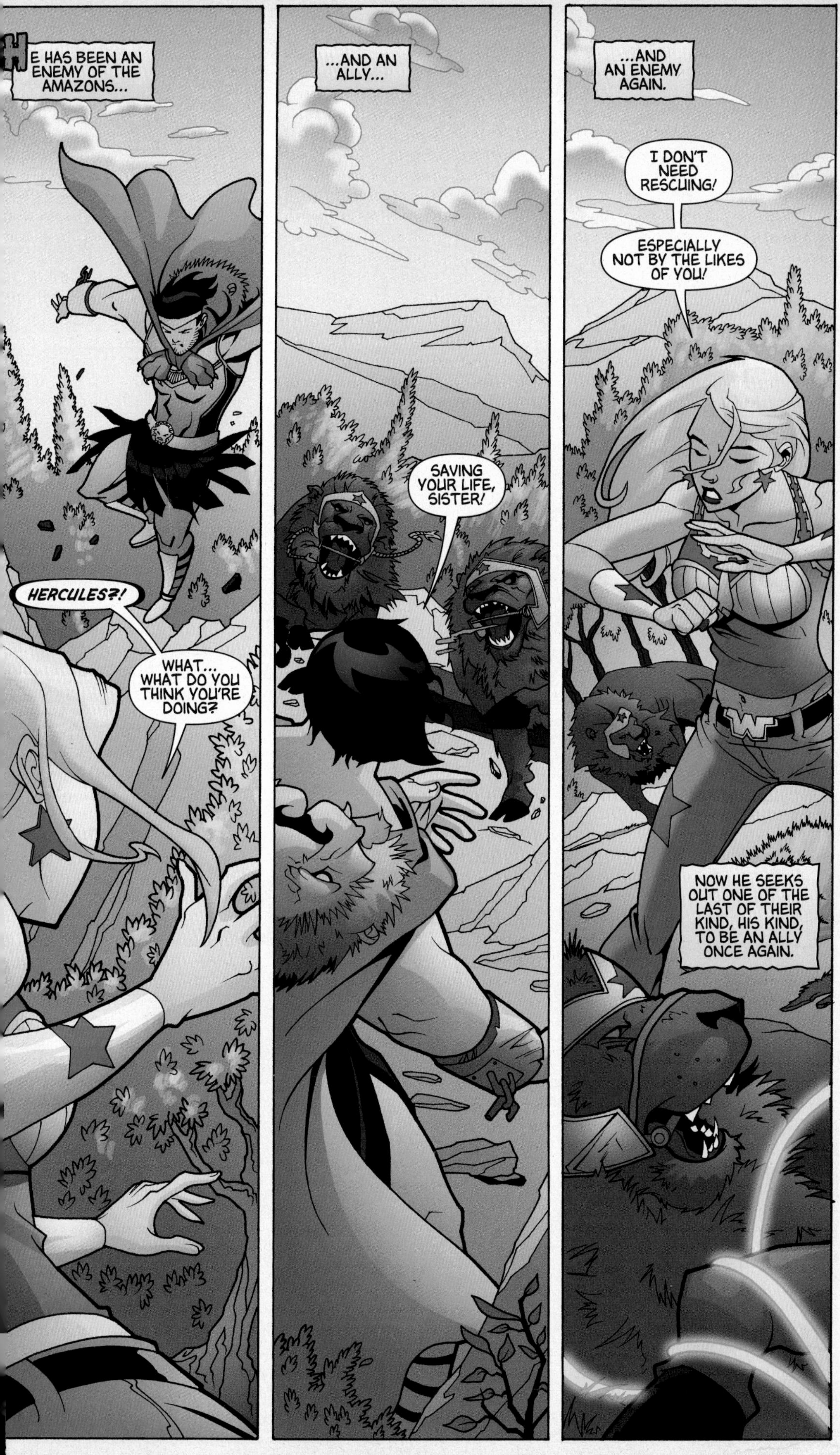
HE HAS BEEN AN ENEMY OF THE AMAZONS...
HERCULES?!
WHAT... WHAT DO YOU THINK YOU'RE DOING?
...AND AN ALLY...
SAVING YOUR LIFE, SISTER!
...AND AN ENEMY AGAIN.
I DON'T NEED RESCUING!
ESPECIALLY NOT BY THE LIKES OF YOU!
NOW HE SEEKS OUT ONE OF THE LAST OF THEIR KIND, HIS KIND, TO BE AN ALLY ONCE AGAIN.

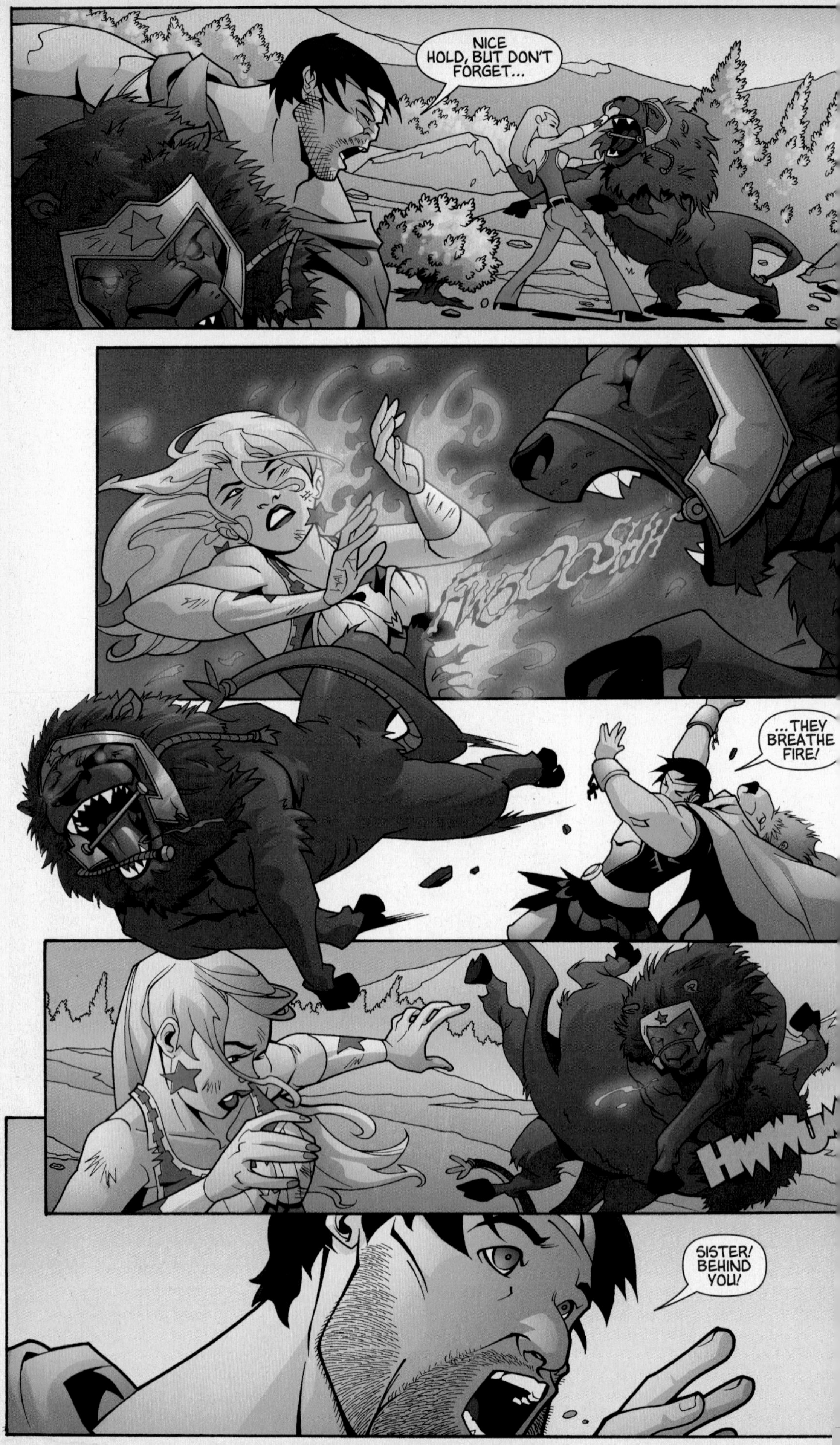
NICE HOLD, BUT DON'T FORGET...
FWOOOSHH
...THEY BREATHE FIRE!
SISTER! BEHIND YOU!

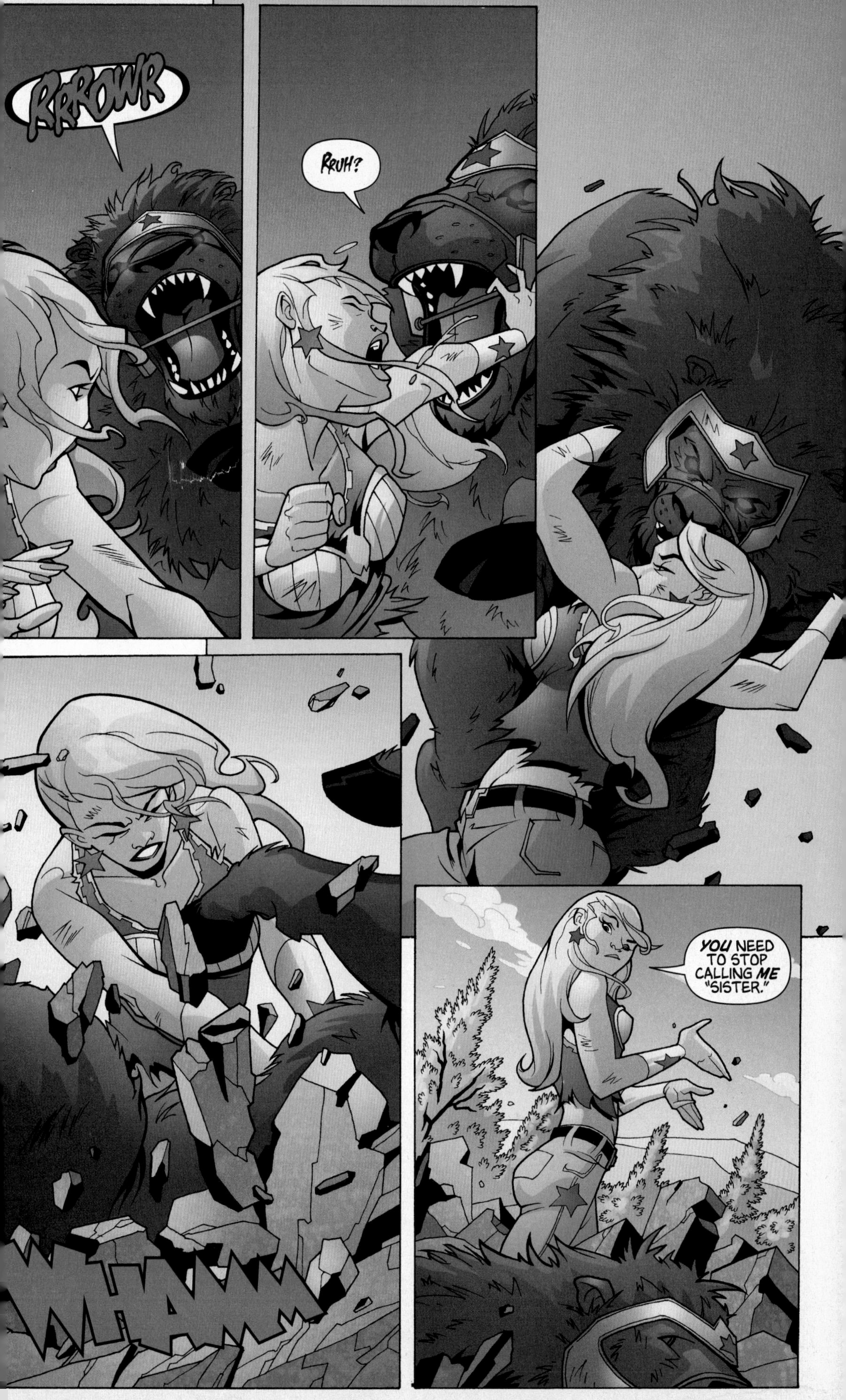
RRROWR
RRUH?
YOU NEED TO STOP CALLING ME "SISTER."
WHAM

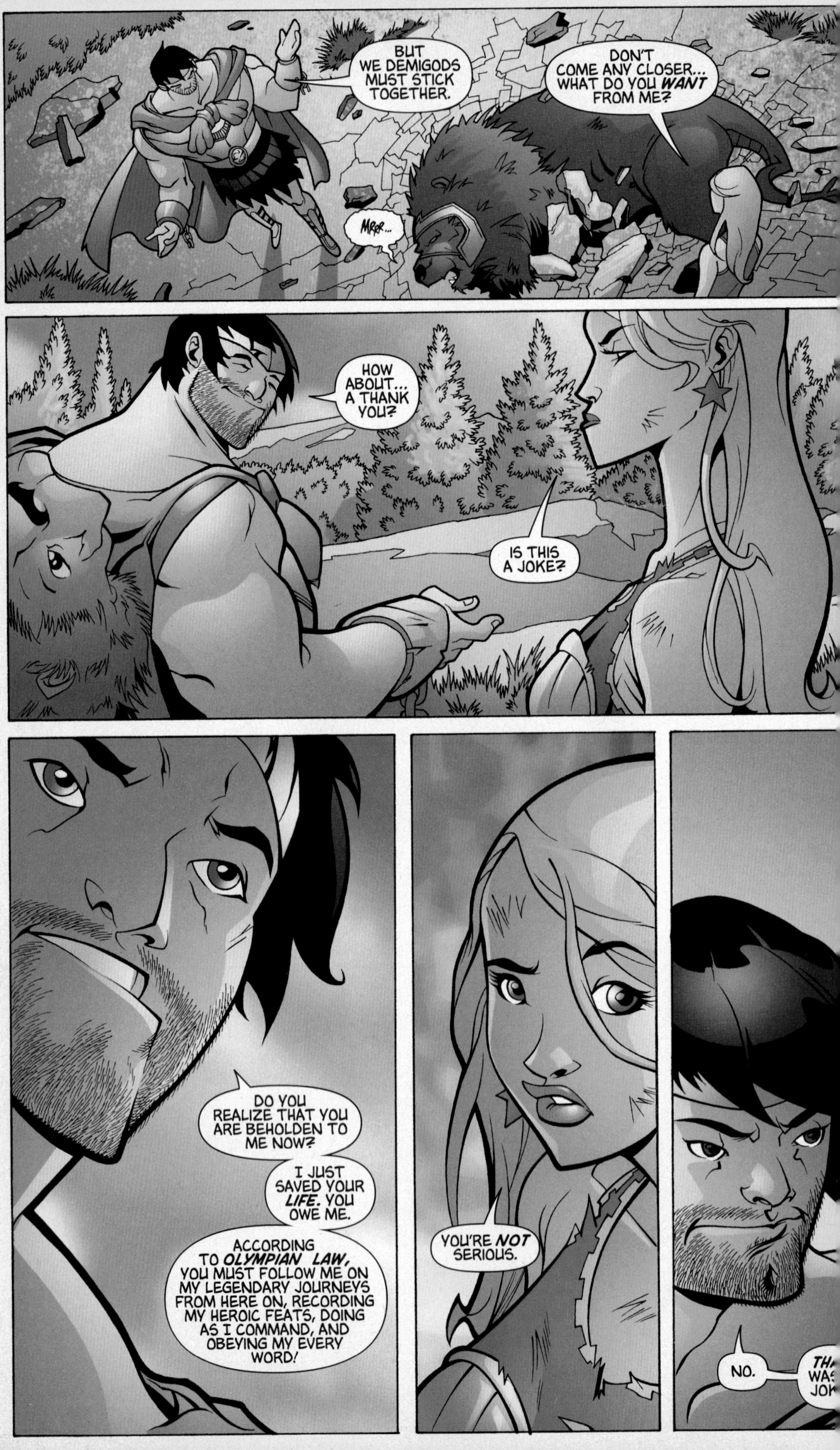
BUT WE DEMIGODS MUST STICK TOGETHER.
DON'T COME ANY CLOSER... WHAT DO YOU *WANT* FROM ME?
MRRR...
HOW ABOUT... A THANK YOU?
IS THIS A JOKE?
DO YOU REALIZE THAT YOU ARE BEHOLDEN TO ME NOW?
I JUST SAVED YOUR *LIFE.* YOU OWE ME.
ACCORDING TO *OLYMPIAN LAW,* YOU MUST FOLLOW ME ON MY LEGENDARY JOURNEYS FROM HERE ON, RECORDING MY HEROIC FEATS, DOING AS I COMMAND, AND OBEYING MY EVERY WORD!
YOU'RE *NOT* SERIOUS.
NO.

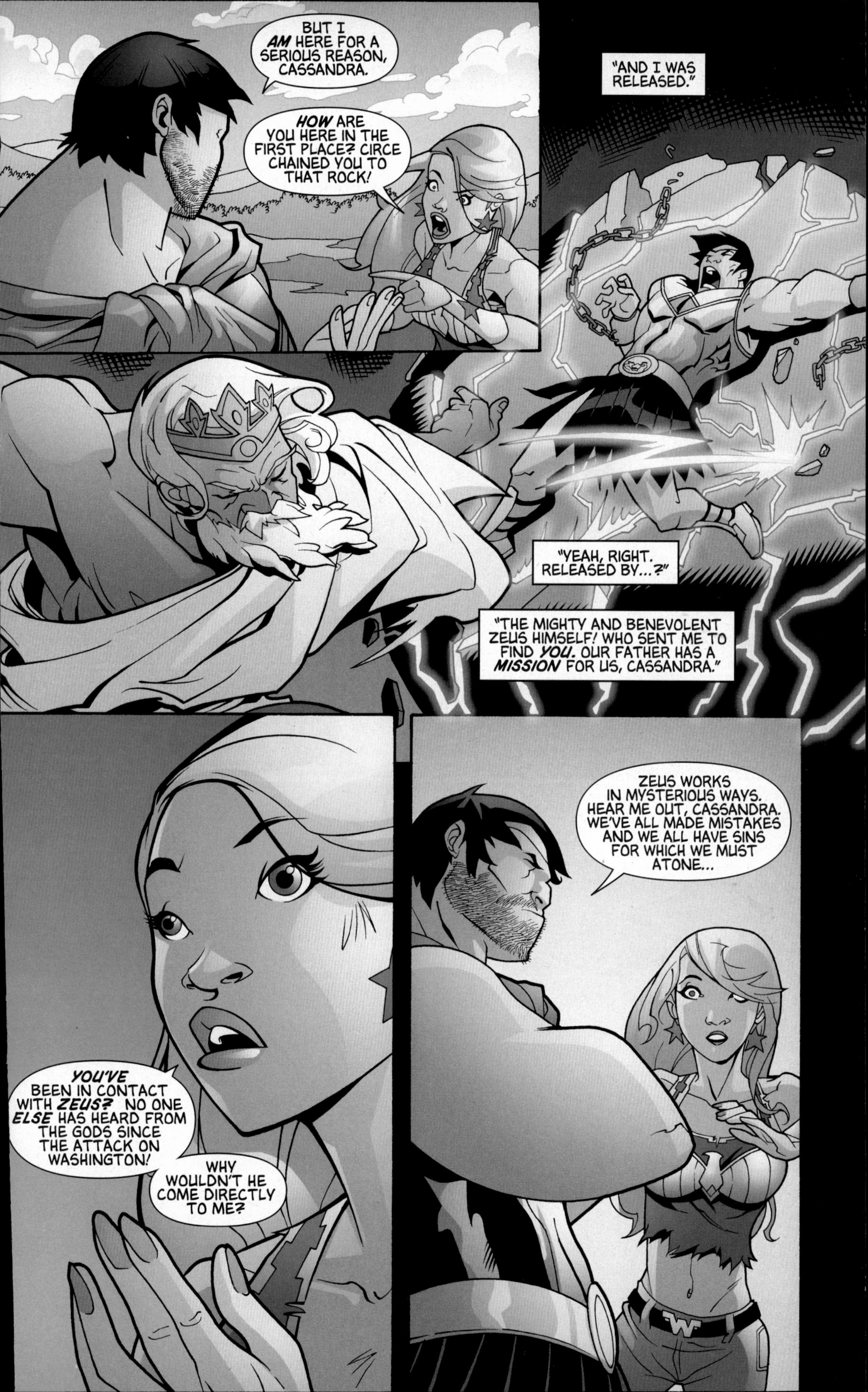
BUT I *AM* HERE FOR A SERIOUS REASON, CASSANDRA.
HOW ARE YOU HERE IN THE FIRST PLACE? CIRCE CHAINED YOU TO THAT ROCK!
"AND I WAS RELEASED."
"YEAH, RIGHT. RELEASED BY...?"
"THE MIGHTY AND BENEVOLENT ZEUS HIMSELF! WHO SENT ME TO FIND *YOU*. OUR FATHER HAS A *MISSION* FOR US, CASSANDRA."
YOU'VE BEEN IN CONTACT WITH *ZEUS?* NO ONE *ELSE* HAS HEARD FROM THE GODS SINCE THE ATTACK ON WASHINGTON!
WHY WOULDN'T HE COME DIRECTLY TO ME?
ZEUS WORKS IN MYSTERIOUS WAYS. HEAR ME OUT, CASSANDRA. WE'VE ALL MADE MISTAKES AND WE ALL HAVE SINS FOR WHICH WE MUST ATONE...

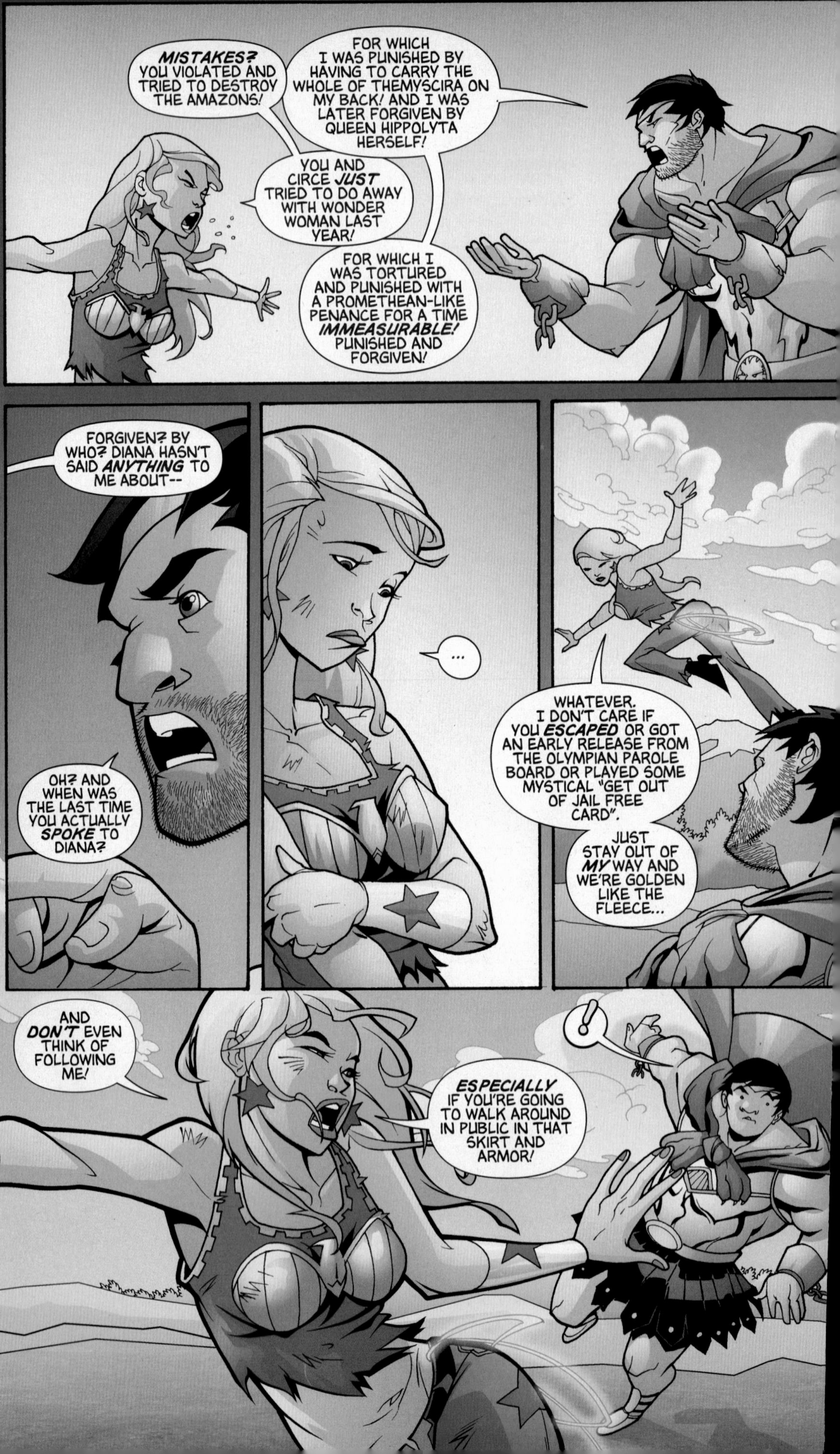
MISTAKES? YOU VIOLATED AND TRIED TO DESTROY THE AMAZONS!
FOR WHICH I WAS PUNISHED BY HAVING TO CARRY THE WHOLE OF THEMYSCIRA ON MY BACK! AND I WAS LATER FORGIVEN BY QUEEN HIPPOLYTA HERSELF!
YOU AND CIRCE JUST TRIED TO DO AWAY WITH WONDER WOMAN LAST YEAR!
FOR WHICH I WAS TORTURED AND PUNISHED WITH A PROMETHEAN-LIKE PENANCE FOR A TIME IMMEASURABLE! PUNISHED AND FORGIVEN!
FORGIVEN? BY WHO? DIANA HASN'T SAID ANYTHING TO ME ABOUT--
OH? AND WHEN WAS THE LAST TIME YOU ACTUALLY SPOKE TO DIANA?
...
WHATEVER. I DON'T CARE IF YOU ESCAPED OR GOT AN EARLY RELEASE FROM THE OLYMPIAN PAROLE BOARD OR PLAYED SOME MYSTICAL "GET OUT OF JAIL FREE CARD".
JUST STAY OUT OF MY WAY AND WE'RE GOLDEN LIKE THE FLEECE...
AND DON'T EVEN THINK OF FOLLOWING ME!
!
ESPECIALLY IF YOU'RE GOING TO WALK AROUND IN PUBLIC IN THAT SKIRT AND ARMOR!

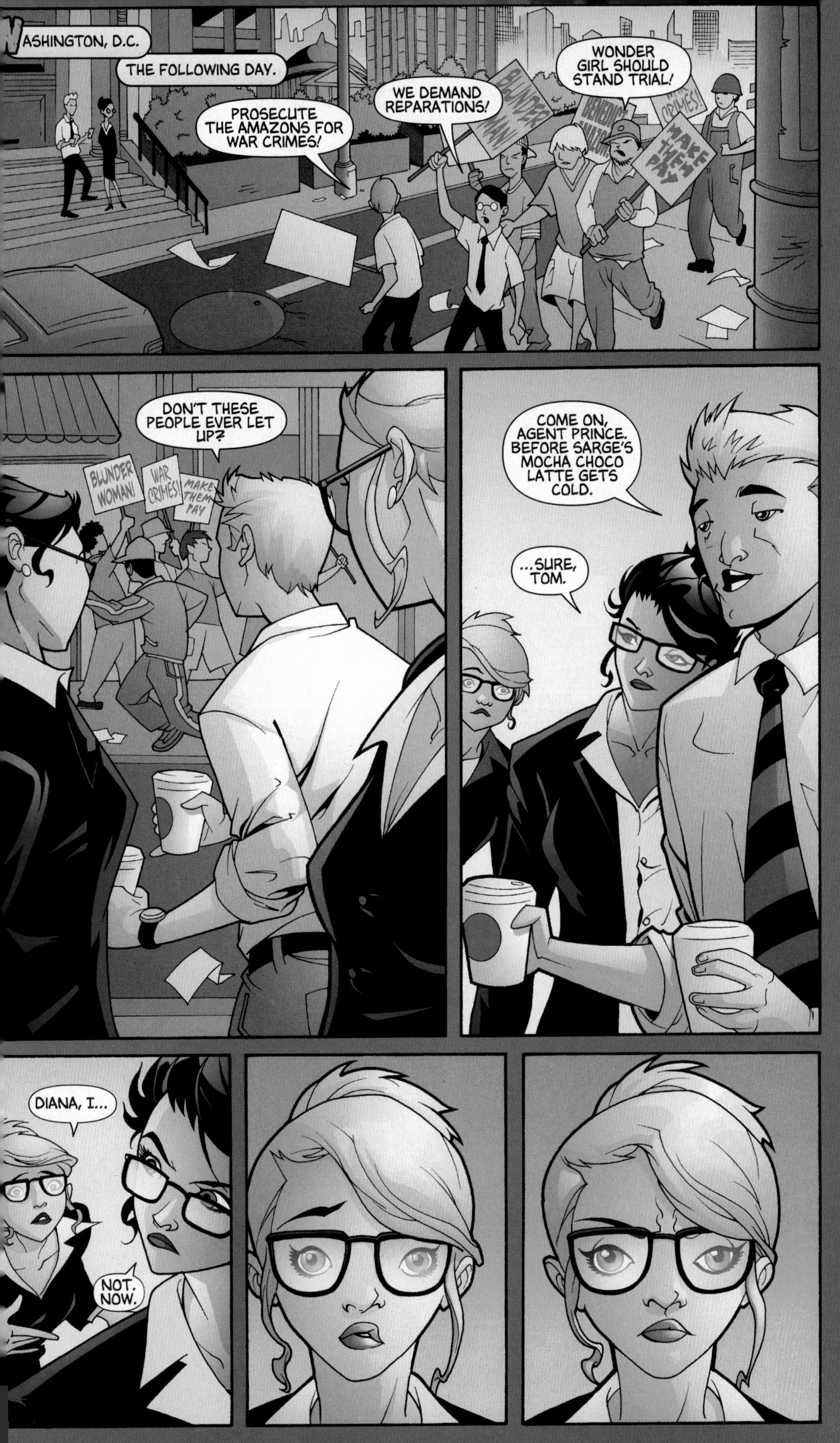

WASHINGTON, D.C.
THE FOLLOWING DAY.
PROSECUTE THE AMAZONS FOR WAR CRIMES!
WE DEMAND REPARATIONS!
BLUNDER WOMAN!
WONDER GIRL SHOULD STAND TRIAL!
MAKE THEM PAY
DON'T THESE PEOPLE EVER LET UP?
BLUNDER WOMAN!
WAR CRIMES!
MAKE THEM PAY
COME ON, AGENT PRINCE. BEFORE SARGE'S MOCHA CHOCO LATTE GETS COLD.
...SURE, TOM.
DIANA, I...
NOT. NOW.

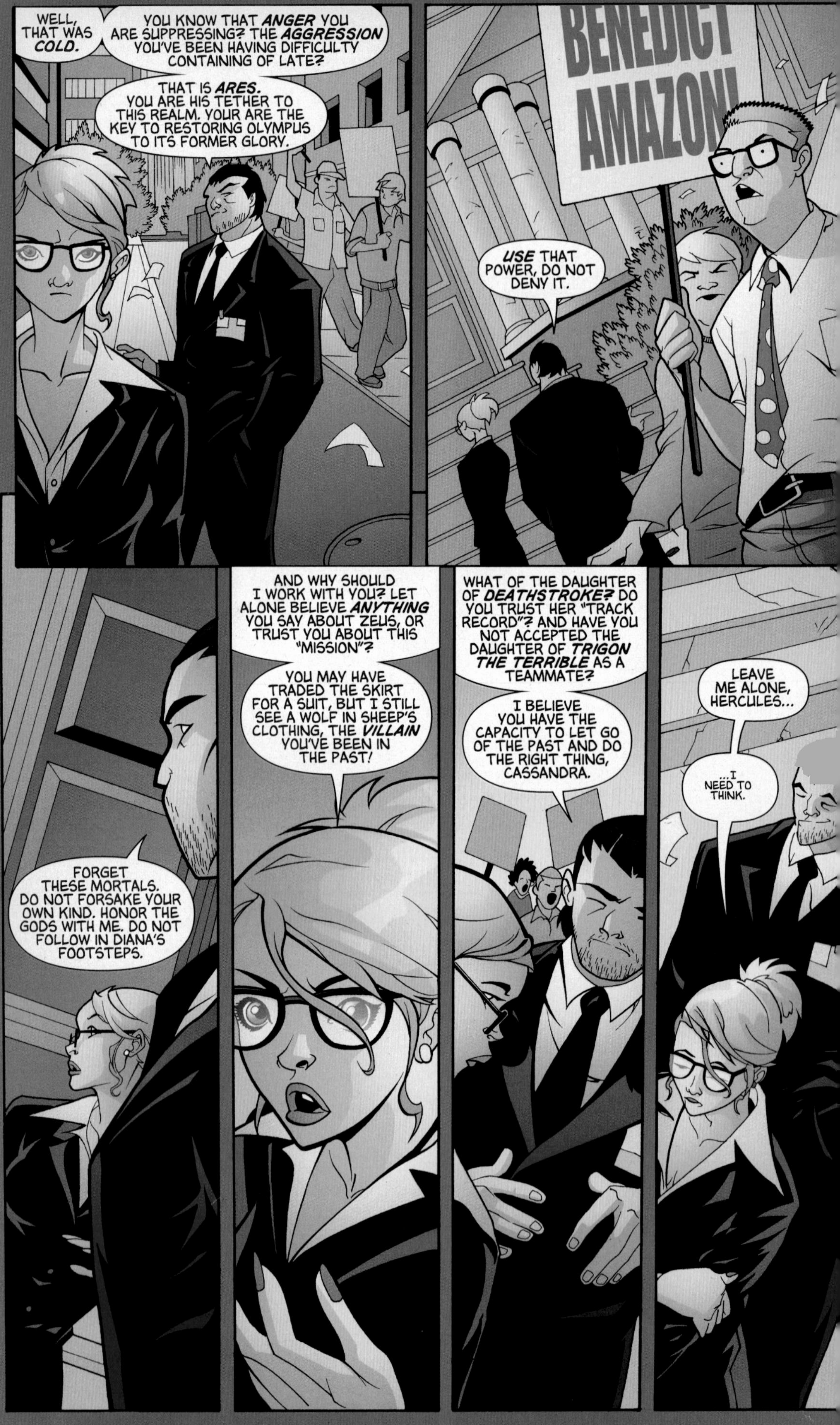
WELL, THAT WAS COLD.
YOU KNOW THAT ANGER YOU ARE SUPPRESSING? THE AGGRESSION YOU'VE BEEN HAVING DIFFICULTY CONTAINING OF LATE?
THAT IS ARES. YOU ARE HIS TETHER TO THIS REALM. YOUR ARE THE KEY TO RESTORING OLYMPUS TO ITS FORMER GLORY.
BENEDICT AMAZON!
USE THAT POWER, DO NOT DENY IT.
FORGET THESE MORTALS. DO NOT FORSAKE YOUR OWN KIND. HONOR THE GODS WITH ME. DO NOT FOLLOW IN DIANA'S FOOTSTEPS.
AND WHY SHOULD I WORK WITH YOU? LET ALONE BELIEVE ANYTHING YOU SAY ABOUT ZEUS, OR TRUST YOU ABOUT THIS "MISSION"?
YOU MAY HAVE TRADED THE SKIRT FOR A SUIT, BUT I STILL SEE A WOLF IN SHEEP'S CLOTHING, THE VILLAIN YOU'VE BEEN IN THE PAST!
WHAT OF THE DAUGHTER OF DEATHSTROKE? DO YOU TRUST HER "TRACK RECORD"? AND HAVE YOU NOT ACCEPTED THE DAUGHTER OF TRIGON THE TERRIBLE AS A TEAMMATE?
I BELIEVE YOU HAVE THE CAPACITY TO LET GO OF THE PAST AND DO THE RIGHT THING, CASSANDRA.
LEAVE ME ALONE, HERCULES...
...I NEED TO THINK.

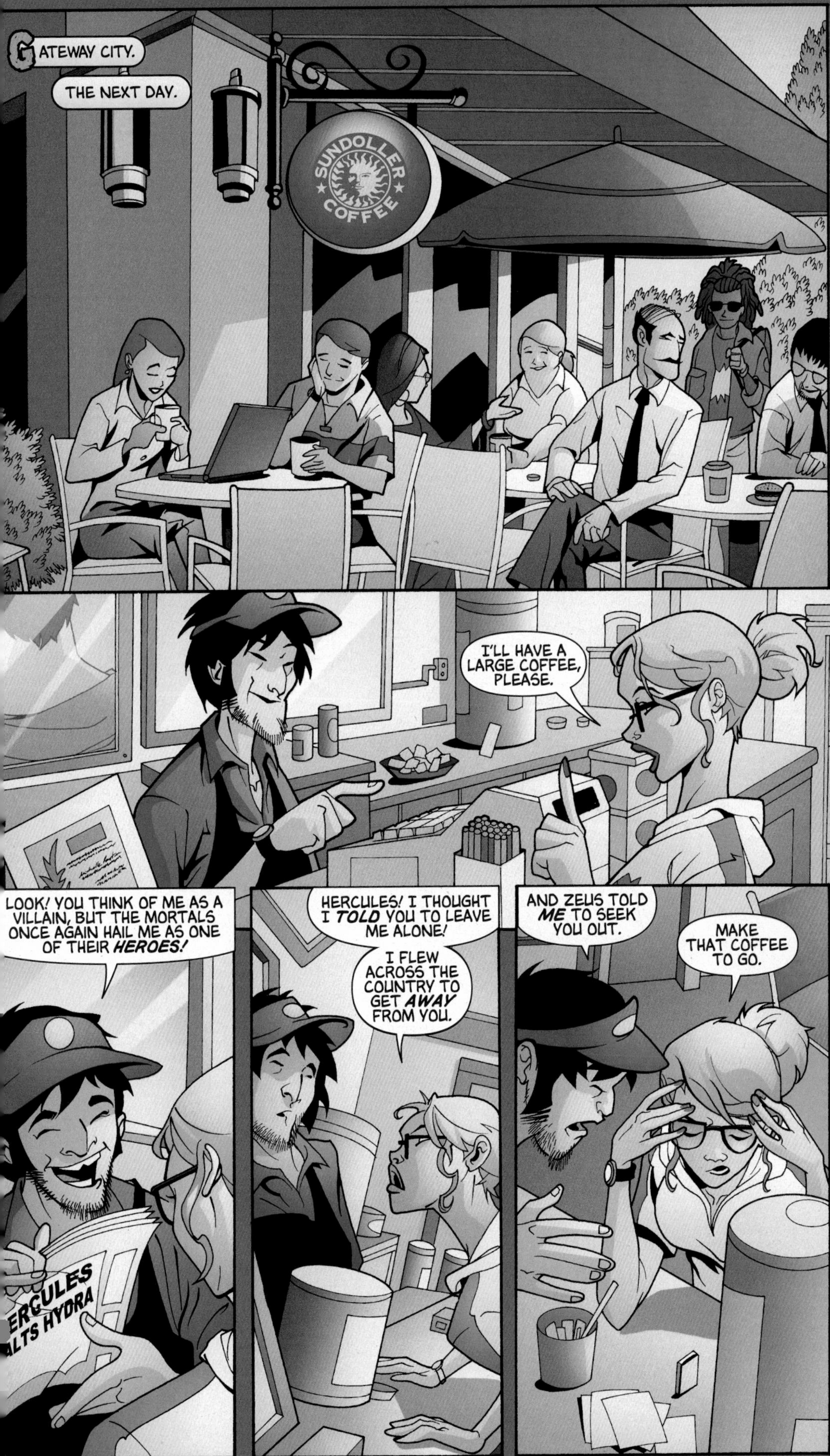
GATEWAY CITY.
THE NEXT DAY.
SUNDOLLER COFFEE
I'LL HAVE A LARGE COFFEE, PLEASE.
LOOK! YOU THINK OF ME AS A VILLAIN, BUT THE MORTALS ONCE AGAIN HAIL ME AS ONE OF THEIR *HEROES!*
ERCULES ALTS HYDRA
HERCULES! I THOUGHT I *TOLD* YOU TO LEAVE ME ALONE!
I FLEW ACROSS THE COUNTRY TO GET *AWAY* FROM YOU.
AND ZEUS TOLD *ME* TO SEEK YOU OUT.
MAKE THAT COFFEE TO GO.

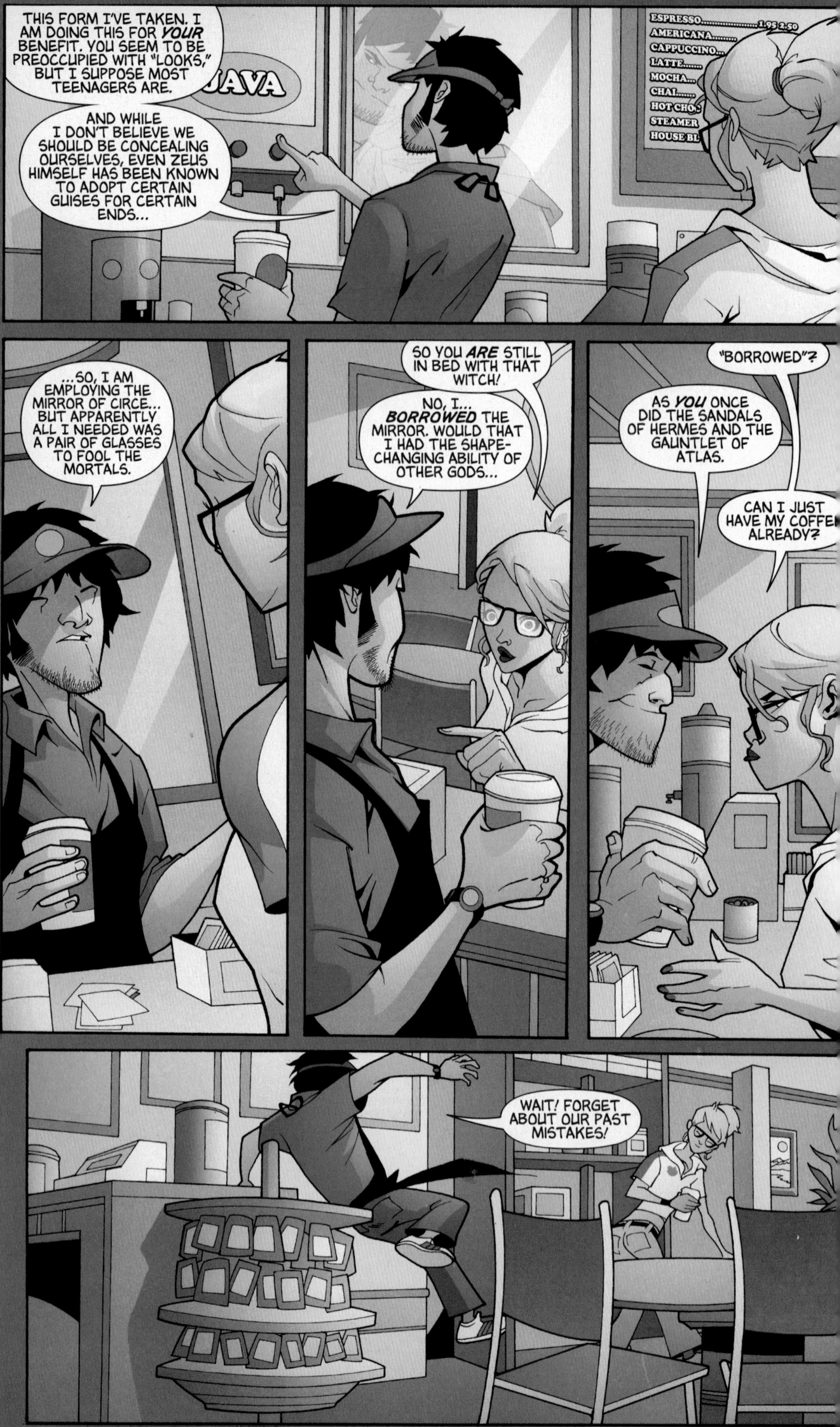
THIS FORM I'VE TAKEN. I AM DOING THIS FOR *YOUR* BENEFIT. YOU SEEM TO BE PREOCCUPIED WITH "LOOKS," BUT I SUPPOSE MOST TEENAGERS ARE.
AND WHILE I DON'T BELIEVE WE SHOULD BE CONCEALING OURSELVES, EVEN ZEUS HIMSELF HAS BEEN KNOWN TO ADOPT CERTAIN GUISES FOR CERTAIN ENDS...
JAVA
ESPRESSO.....1.95 2.50
AMERICANA
CAPPUCCINO
LATTE
MOCHA
CHAI
STEAMER
...SO, I AM EMPLOYING THE MIRROR OF CIRCE... BUT APPARENTLY ALL I NEEDED WAS A PAIR OF GLASSES TO FOOL THE MORTALS.
SO YOU *ARE* STILL IN BED WITH THAT WITCH!
NO, I... *BORROWED* THE MIRROR. WOULD THAT I HAD THE SHAPE-CHANGING ABILITY OF OTHER GODS...
"BORROWED"?
AS *YOU* ONCE DID THE SANDALS OF HERMES AND THE GAUNTLET OF ATLAS.
CAN I JUST HAVE MY COFFE ALREADY?
WAIT! FORGET ABOUT OUR PAST MISTAKES!

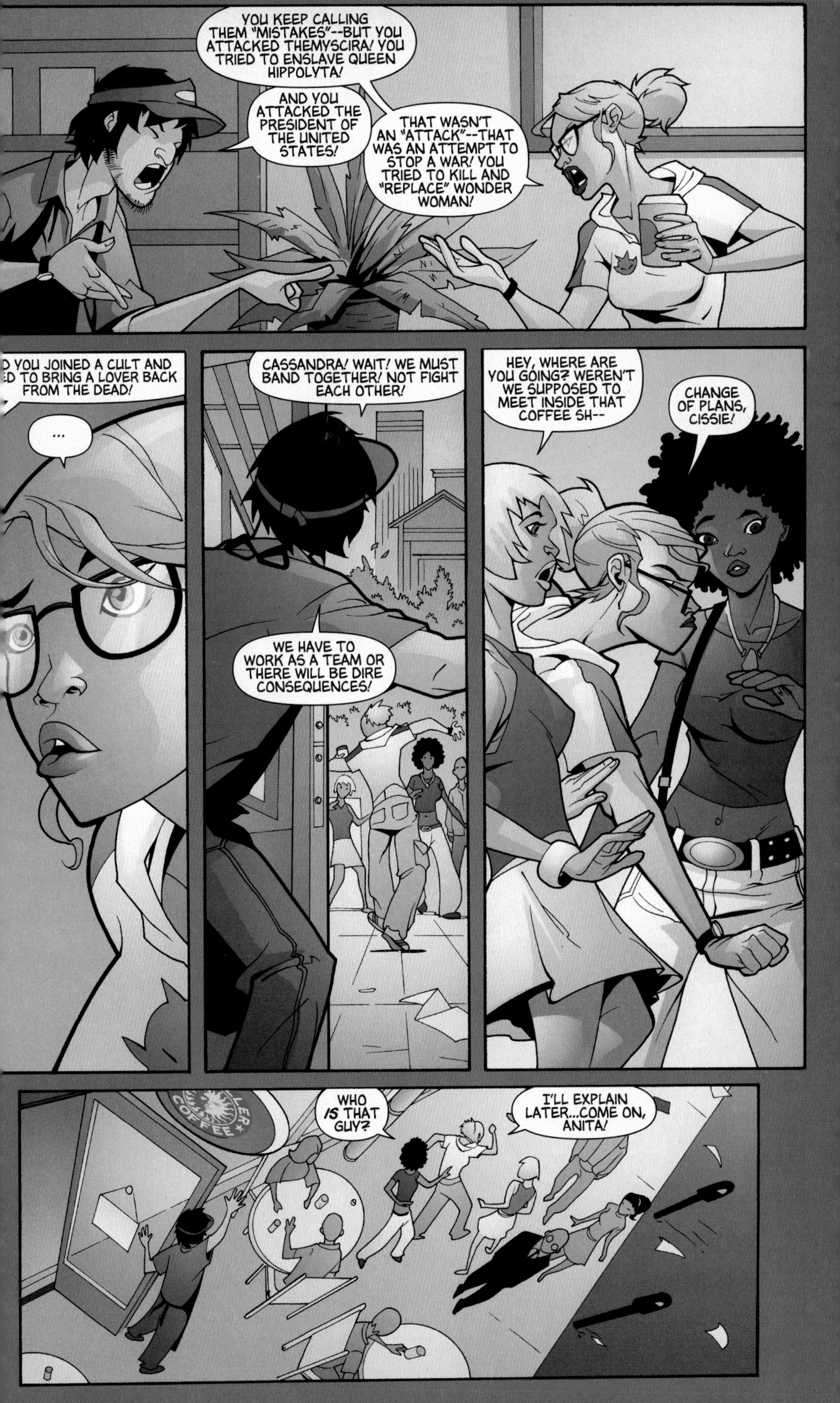
YOU KEEP CALLING THEM "MISTAKES"--BUT YOU ATTACKED THEMYSCIRA! YOU TRIED TO ENSLAVE QUEEN HIPPOLYTA!
AND YOU ATTACKED THE PRESIDENT OF THE UNITED STATES!
THAT WASN'T AN "ATTACK"--THAT WAS AN ATTEMPT TO STOP A WAR! YOU TRIED TO KILL AND "REPLACE" WONDER WOMAN!
D YOU JOINED A CULT AND ED TO BRING A LOVER BACK FROM THE DEAD!
...
CASSANDRA! WAIT! WE MUST BAND TOGETHER! NOT FIGHT EACH OTHER!
WE HAVE TO WORK AS A TEAM OR THERE WILL BE DIRE CONSEQUENCES!
HEY, WHERE ARE YOU GOING? WEREN'T WE SUPPOSED TO MEET INSIDE THAT COFFEE SH--
CHANGE OF PLANS, CISSIE!
COFFEE
WHO *IS* THAT GUY?
I'LL EXPLAIN LATER...COME ON, ANITA!

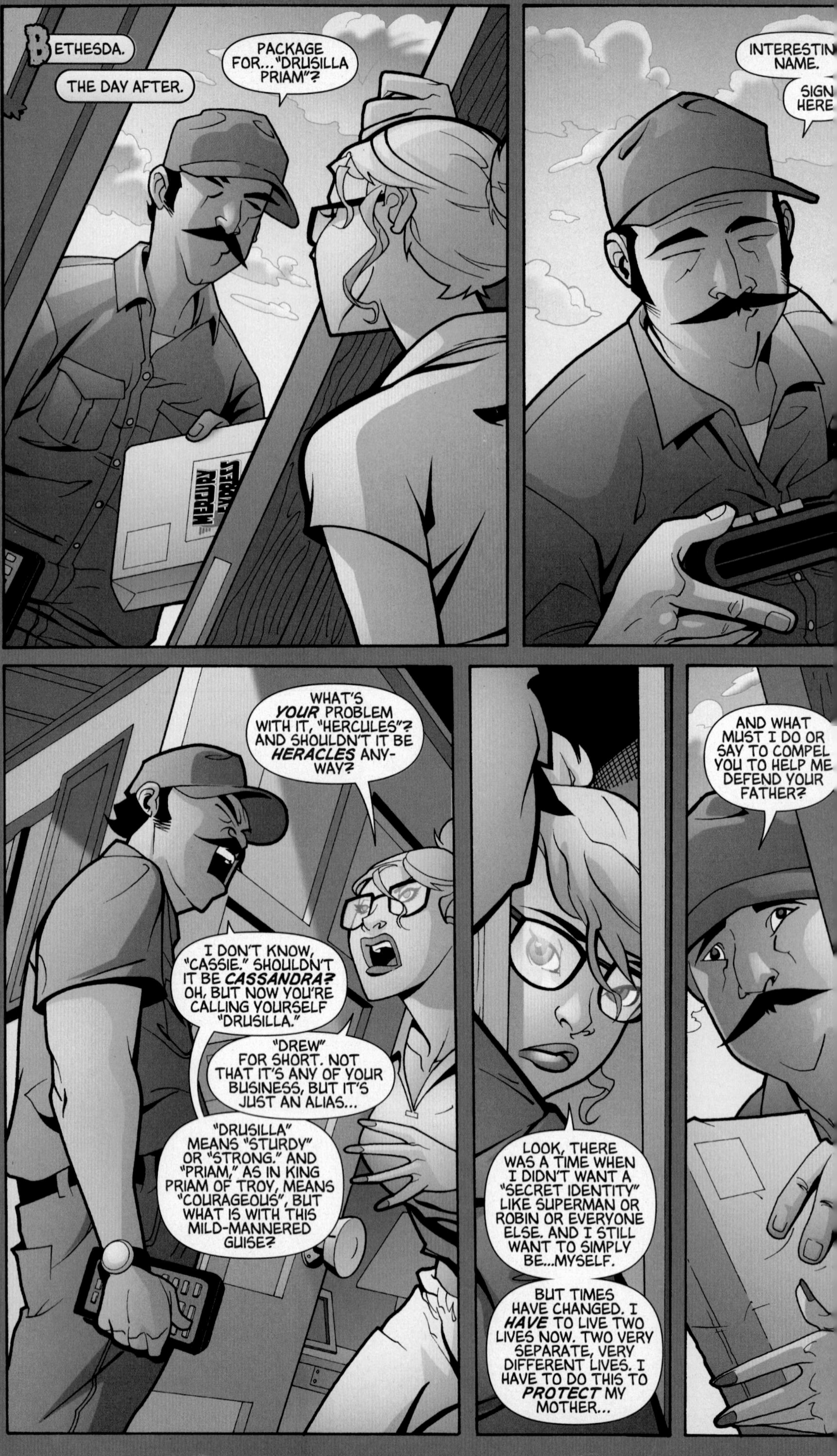
BETHESDA.
THE DAY AFTER.
PACKAGE FOR..."DRUSILLA PRIAM"?
INTERESTIN NAME.
SIGN HERE
WHAT'S YOUR PROBLEM WITH IT, "HERCULES"? AND SHOULDN'T IT BE HERACLES ANYWAY?
I DON'T KNOW, "CASSIE." SHOULDN'T IT BE CASSANDRA? OH, BUT NOW YOU'RE CALLING YOURSELF "DRUSILLA."
"DREW" FOR SHORT. NOT THAT IT'S ANY OF YOUR BUSINESS, BUT IT'S JUST AN ALIAS...
"DRUSILLA" MEANS "STURDY" OR "STRONG." AND "PRIAM," AS IN KING PRIAM OF TROY, MEANS "COURAGEOUS", BUT WHAT IS WITH THIS MILD-MANNERED GUISE?
LOOK, THERE WAS A TIME WHEN I DIDN'T WANT A "SECRET IDENTITY" LIKE SUPERMAN OR ROBIN OR EVERYONE ELSE. AND I STILL WANT TO SIMPLY BE...MYSELF.
BUT TIMES HAVE CHANGED. I HAVE TO LIVE TWO LIVES NOW. TWO VERY SEPARATE, VERY DIFFERENT LIVES. I HAVE TO DO THIS TO PROTECT MY MOTHER...
AND WHAT MUST I DO OR SAY TO COMPEL YOU TO HELP ME DEFEND YOUR FATHER?

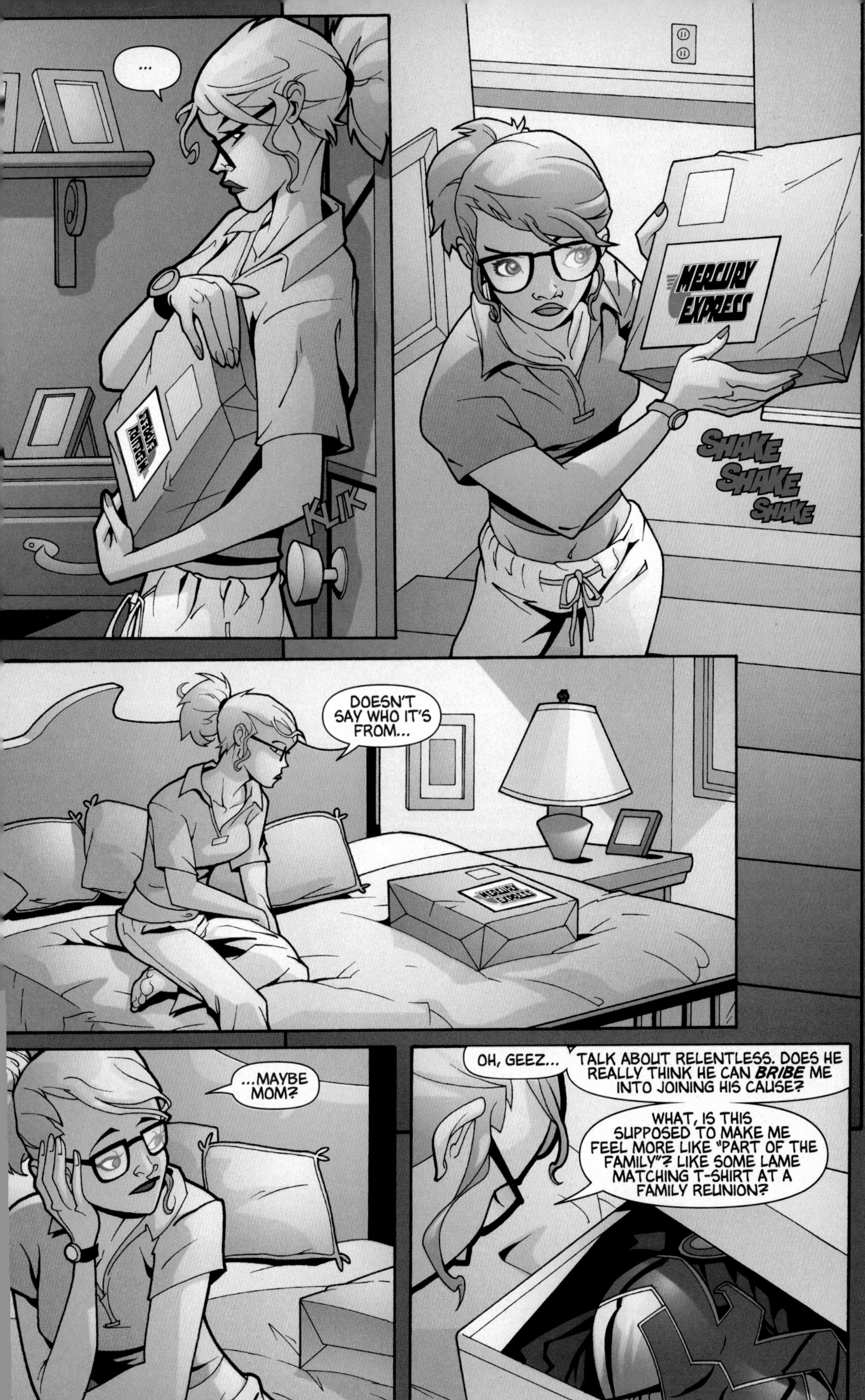
...
MERCURY EXPRESS
KLIK
MERCURY EXPRESS
SHAKE SHAKE SHAKE
DOESN'T SAY WHO IT'S FROM...
MERCURY EXPRESS
...MAYBE MOM?
OH, GEEZ...
TALK ABOUT RELENTLESS. DOES HE REALLY THINK HE CAN *BRIBE* ME INTO JOINING HIS CAUSE?
WHAT, IS THIS SUPPOSED TO MAKE ME FEEL MORE LIKE "PART OF THE FAMILY"? LIKE SOME LAME MATCHING T-SHIRT AT A FAMILY REUNION?

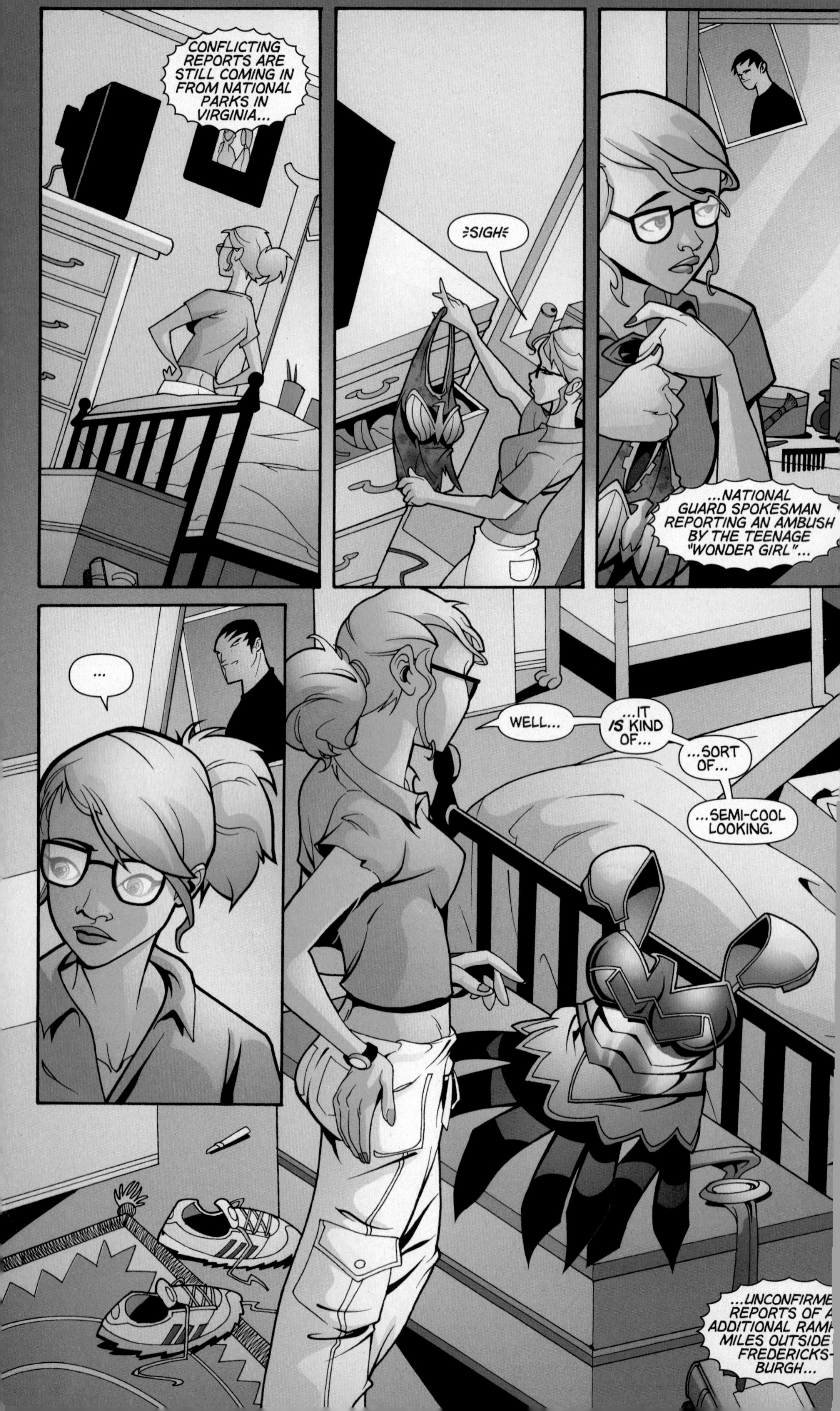
CONFLICTING REPORTS ARE STILL COMING IN FROM NATIONAL PARKS IN VIRGINIA...
SIGH
...NATIONAL GUARD SPOKESMAN REPORTING AN AMBUSH BY THE TEENAGE "WONDER GIRL"...
...
WELL...
...IT IS KIND OF...
...SORT OF...
...SEMI-COOL LOOKING.
...UNCONFIRME REPORTS OF A ADDITIONAL RAMP MILES OUTSIDE FREDERICKS-BURGH...

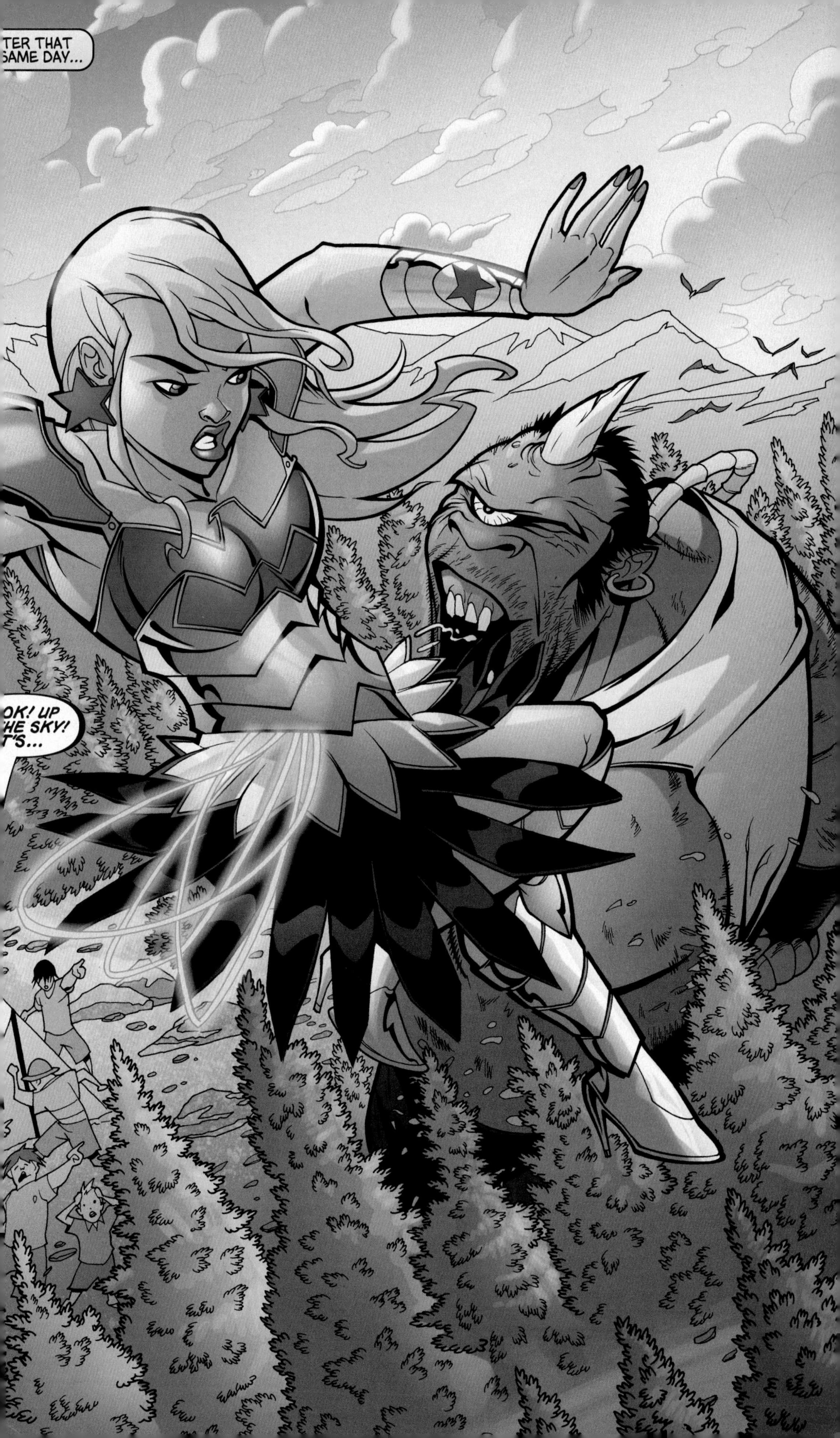
TER THAT
SAME DAY...
OK! UP
HE SKY!
T'S...

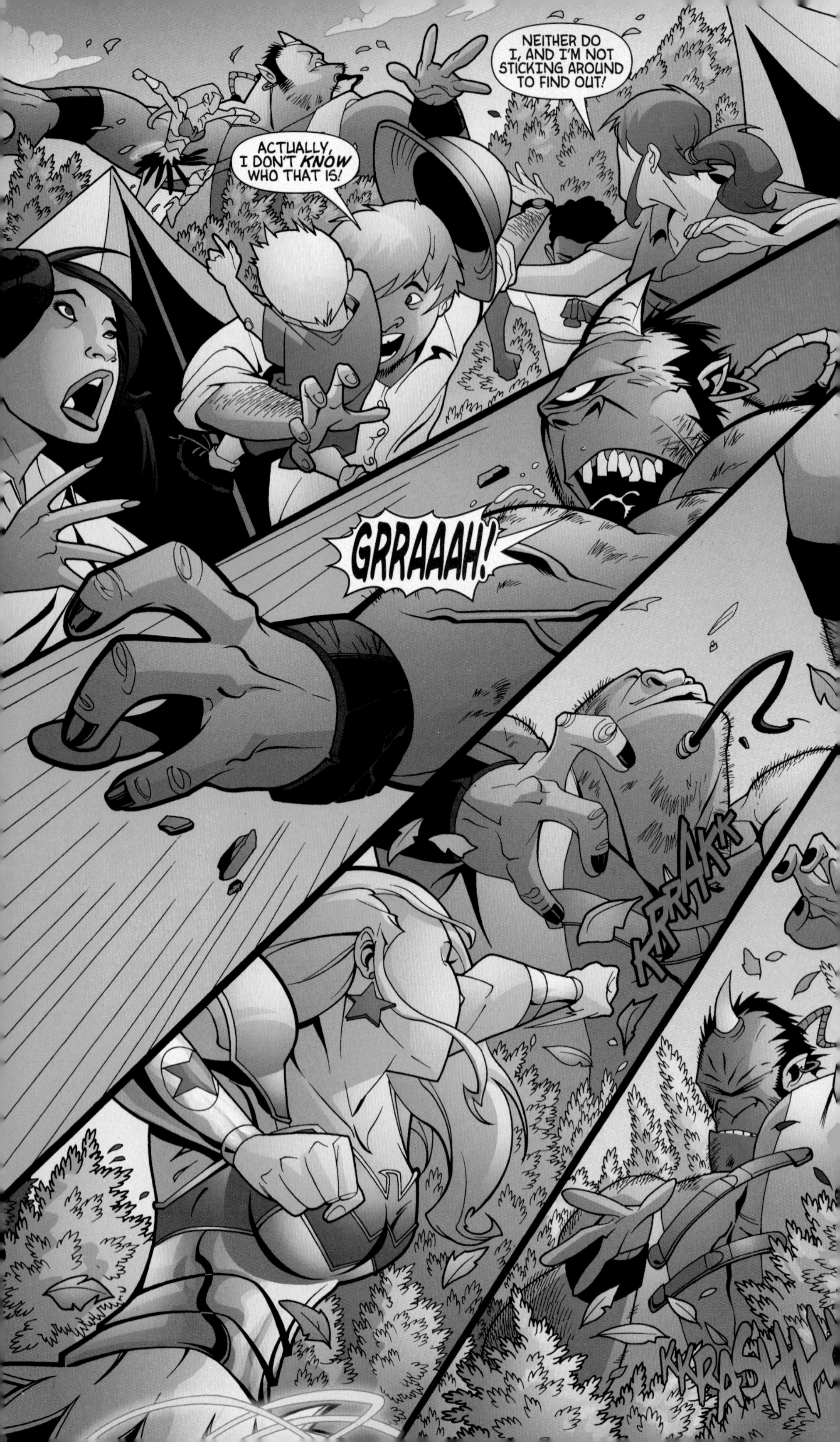
ACTUALLY, I DON'T KNOW WHO THAT IS!
NEITHER DO I, AND I'M NOT STICKING AROUND TO FIND OUT!
GRRAAAH!
KRRAKK
KKRASH

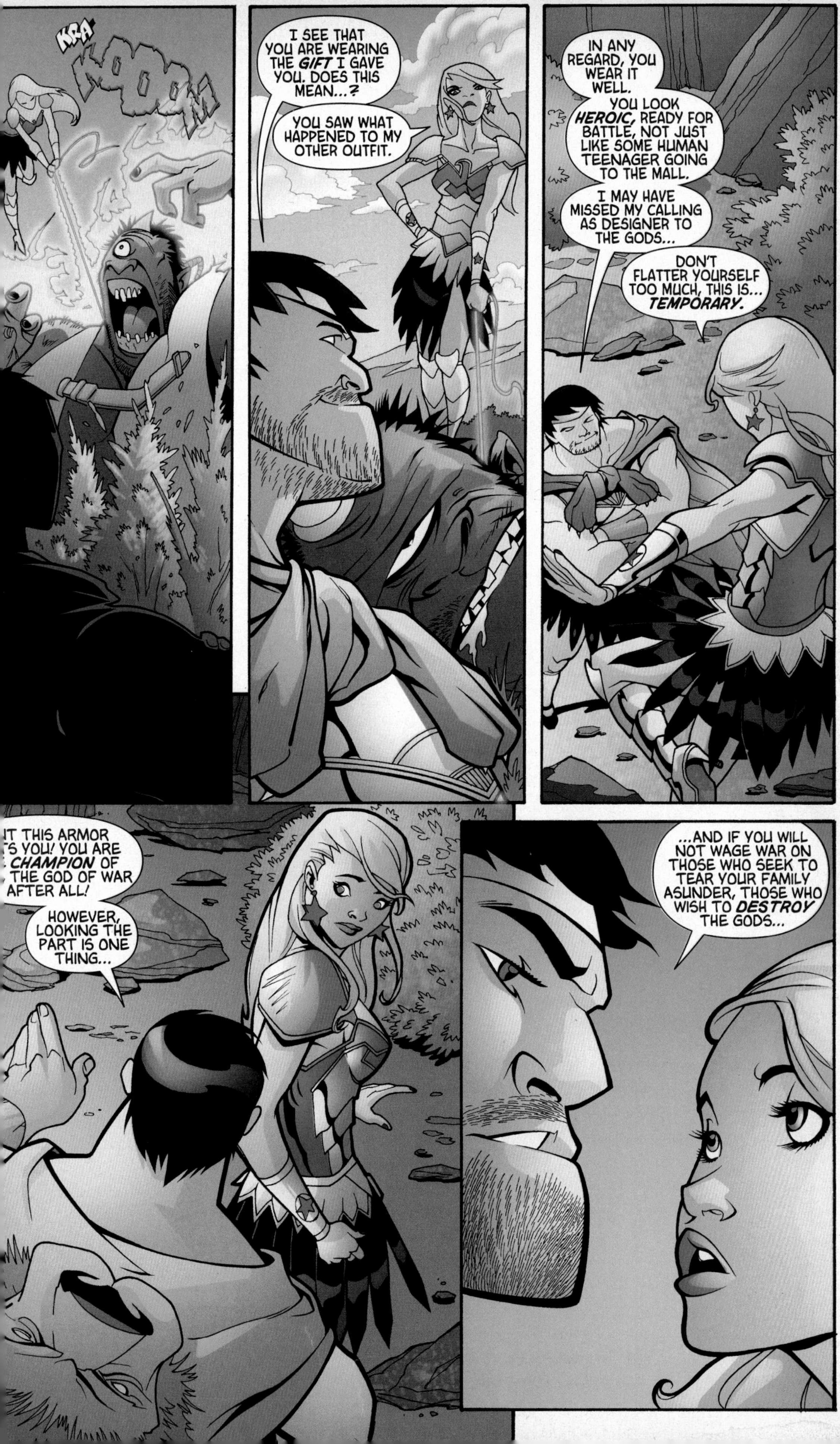
KRA-KOOOM
I SEE THAT YOU ARE WEARING THE *GIFT* I GAVE YOU. DOES THIS MEAN...?
YOU SAW WHAT HAPPENED TO MY OTHER OUTFIT.
IN ANY REGARD, YOU WEAR IT WELL.
YOU LOOK *HEROIC*, READY FOR BATTLE, NOT JUST LIKE SOME HUMAN TEENAGER GOING TO THE MALL.
I MAY HAVE MISSED MY CALLING AS DESIGNER TO THE GODS...
DON'T FLATTER YOURSELF TOO MUCH, THIS IS... ***TEMPORARY.***
IT THIS ARMOR 'S YOU! YOU ARE *CHAMPION* OF THE GOD OF WAR AFTER ALL!
HOWEVER, LOOKING THE PART IS ONE THING...
...AND IF YOU WILL NOT WAGE WAR ON THOSE WHO SEEK TO TEAR YOUR FAMILY ASUNDER, THOSE WHO WISH TO *DESTROY* THE GODS...

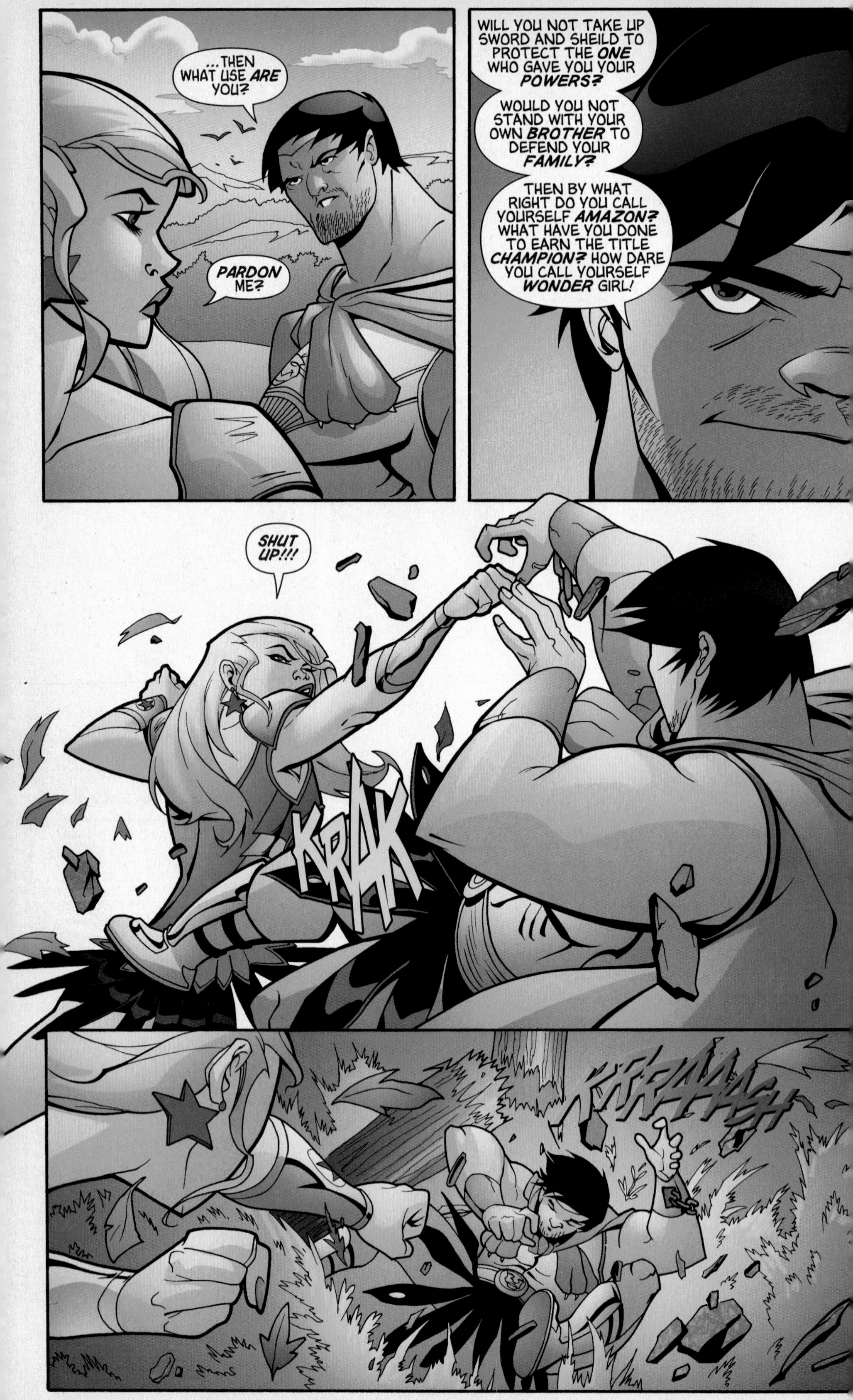

...THEN WHAT USE ARE YOU?
PARDON ME?
WILL YOU NOT TAKE UP SWORD AND SHEILD TO PROTECT THE ONE WHO GAVE YOU YOUR POWERS?
WOULD YOU NOT STAND WITH YOUR OWN BROTHER TO DEFEND YOUR FAMILY?
THEN BY WHAT RIGHT DO YOU CALL YOURSELF AMAZON? WHAT HAVE YOU DONE TO EARN THE TITLE CHAMPION? HOW DARE YOU CALL YOURSELF WONDER GIRL!
SHUT UP!!!
KRAK
KRAAASH

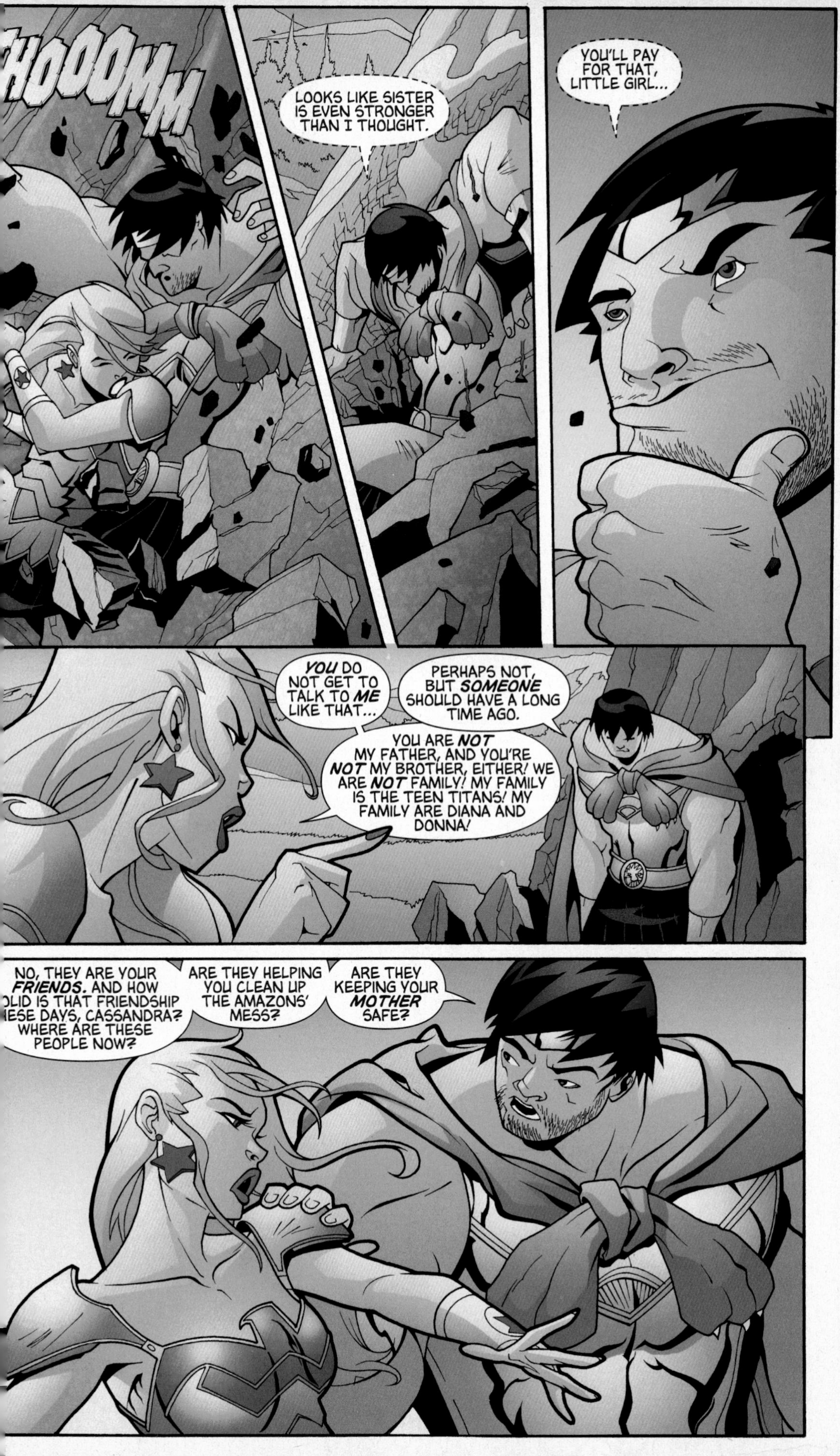

HOOOMM
LOOKS LIKE SISTER IS EVEN STRONGER THAN I THOUGHT.
YOU'LL PAY FOR THAT, LITTLE GIRL...
YOU DO NOT GET TO TALK TO ME LIKE THAT...
PERHAPS NOT, BUT SOMEONE SHOULD HAVE A LONG TIME AGO.
YOU ARE NOT MY FATHER, AND YOU'RE NOT MY BROTHER, EITHER! WE ARE NOT FAMILY! MY FAMILY IS THE TEEN TITANS! MY FAMILY ARE DIANA AND DONNA!
NO, THEY ARE YOUR FRIENDS. AND HOW OLID IS THAT FRIENDSHIP HESE DAYS, CASSANDRA? WHERE ARE THESE PEOPLE NOW?
ARE THEY HELPING YOU CLEAN UP THE AMAZONS' MESS?
ARE THEY KEEPING YOUR MOTHER SAFE?

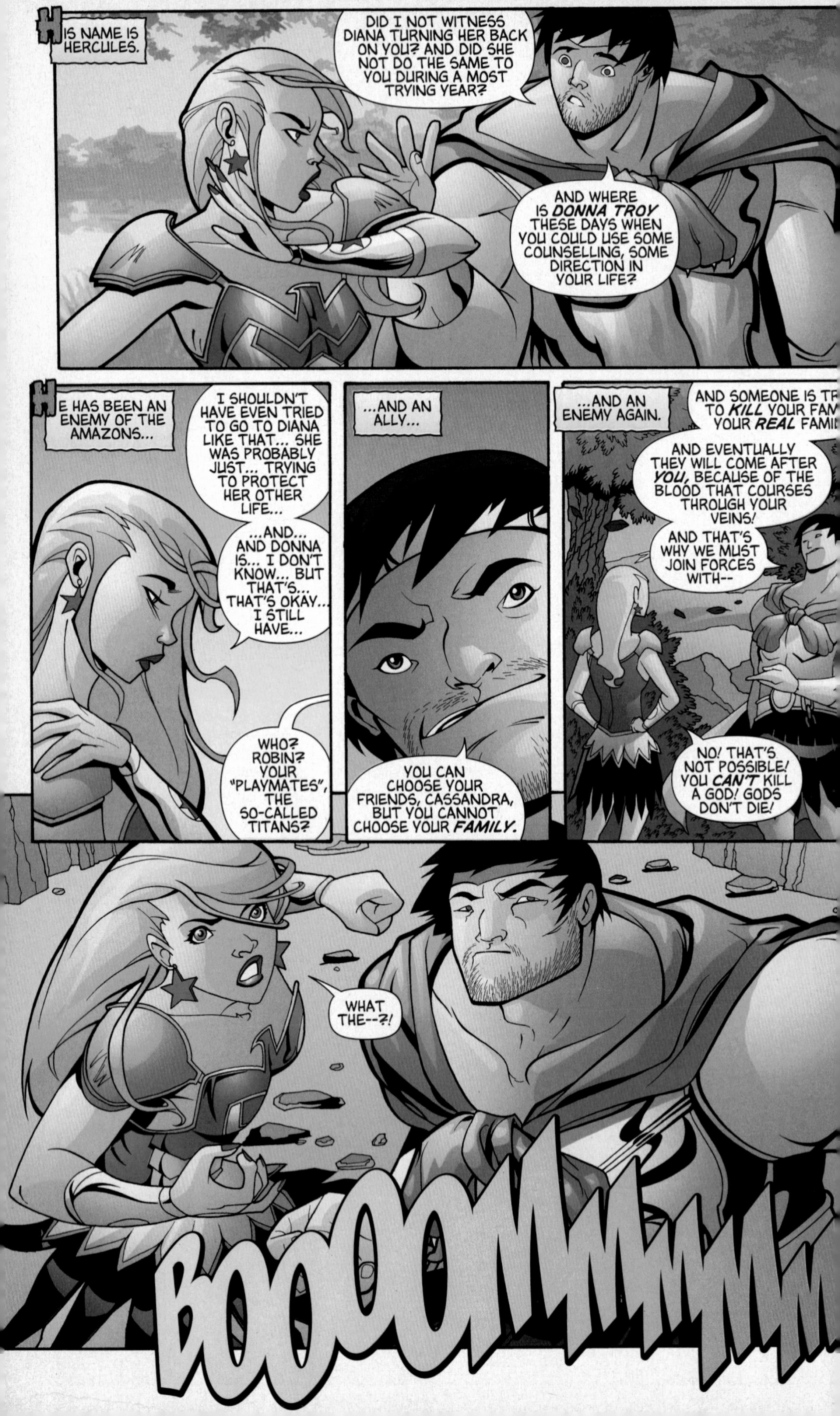
HIS NAME IS HERCULES.
DID I NOT WITNESS DIANA TURNING HER BACK ON YOU? AND DID SHE NOT DO THE SAME TO YOU DURING A MOST TRYING YEAR?
AND WHERE IS DONNA TROY THESE DAYS WHEN YOU COULD USE SOME COUNSELLING, SOME DIRECTION IN YOUR LIFE?
HE HAS BEEN AN ENEMY OF THE AMAZONS...
I SHOULDN'T HAVE EVEN TRIED TO GO TO DIANA LIKE THAT... SHE WAS PROBABLY JUST... TRYING TO PROTECT HER OTHER LIFE...
...AND... AND DONNA IS... I DON'T KNOW... BUT THAT'S... THAT'S OKAY... I STILL HAVE...
WHO? ROBIN? YOUR "PLAYMATES", THE SO-CALLED TITANS?
...AND AN ALLY...
YOU CAN CHOOSE YOUR FRIENDS, CASSANDRA, BUT YOU CANNOT CHOOSE YOUR FAMILY.
...AND AN ENEMY AGAIN.
AND EVENTUALLY THEY WILL COME AFTER YOU, BECAUSE OF THE BLOOD THAT COURSES THROUGH YOUR VEINS!
AND THAT'S WHY WE MUST JOIN FORCES WITH--
NO! THAT'S NOT POSSIBLE! YOU CAN'T KILL A GOD! GODS DON'T DIE!
WHAT THE--?!
BOOOOMMMMM

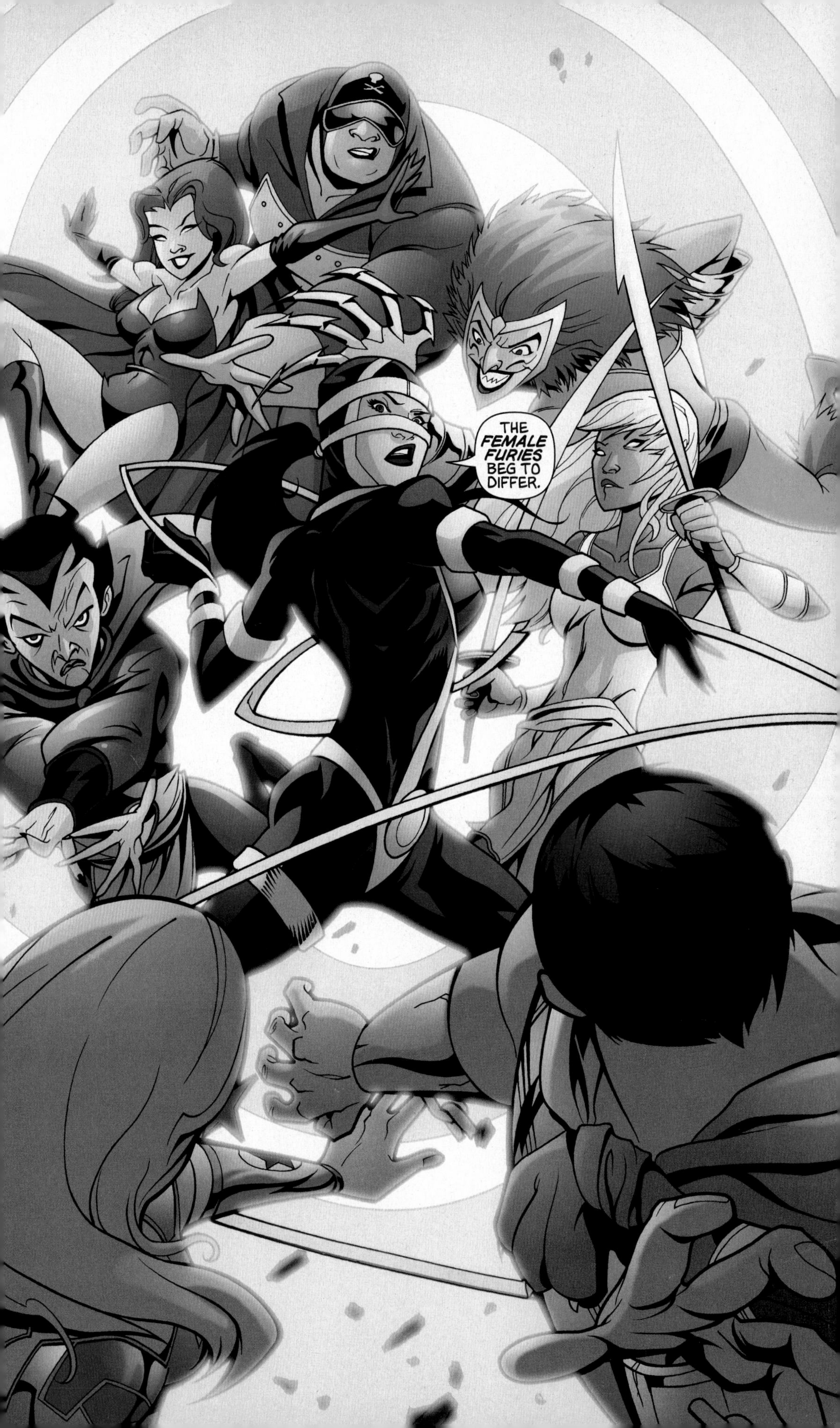
THE FEMALE FURIES BEG TO DIFFER.

Part 3: Furies Unleashed

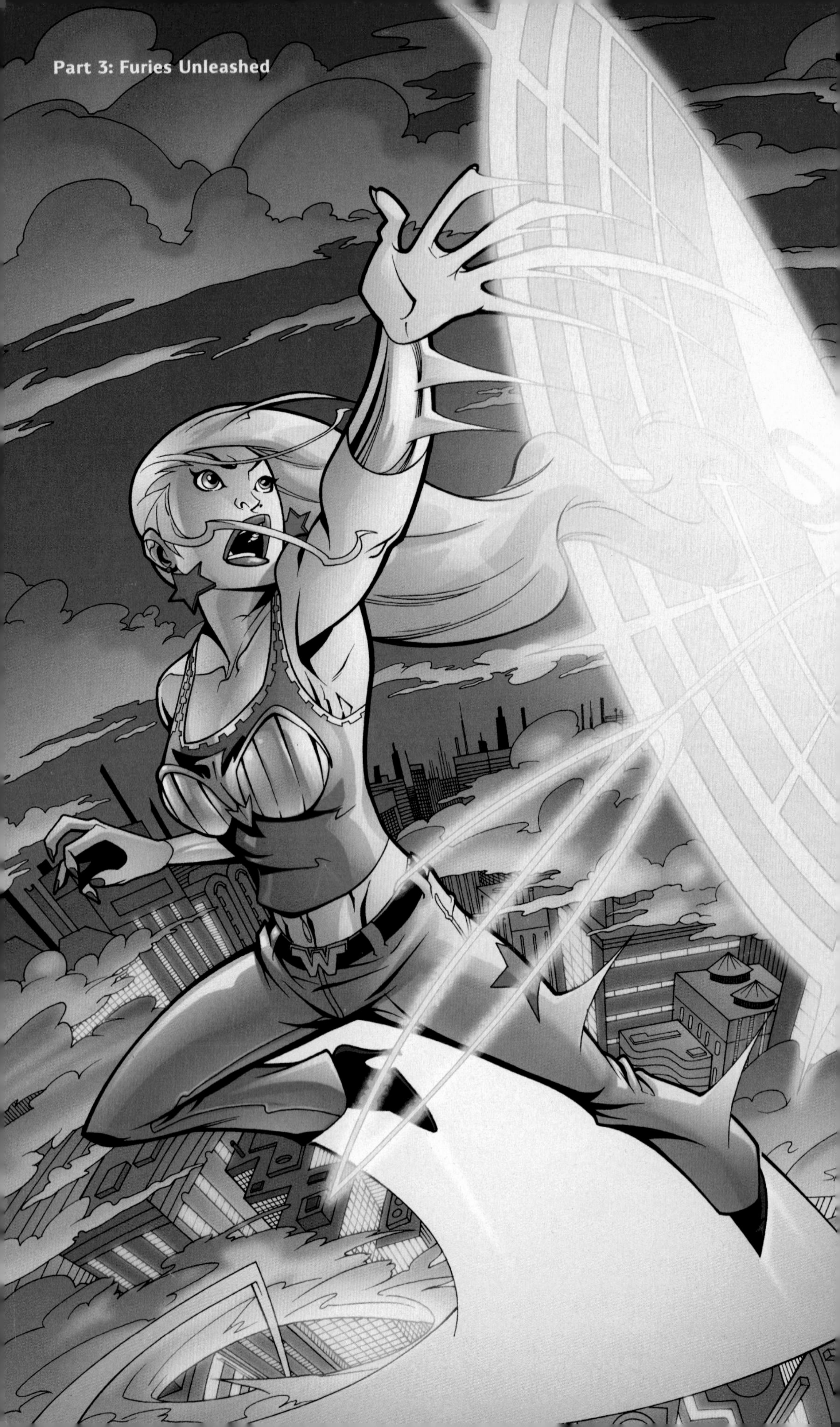

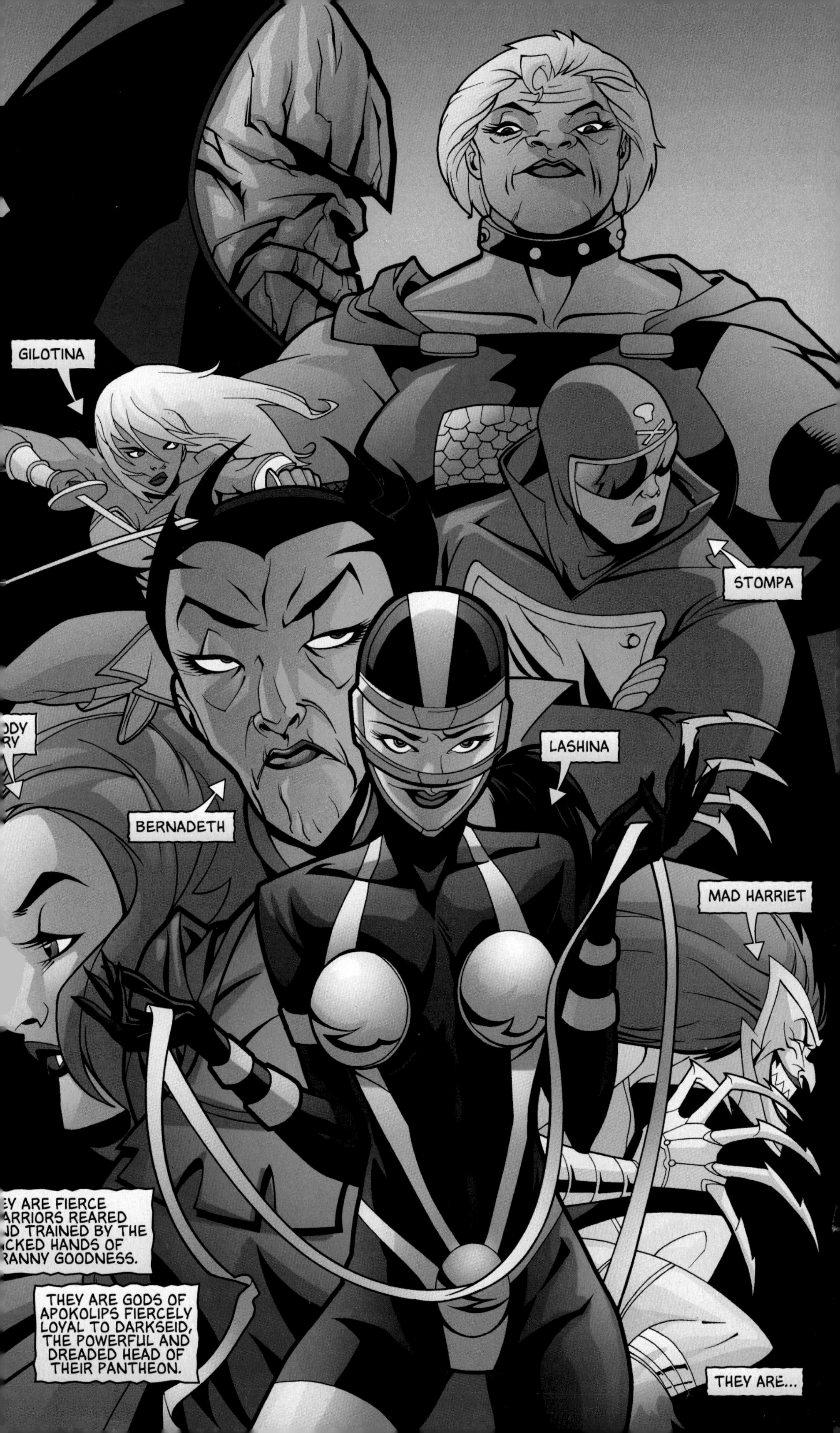
GILOTINA
STOMPA
ODY
RY
BERNADETH
LASHINA
MAD HARRIET
EY ARE FIERCE
ARRIORS REARED
ND TRAINED BY THE
CKED HANDS OF
RANNY GOODNESS.
THEY ARE GODS OF APOKOLIPS FIERCELY LOYAL TO DARKSEID, THE POWERFUL AND DREADED HEAD OF THEIR PANTHEON.
THEY ARE...

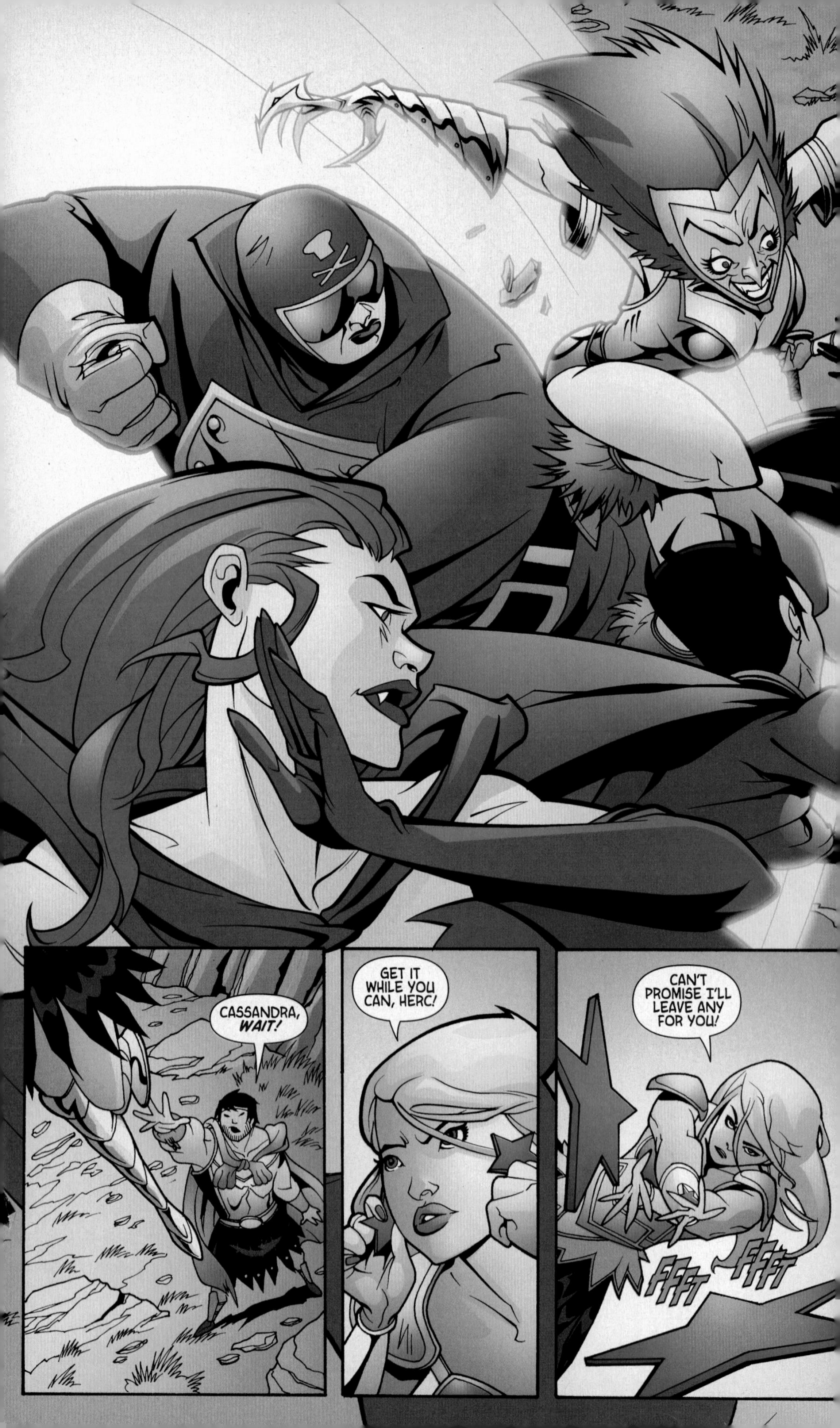
CASSANDRA, WAIT!
GET IT WHILE YOU CAN, HERC!
CAN'T PROMISE I'LL LEAVE ANY FOR YOU!
FFFT
FFFT

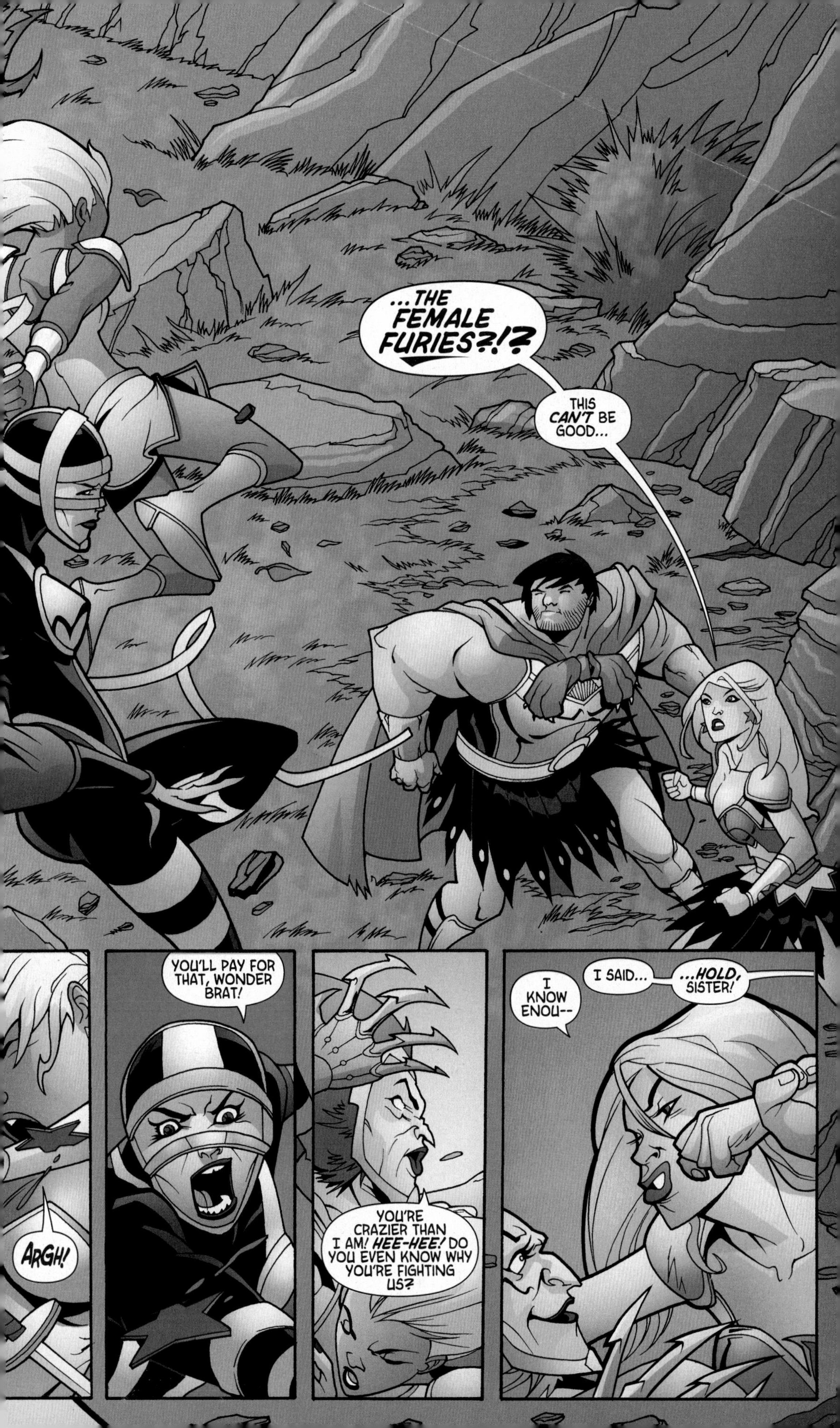
...THE FEMALE FURIES?!?
THIS CAN'T BE GOOD...
ARGH!
YOU'LL PAY FOR THAT, WONDER BRAT!
YOU'RE CRAZIER THAN I AM! HEE-HEE! DO YOU EVEN KNOW WHY YOU'RE FIGHTING US?
I KNOW ENOU--
I SAID...
...HOLD, SISTER!

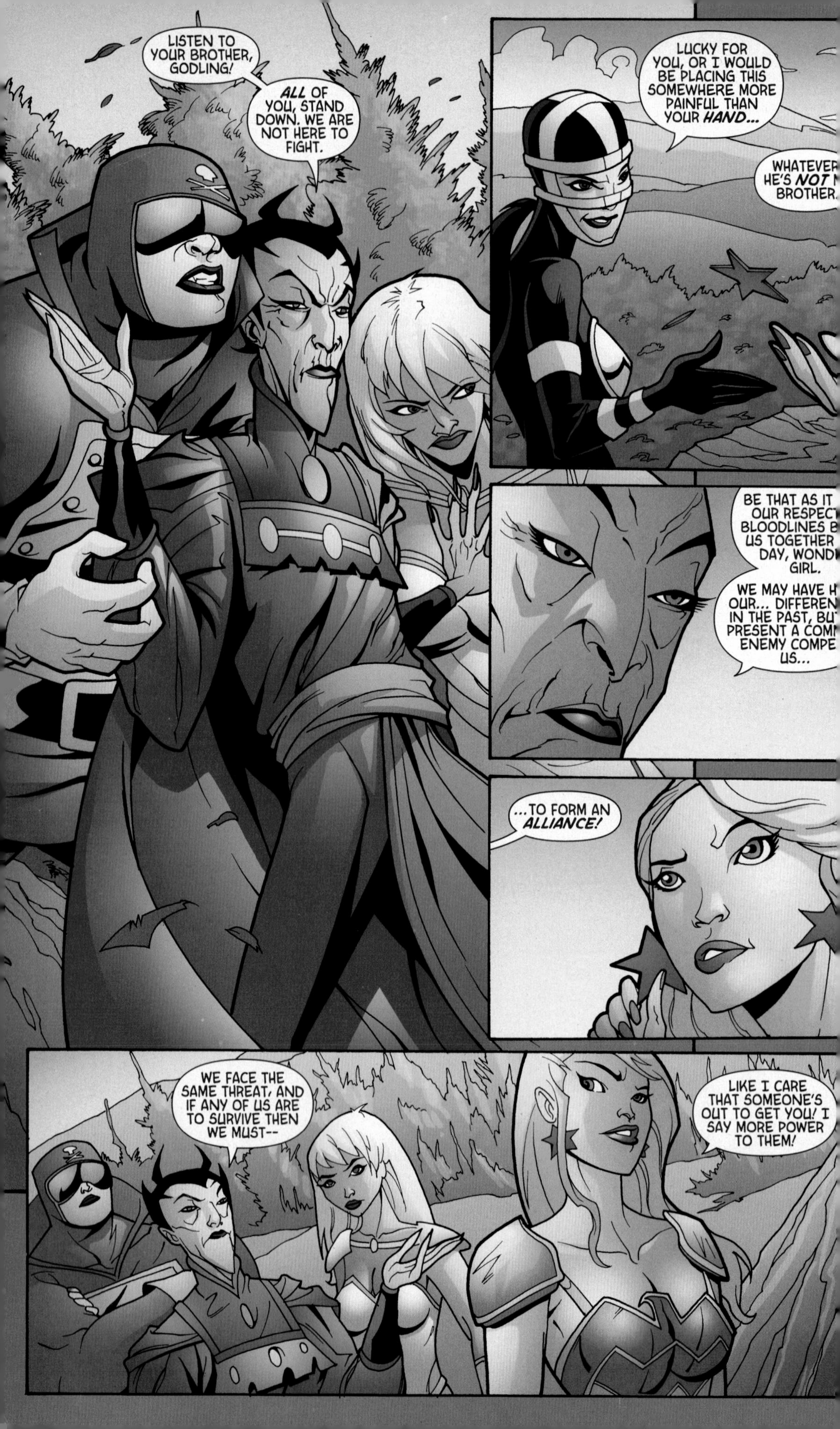
LISTEN TO YOUR BROTHER, GODLING!
ALL OF YOU, STAND DOWN. WE ARE NOT HERE TO FIGHT.
LUCKY FOR YOU, OR I WOULD BE PLACING THIS SOMEWHERE MORE PAINFUL THAN YOUR HAND...
WHATEVER HE'S NOT BROTHER.
BE THAT AS IT OUR RESPECT BLOODLINES B US TOGETHER DAY, WOND GIRL.
WE MAY HAVE H OUR... DIFFEREN IN THE PAST, BU PRESENT A COM ENEMY COMPE US...
...TO FORM AN ALLIANCE!
WE FACE THE SAME THREAT, AND IF ANY OF US ARE TO SURVIVE THEN WE MUST--
LIKE I CARE THAT SOMEONE'S OUT TO GET YOU! I SAY MORE POWER TO THEM!

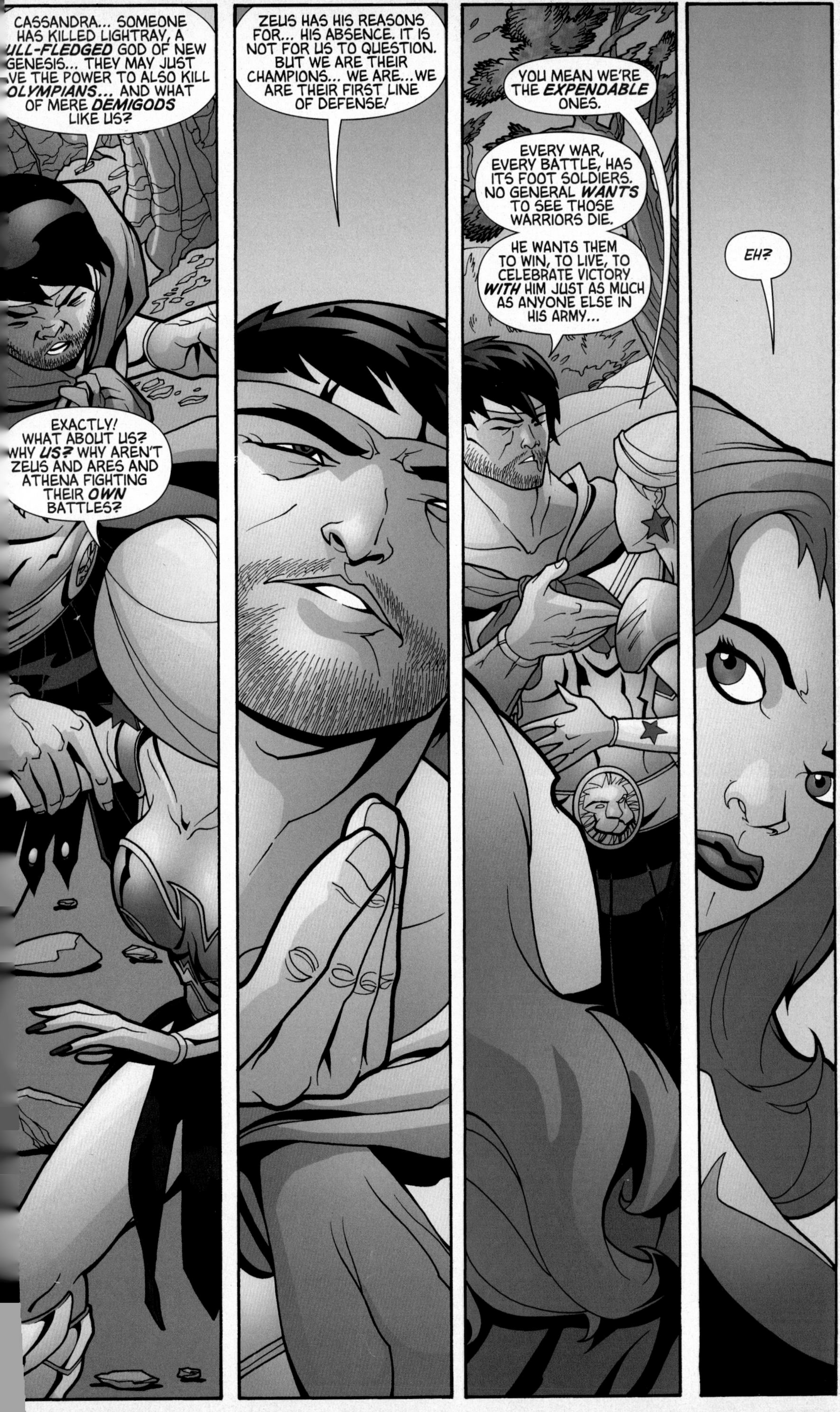
CASSANDRA... SOMEONE HAS KILLED LIGHTRAY, A ULL-FLEDGED GOD OF NEW GENESIS... THEY MAY JUST VE THE POWER TO ALSO KILL OLYMPIANS... AND WHAT OF MERE DEMIGODS LIKE US?
EXACTLY! WHAT ABOUT US? WHY US? WHY AREN'T ZEUS AND ARES AND ATHENA FIGHTING THEIR OWN BATTLES?
ZEUS HAS HIS REASONS FOR... HIS ABSENCE. IT IS NOT FOR US TO QUESTION. BUT WE ARE THEIR CHAMPIONS... WE ARE...WE ARE THEIR FIRST LINE OF DEFENSE!
YOU MEAN WE'RE THE EXPENDABLE ONES.
EVERY WAR, EVERY BATTLE, HAS ITS FOOT SOLDIERS. NO GENERAL WANTS TO SEE THOSE WARRIORS DIE.
HE WANTS THEM TO WIN, TO LIVE, TO CELEBRATE VICTORY WITH HIM JUST AS MUCH AS ANYONE ELSE IN HIS ARMY...
EH?

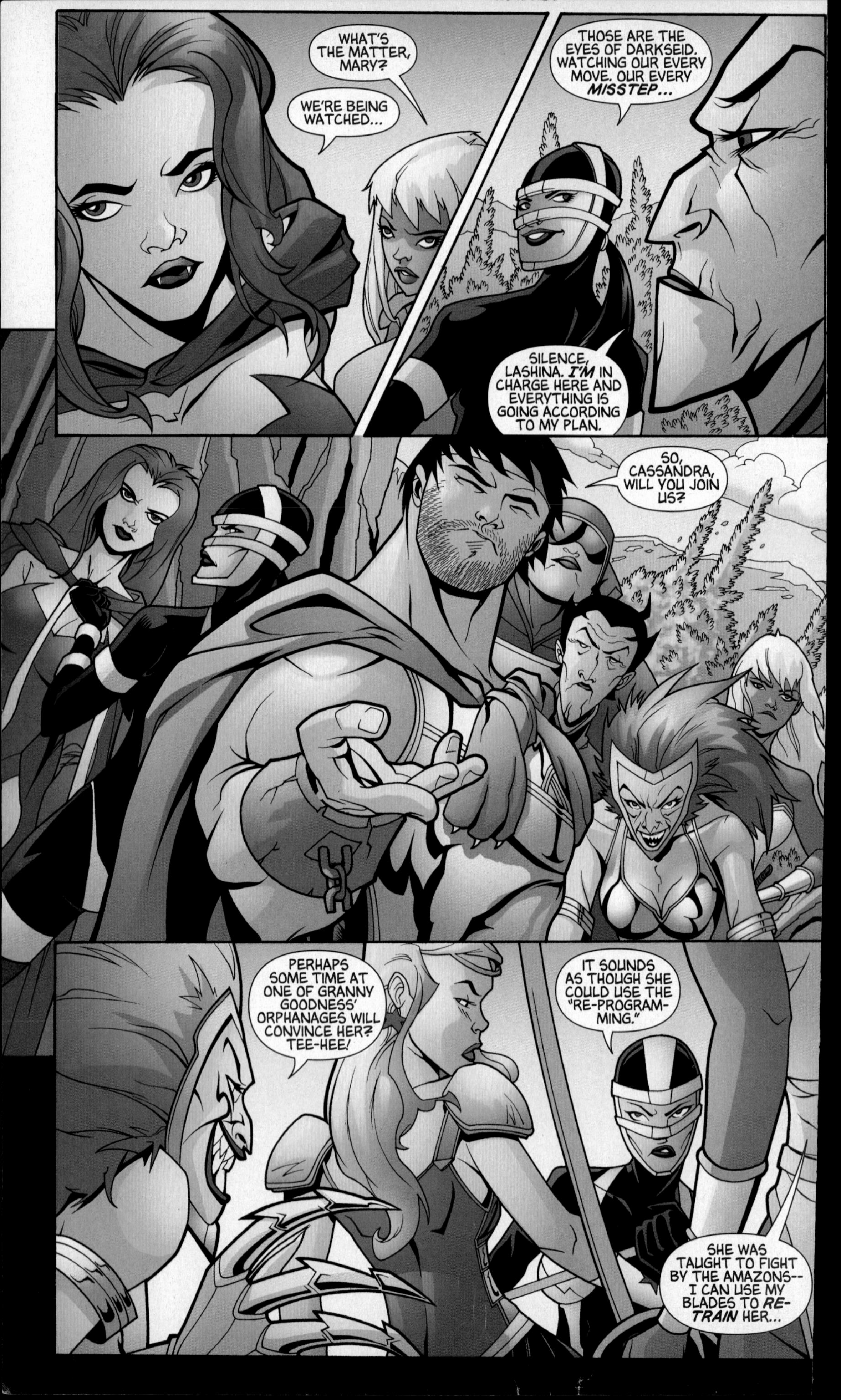
WHAT'S THE MATTER, MARY?
WE'RE BEING WATCHED...
THOSE ARE THE EYES OF DARKSEID. WATCHING OUR EVERY MOVE. OUR EVERY *MISSTEP*...
SILENCE, LASHINA. *I'M* IN CHARGE HERE AND EVERYTHING IS GOING ACCORDING TO MY PLAN.
SO, CASSANDRA, WILL YOU JOIN US?
PERHAPS SOME TIME AT ONE OF GRANNY GOODNESS' ORPHANAGES WILL CONVINCE HER? TEE-HEE!
IT SOUNDS AS THOUGH SHE COULD USE THE "RE-PROGRAMMING."
SHE WAS TAUGHT TO FIGHT BY THE AMAZONS-- I CAN USE MY BLADES TO *RE-TRAIN* HER...

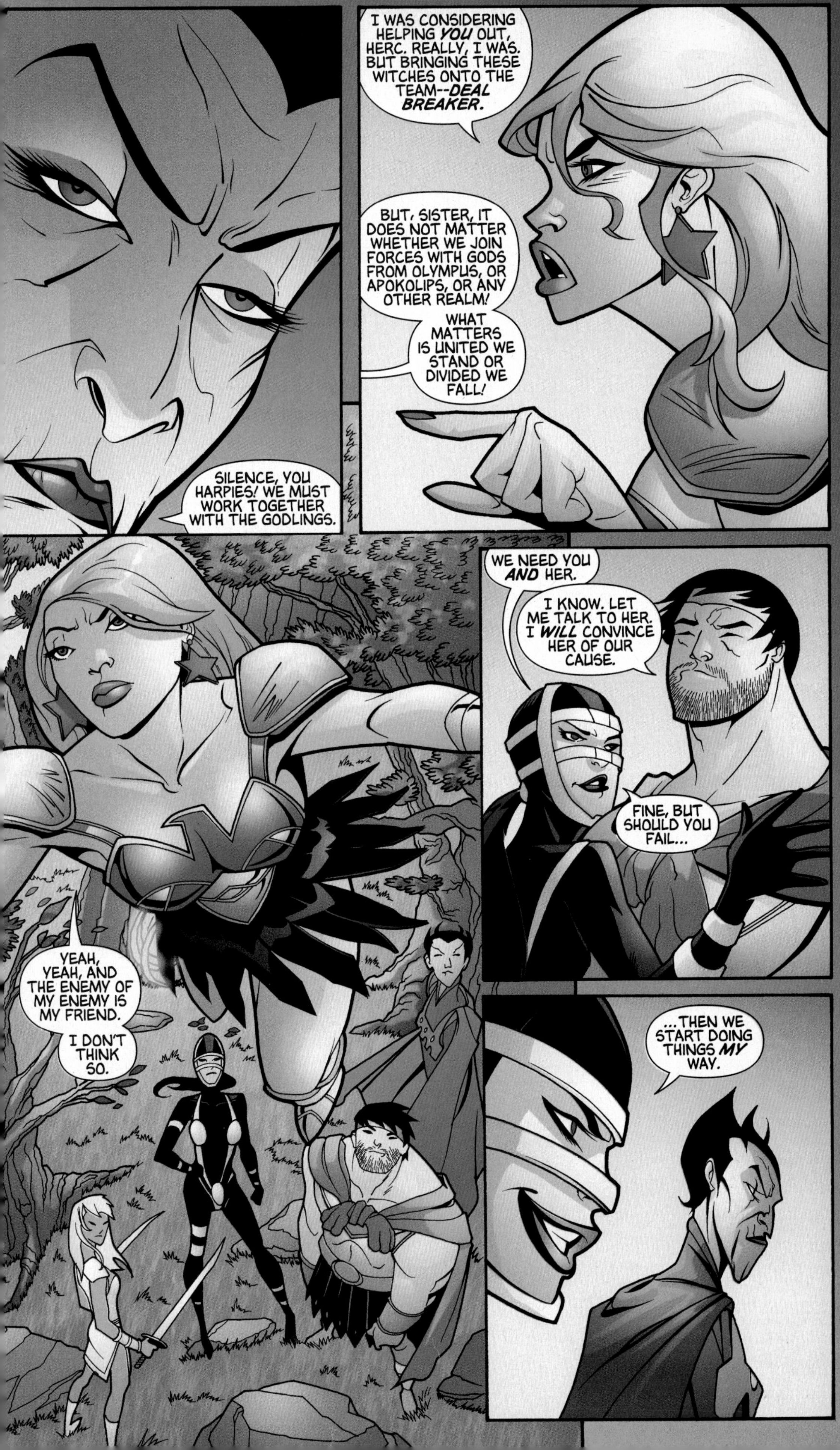
I WAS CONSIDERING HELPING YOU OUT, HERC. REALLY, I WAS. BUT BRINGING THESE WITCHES ONTO THE TEAM--DEAL BREAKER.
BUT, SISTER, IT DOES NOT MATTER WHETHER WE JOIN FORCES WITH GODS FROM OLYMPUS, OR APOKOLIPS, OR ANY OTHER REALM!
WHAT MATTERS IS UNITED WE STAND OR DIVIDED WE FALL!
SILENCE, YOU HARPIES! WE MUST WORK TOGETHER WITH THE GODLINGS.
YEAH, YEAH, AND THE ENEMY OF MY ENEMY IS MY FRIEND.
I DON'T THINK SO.
WE NEED YOU AND HER.
I KNOW. LET ME TALK TO HER. I WILL CONVINCE HER OF OUR CAUSE.
FINE, BUT SHOULD YOU FAIL...
...THEN WE START DOING THINGS MY WAY.

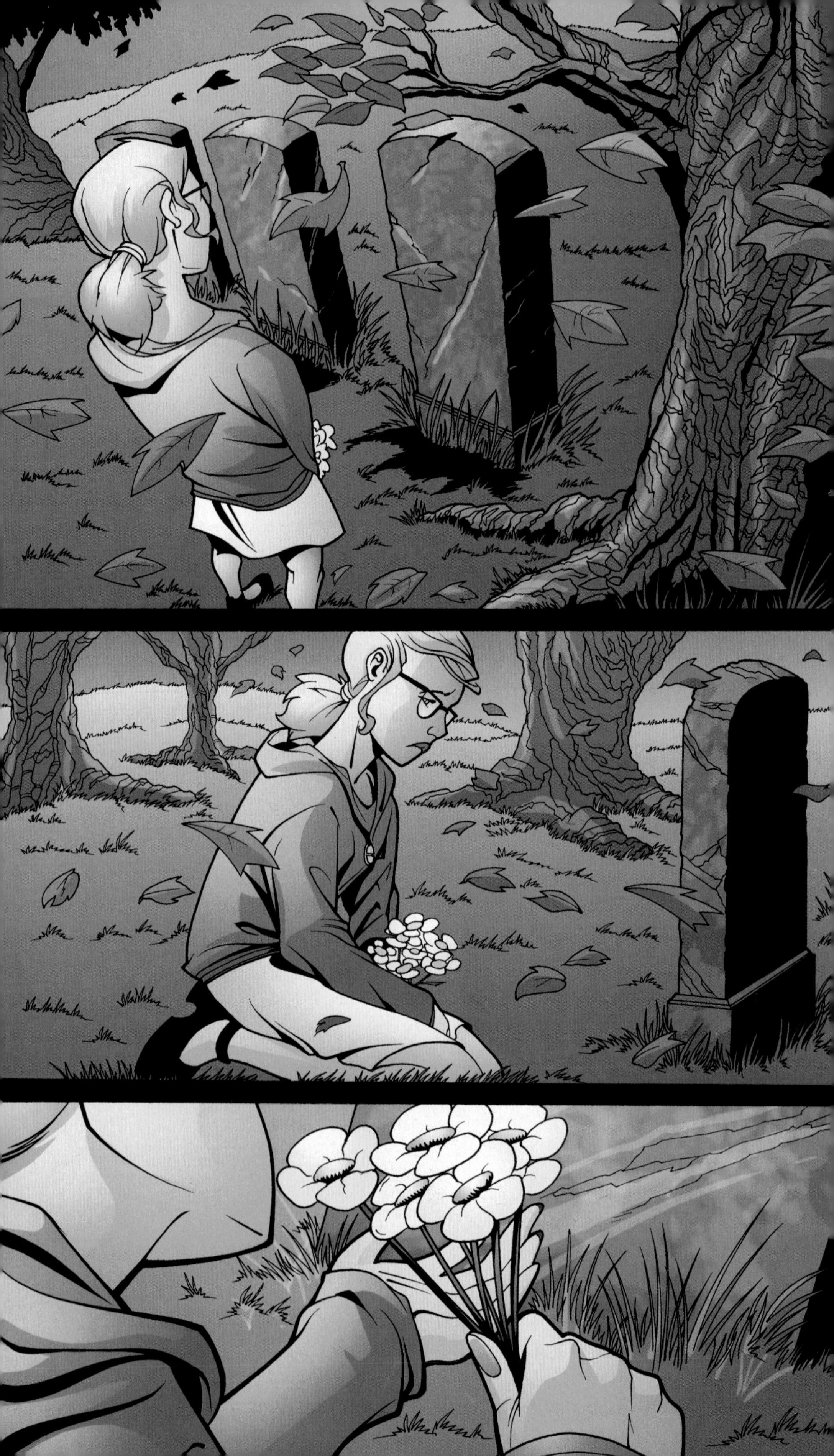

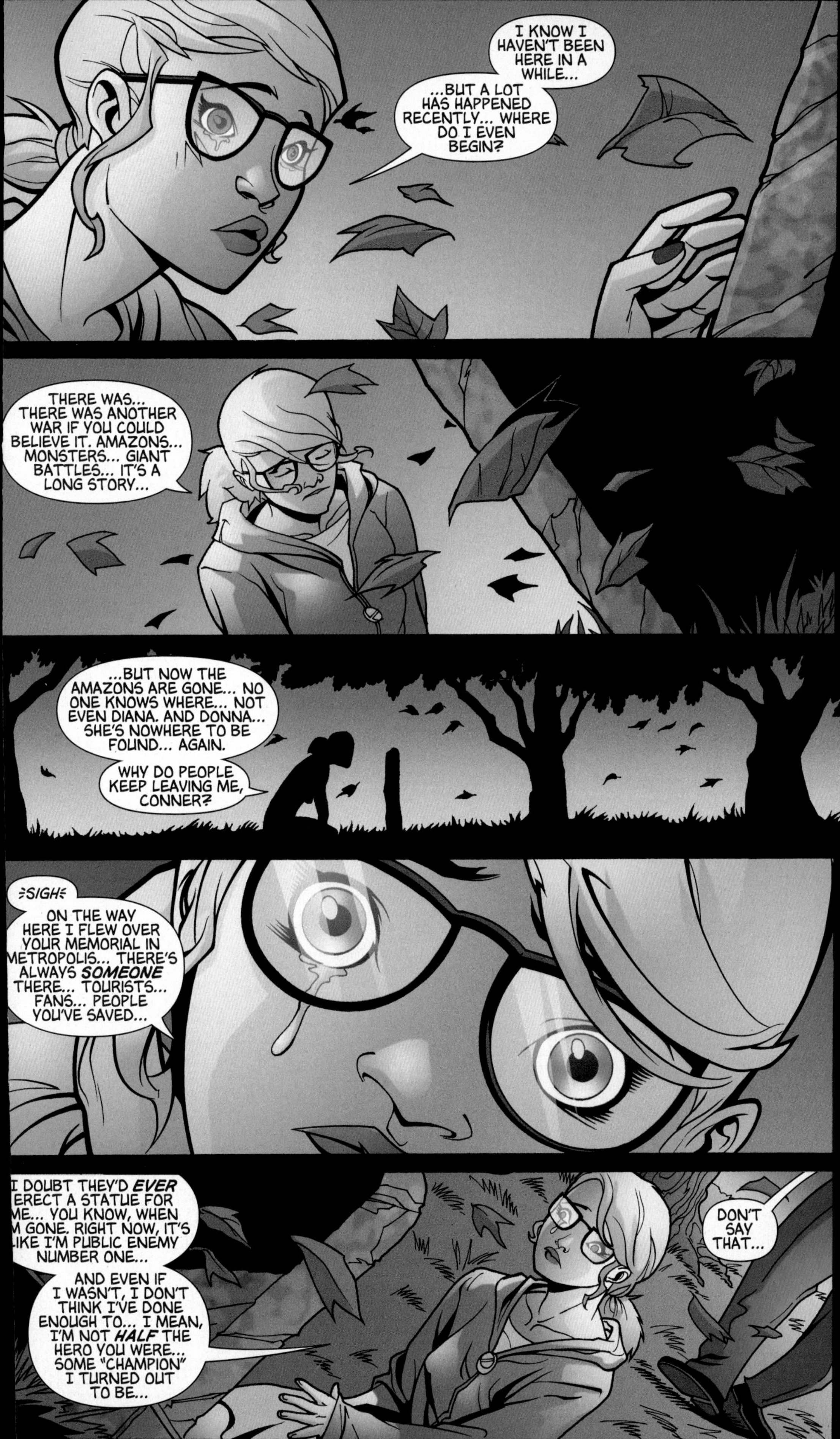
I KNOW I HAVEN'T BEEN HERE IN A WHILE...
...BUT A LOT HAS HAPPENED RECENTLY... WHERE DO I EVEN BEGIN?
THERE WAS... THERE WAS ANOTHER WAR IF YOU COULD BELIEVE IT. AMAZONS... MONSTERS... GIANT BATTLES... IT'S A LONG STORY...
...BUT NOW THE AMAZONS ARE GONE... NO ONE KNOWS WHERE... NOT EVEN DIANA. AND DONNA... SHE'S NOWHERE TO BE FOUND... AGAIN.
WHY DO PEOPLE KEEP LEAVING ME, CONNER?
SIGH
ON THE WAY HERE I FLEW OVER YOUR MEMORIAL IN METROPOLIS... THERE'S ALWAYS SOMEONE THERE... TOURISTS... FANS... PEOPLE YOU'VE SAVED...
I DOUBT THEY'D EVER ERECT A STATUE FOR ME... YOU KNOW, WHEN I'M GONE. RIGHT NOW, IT'S LIKE I'M PUBLIC ENEMY NUMBER ONE...
AND EVEN IF I WASN'T, I DON'T THINK I'VE DONE ENOUGH TO... I MEAN, I'M NOT HALF THE HERO YOU WERE... SOME "CHAMPION" I TURNED OUT TO BE...
DON'T SAY THAT...

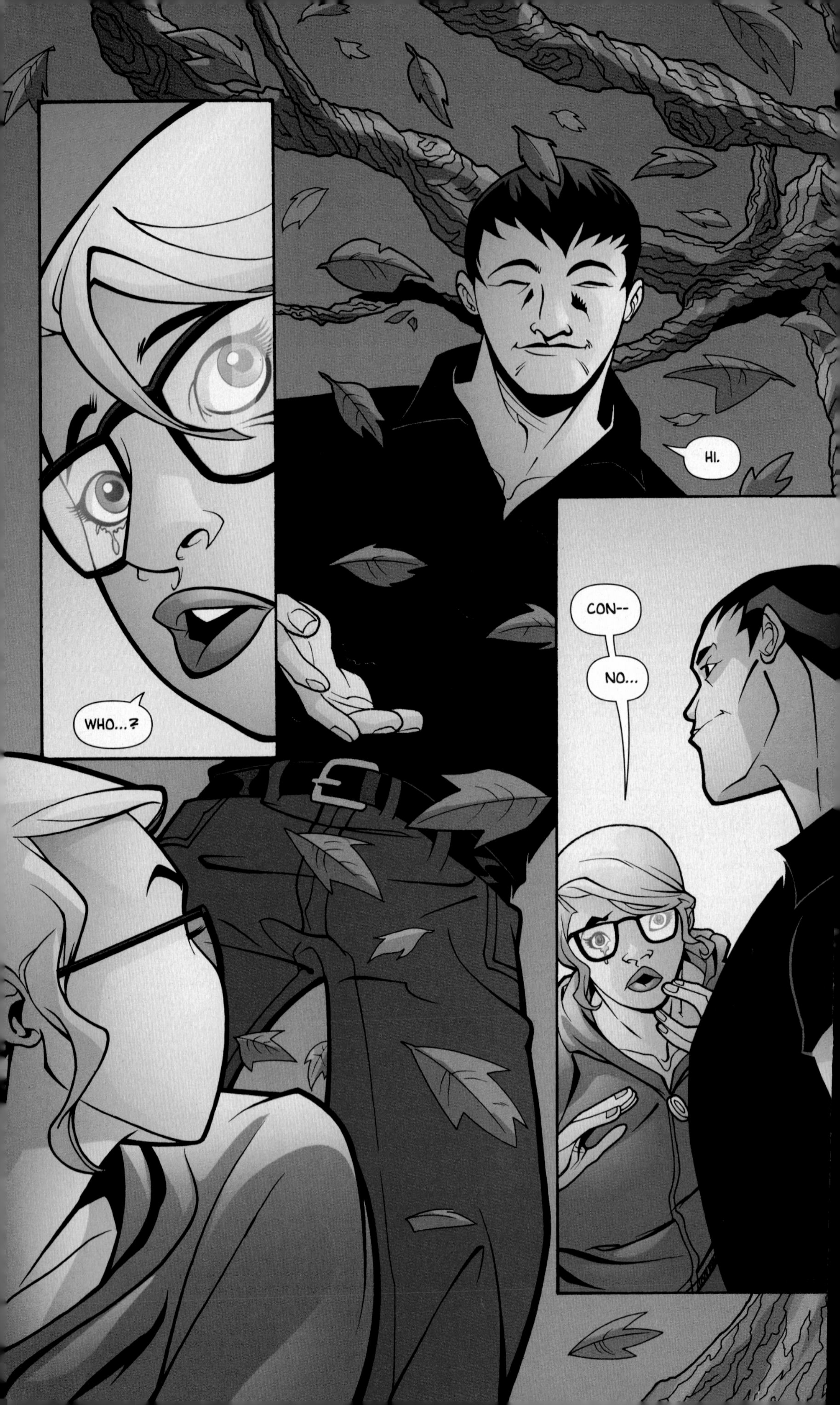
HI.
WHO...?
CON--
NO...

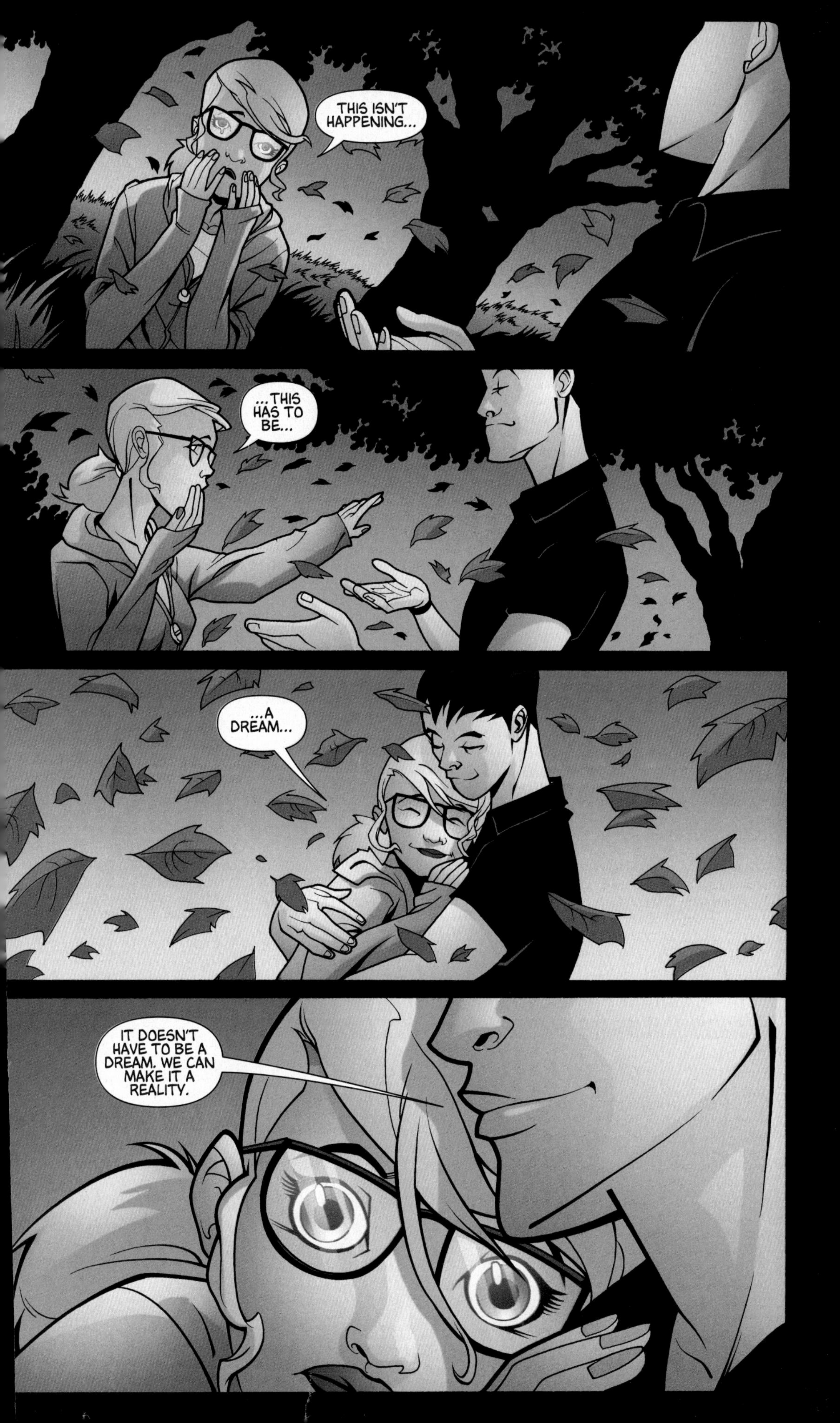
THIS ISN'T HAPPENING...
...THIS HAS TO BE...
...A DREAM...
IT DOESN'T HAVE TO BE A DREAM. WE CAN MAKE IT A REALITY.

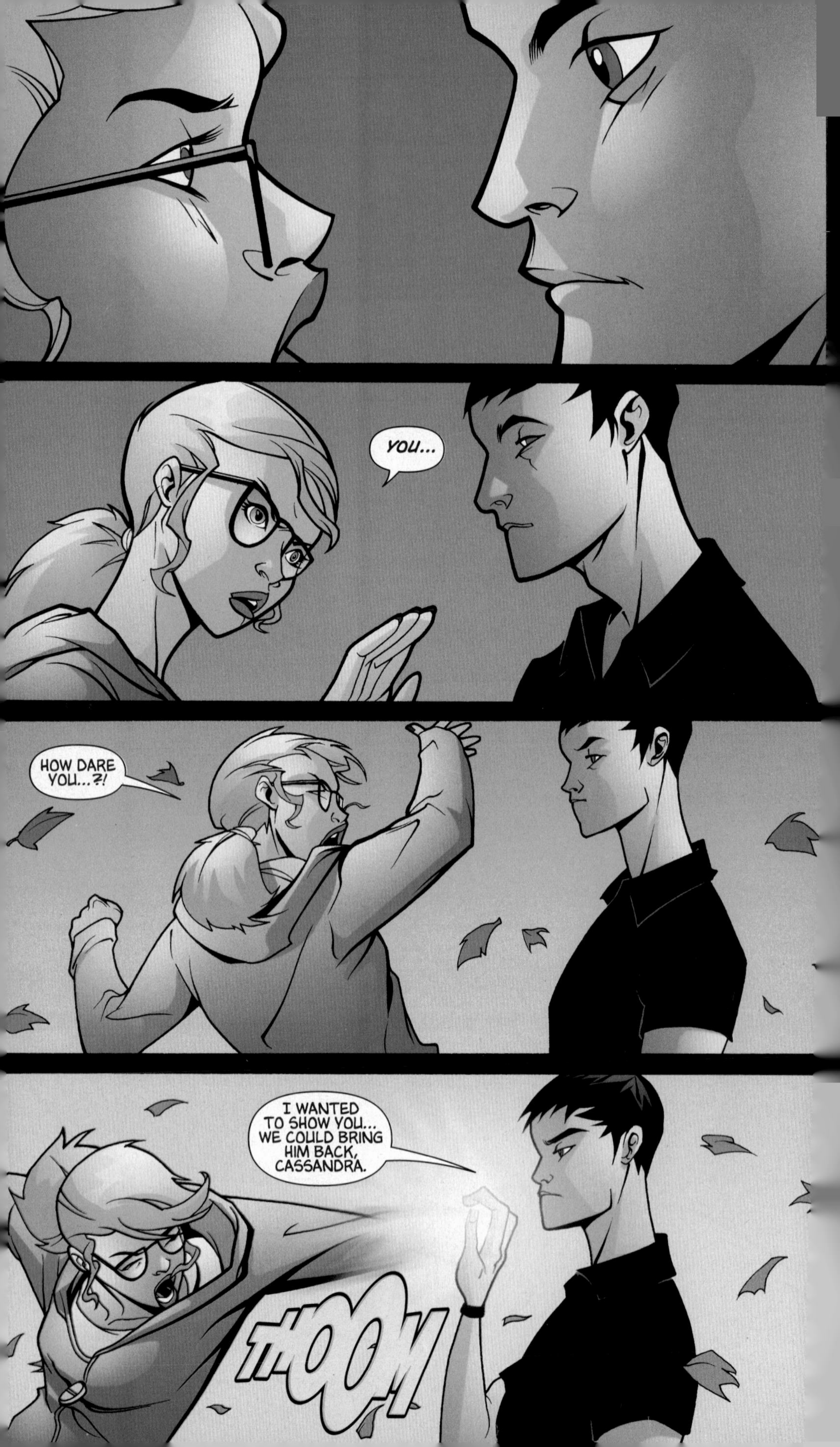
YOU...
HOW DARE YOU...?!
I WANTED TO SHOW YOU... WE COULD BRING HIM BACK, CASSANDRA.
THOOM

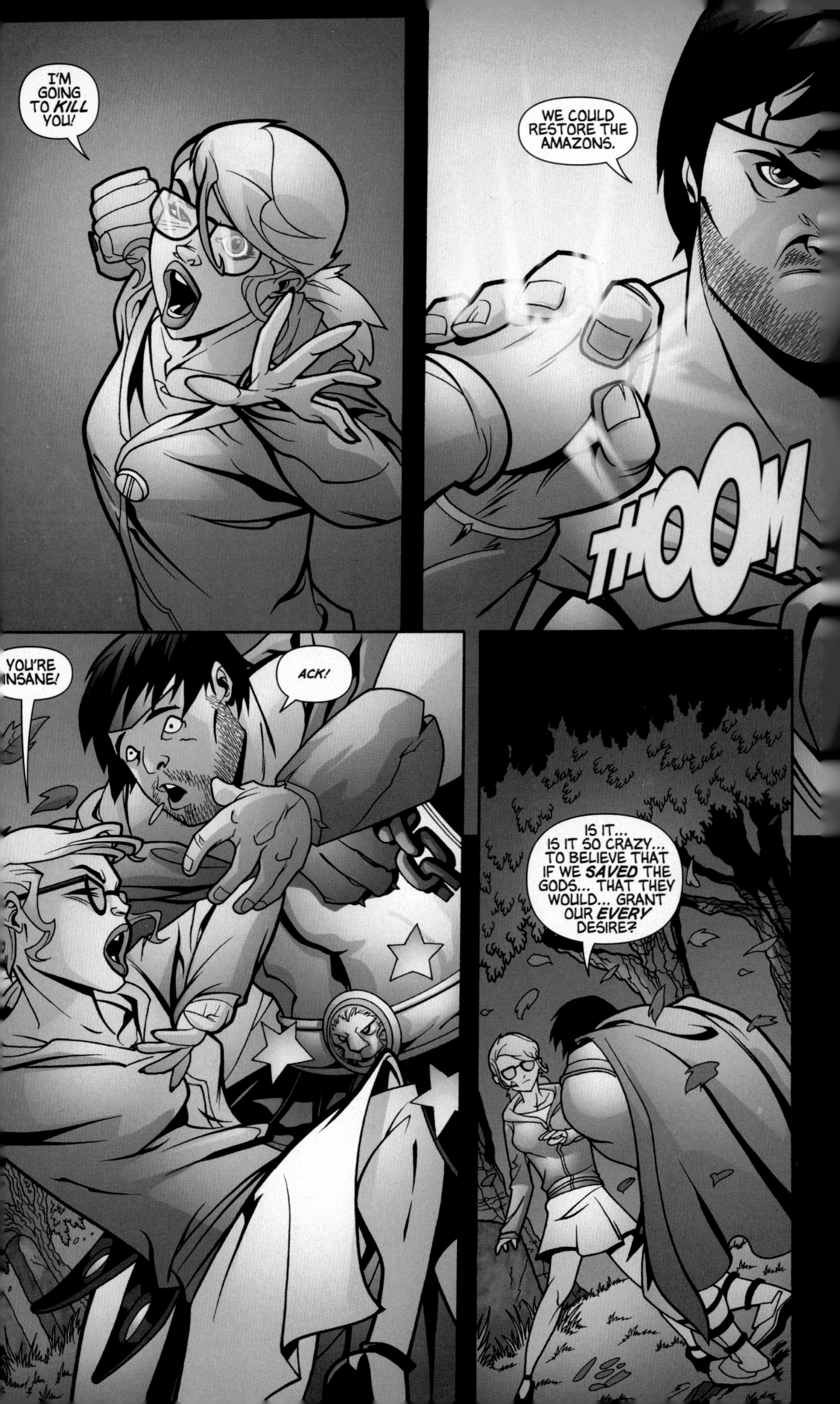
I'M GOING TO *KILL* YOU!
WE COULD RESTORE THE AMAZONS.
THOOM
YOU'RE INSANE!
ACK!
IS IT... IS IT SO CRAZY... TO BELIEVE THAT IF WE *SAVED* THE GODS... THAT THEY WOULD... GRANT OUR *EVERY* DESIRE?

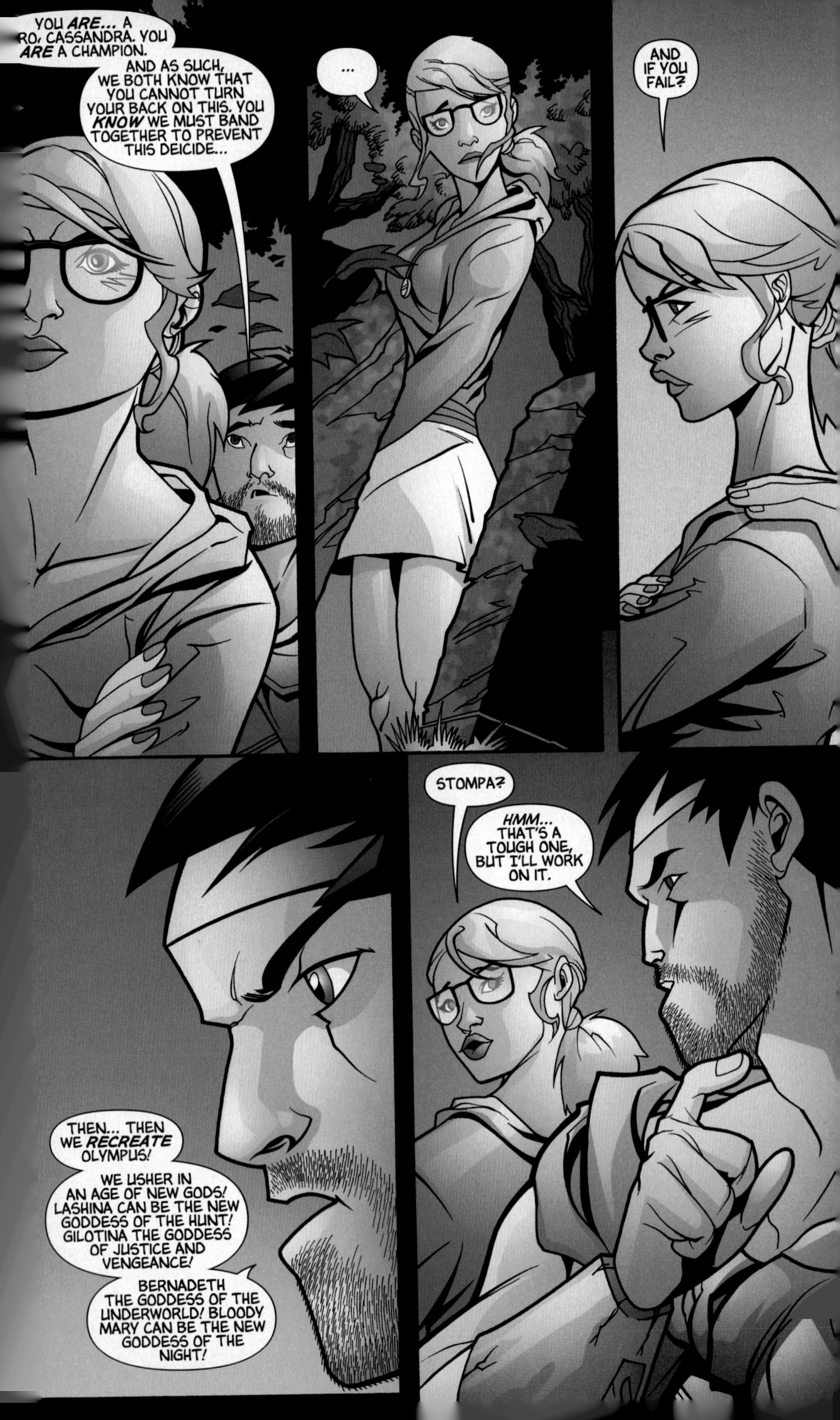
YOU *ARE*... A
RO, CASSANDRA. YOU *ARE* A CHAMPION.
AND AS SUCH, WE BOTH KNOW THAT YOU CANNOT TURN YOUR BACK ON THIS. YOU *KNOW* WE MUST BAND TOGETHER TO PREVENT THIS DEICIDE...
...
AND IF YOU FAIL?
THEN... THEN WE *RECREATE* OLYMPUS!
WE USHER IN AN AGE OF NEW GODS! LASHINA CAN BE THE NEW GODDESS OF THE HUNT! GILOTINA THE GODDESS OF JUSTICE AND VENGEANCE!
BERNADETH THE GODDESS OF THE UNDERWORLD! BLOODY MARY CAN BE THE NEW GODDESS OF THE NIGHT!
STOMPA?
HMM... THAT'S A TOUGH ONE, BUT I'LL WORK ON IT.

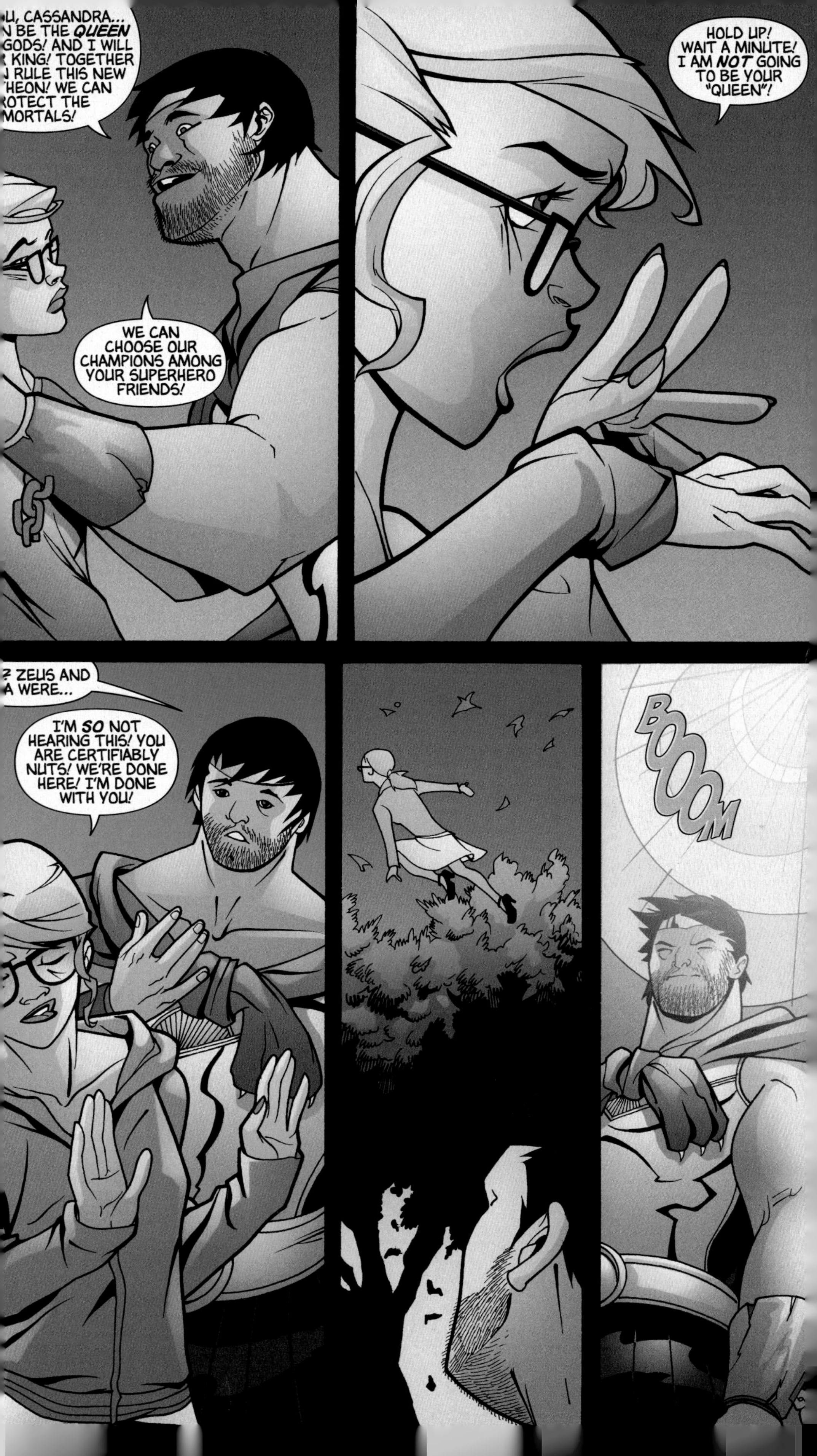

U, CASSANDRA... N BE THE QUEEN GODS! AND I WILL R KING! TOGETHER N RULE THIS NEW THEON! WE CAN ROTECT THE MORTALS!
WE CAN CHOOSE OUR CHAMPIONS AMONG YOUR SUPERHERO FRIENDS!
HOLD UP! WAIT A MINUTE! I AM NOT GOING TO BE YOUR "QUEEN"!
ZEUS AND A WERE...
I'M SO NOT HEARING THIS! YOU ARE CERTIFIABLY NUTS! WE'RE DONE HERE! I'M DONE WITH YOU!
BOOOM

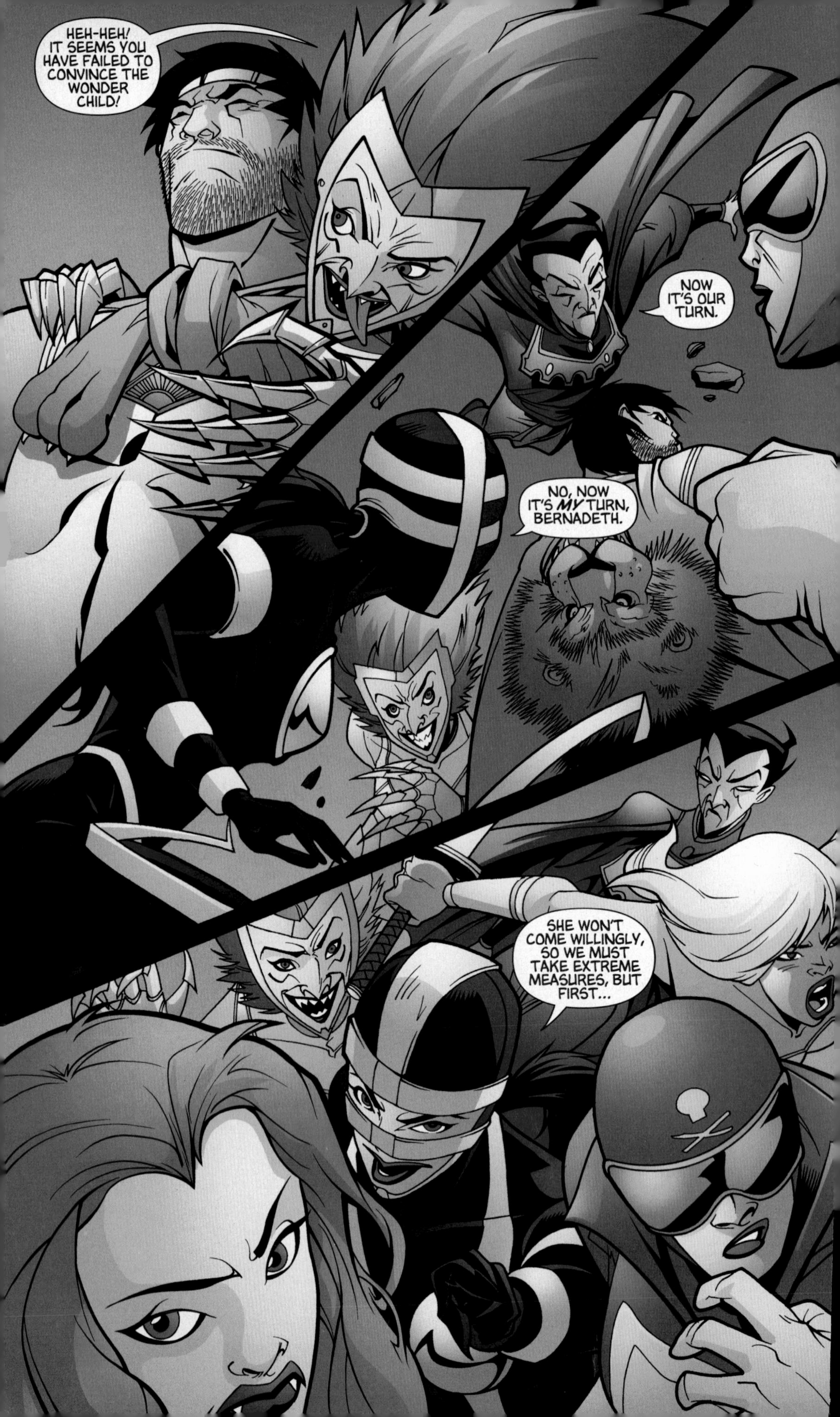
HEH-HEH! IT SEEMS YOU HAVE FAILED TO CONVINCE THE WONDER CHILD!
NOW IT'S OUR TURN.
NO, NOW IT'S *MY* TURN, BERNADETH.
SHE WON'T COME WILLINGLY, SO WE MUST TAKE EXTREME MEASURES, BUT FIRST...

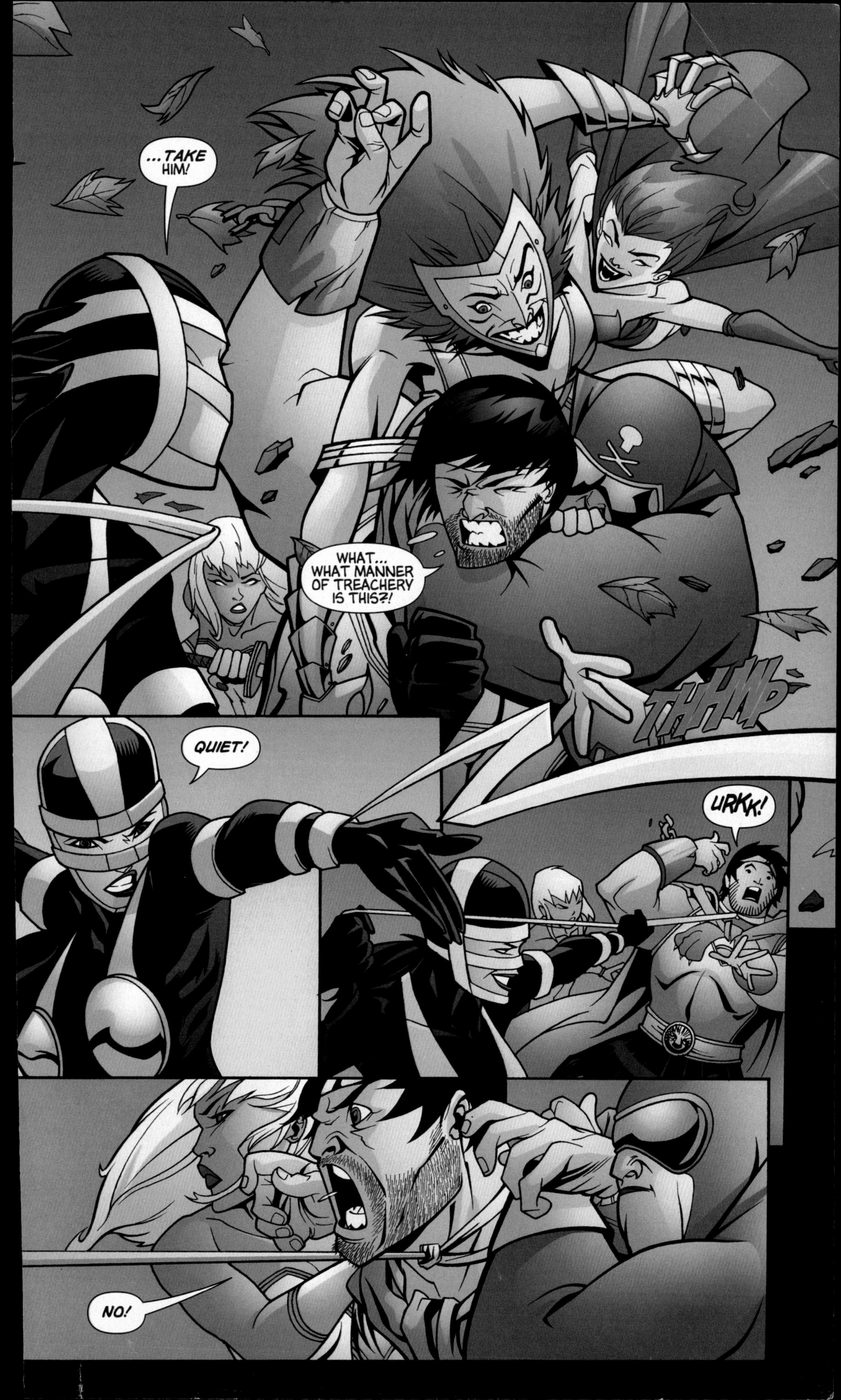
...TAKE HIM!
WHAT... WHAT MANNER OF TREACHERY IS THIS?!
THHMP
QUIET!
URKK!
NO!

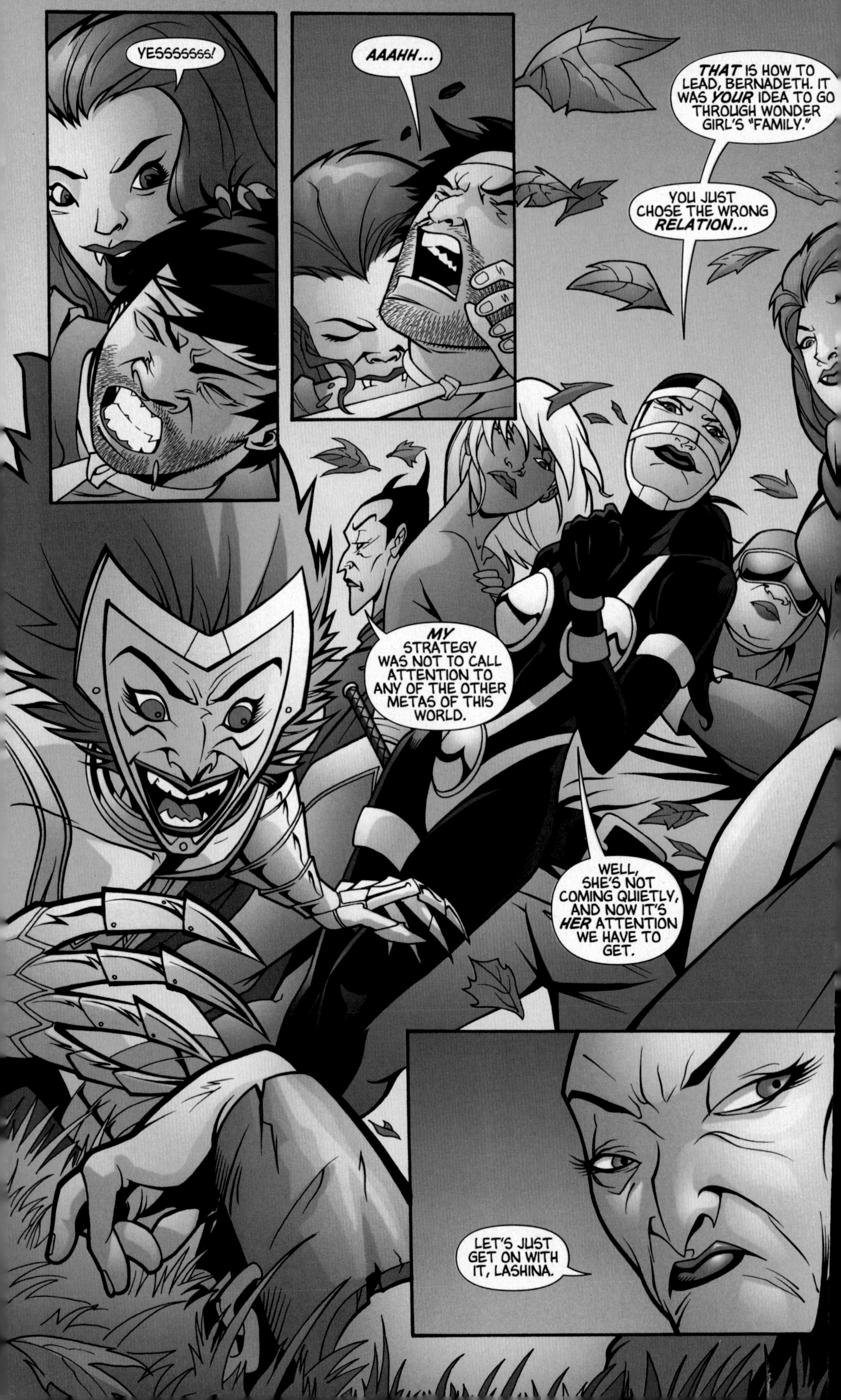
YESSSSSSS!
AAAHH...
THAT IS HOW TO LEAD, BERNADETH. IT WAS YOUR IDEA TO GO THROUGH WONDER GIRL'S "FAMILY."
YOU JUST CHOSE THE WRONG RELATION...
MY STRATEGY WAS NOT TO CALL ATTENTION TO ANY OF THE OTHER METAS OF THIS WORLD.
WELL, SHE'S NOT COMING QUIETLY, AND NOW IT'S HER ATTENTION WE HAVE TO GET.
LET'S JUST GET ON WITH IT, LASHINA.

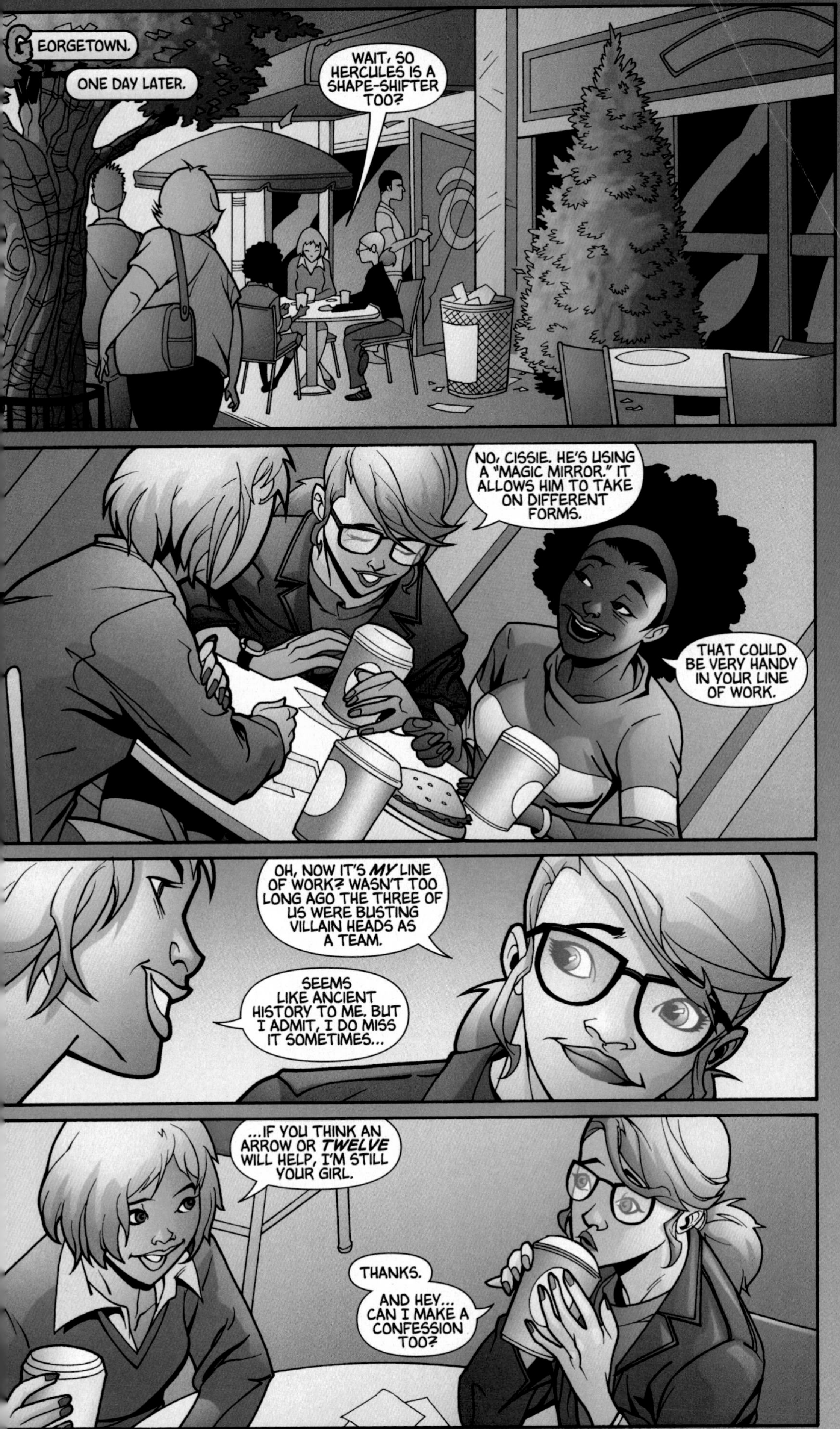
GEORGETOWN.
ONE DAY LATER.
WAIT, SO HERCULES IS A SHAPE-SHIFTER TOO?
NO, CISSIE. HE'S USING A "MAGIC MIRROR." IT ALLOWS HIM TO TAKE ON DIFFERENT FORMS.
THAT COULD BE VERY HANDY IN YOUR LINE OF WORK.
OH, NOW IT'S MY LINE OF WORK? WASN'T TOO LONG AGO THE THREE OF US WERE BUSTING VILLAIN HEADS AS A TEAM.
SEEMS LIKE ANCIENT HISTORY TO ME. BUT I ADMIT, I DO MISS IT SOMETIMES...
...IF YOU THINK AN ARROW OR TWELVE WILL HELP, I'M STILL YOUR GIRL.
THANKS.
AND HEY... CAN I MAKE A CONFESSION TOO?

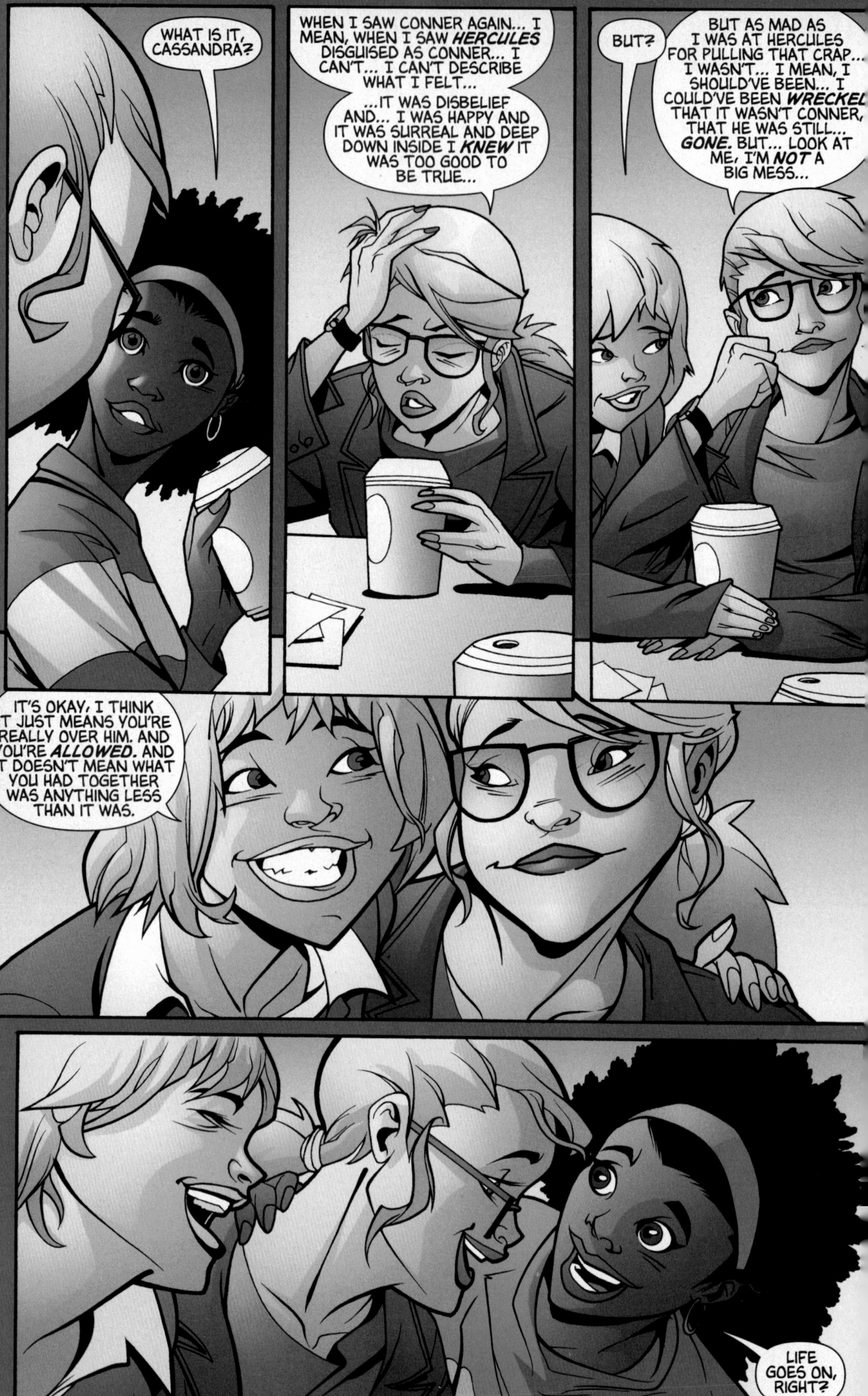
WHAT IS IT, CASSANDRA?
WHEN I SAW CONNER AGAIN... I MEAN, WHEN I SAW HERCULES DISGUISED AS CONNER... I CAN'T... I CAN'T DESCRIBE WHAT I FELT...
...IT WAS DISBELIEF AND... I WAS HAPPY AND IT WAS SURREAL AND DEEP DOWN INSIDE I KNEW IT WAS TOO GOOD TO BE TRUE...
BUT?
BUT AS MAD AS I WAS AT HERCULES FOR PULLING THAT CRAP... I WASN'T... I MEAN, I SHOULD'VE BEEN... I COULD'VE BEEN WRECKED THAT IT WASN'T CONNER, THAT HE WAS STILL... GONE. BUT... LOOK AT ME, I'M NOT A BIG MESS...
IT'S OKAY, I THINK IT JUST MEANS YOU'RE REALLY OVER HIM. AND YOU'RE ALLOWED. AND IT DOESN'T MEAN WHAT YOU HAD TOGETHER WAS ANYTHING LESS THAN IT WAS.
LIFE GOES ON, RIGHT?

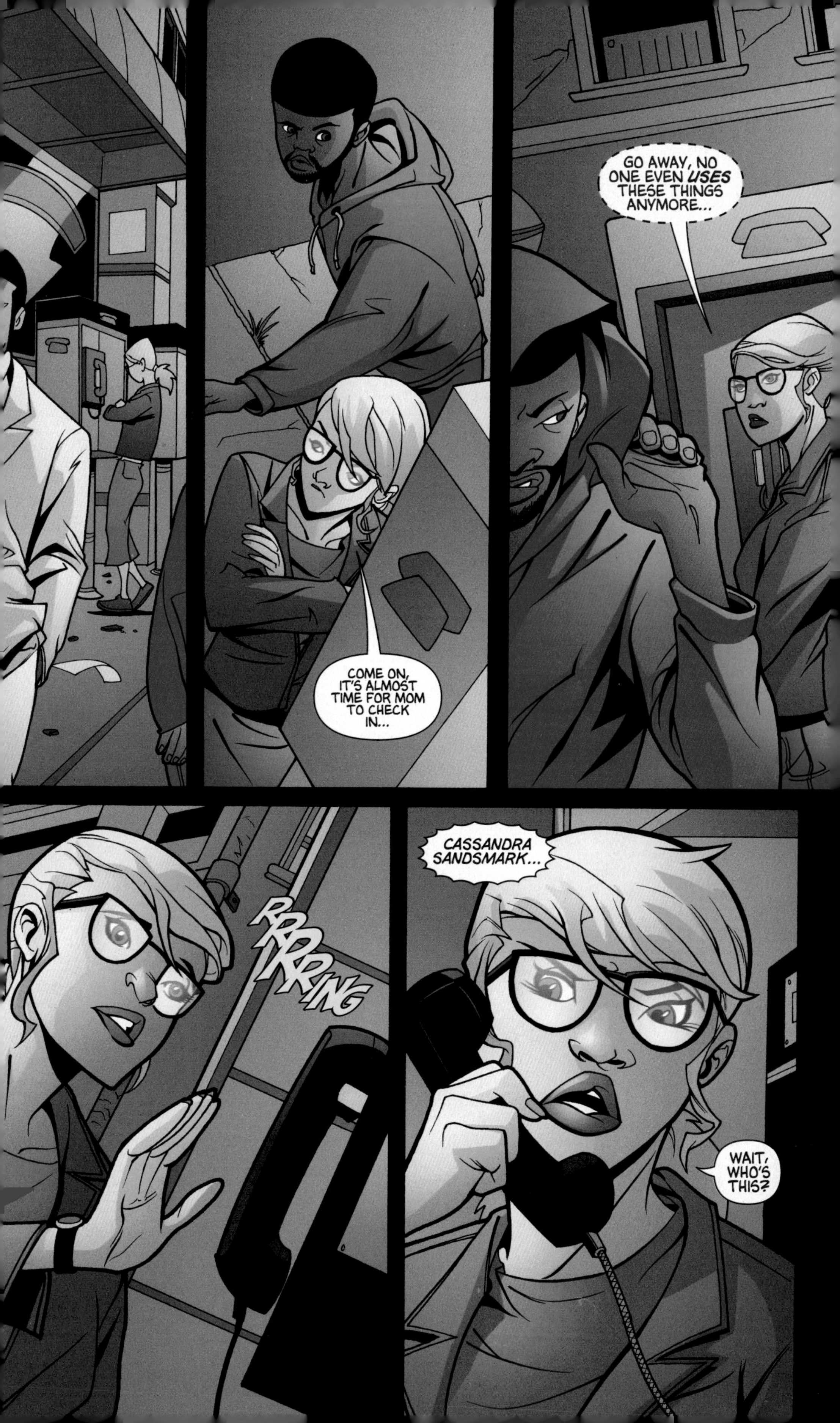
COME ON, IT'S ALMOST TIME FOR MOM TO CHECK IN...
GO AWAY, NO ONE EVEN USES THESE THINGS ANYMORE...
RRRRING
CASSANDRA SANDSMARK...
WAIT, WHO'S THIS?

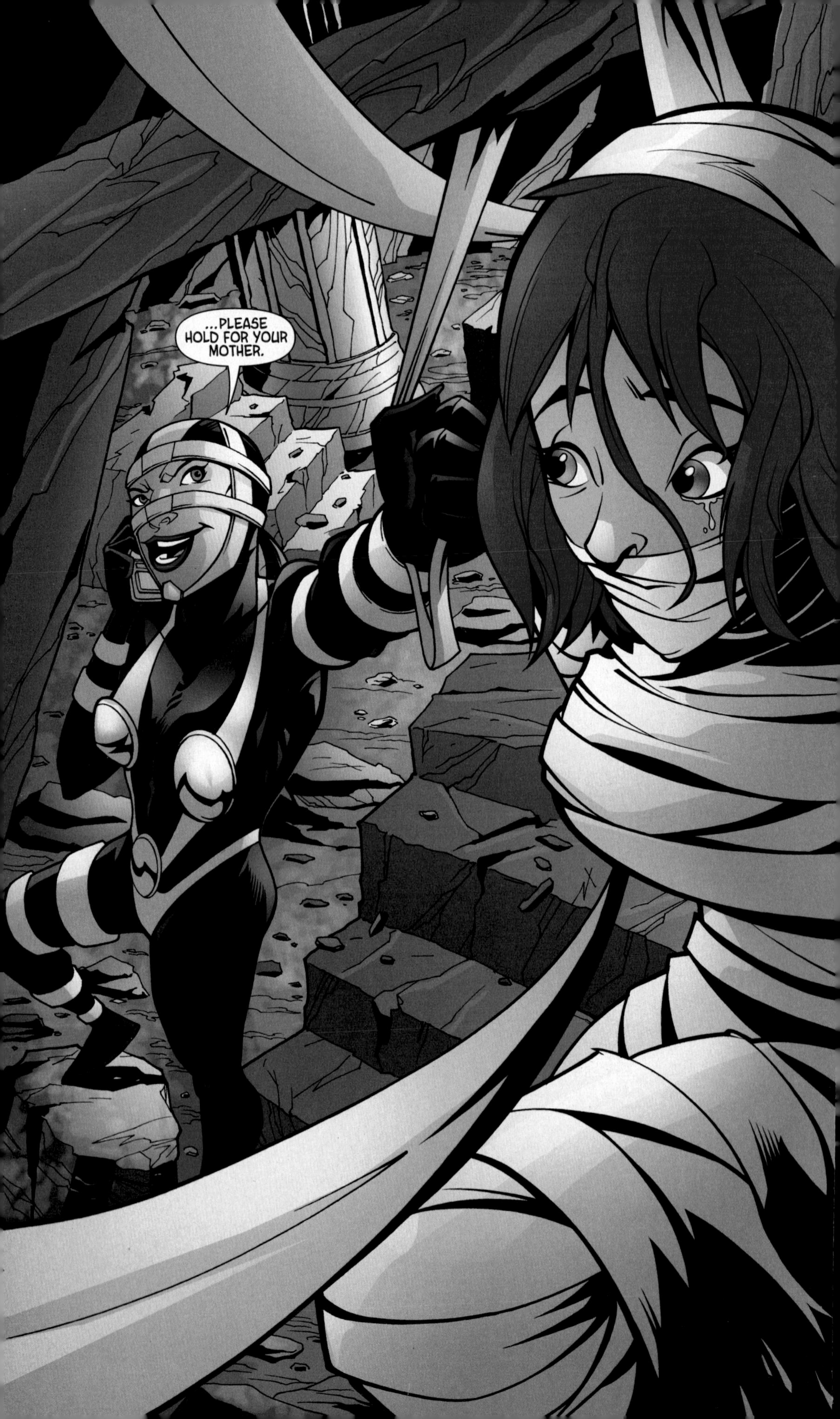
...PLEASE HOLD FOR YOUR MOTHER.

art 4: Enter the Olympian

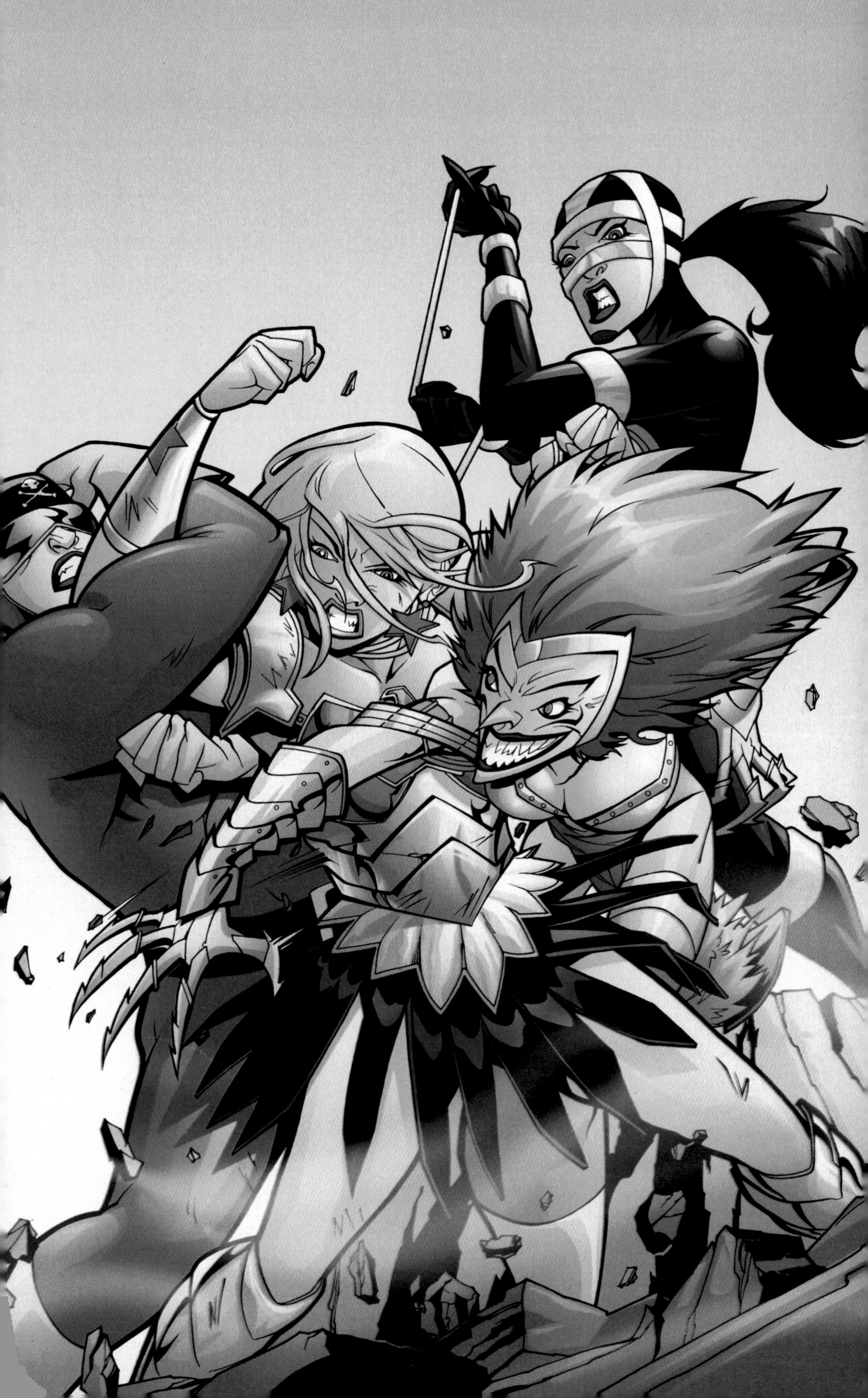

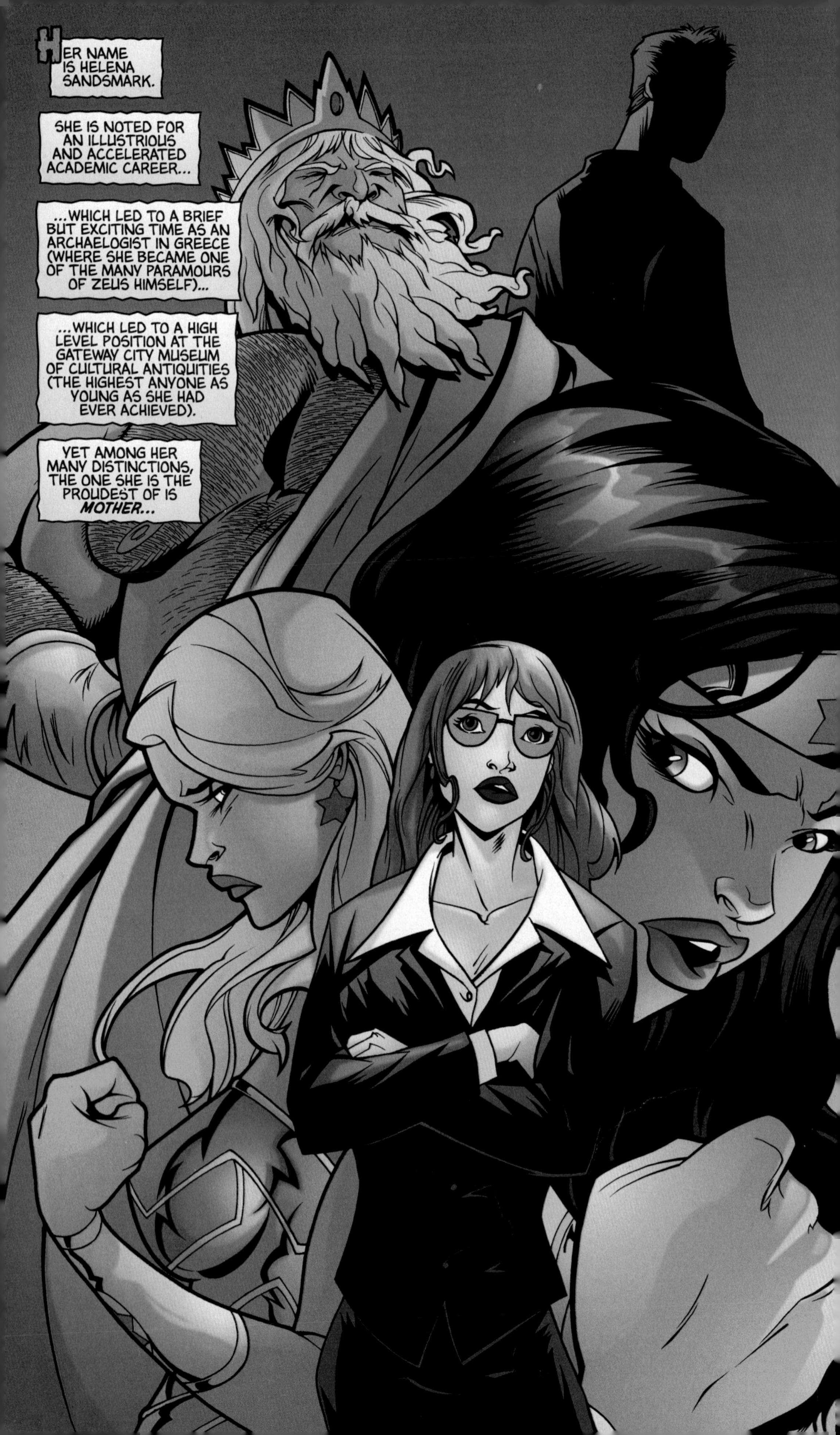

HER NAME IS HELENA SANDSMARK.
SHE IS NOTED FOR AN ILLUSTRIOUS AND ACCELERATED ACADEMIC CAREER...
...WHICH LED TO A BRIEF BUT EXCITING TIME AS AN ARCHAELOGIST IN GREECE (WHERE SHE BECAME ONE OF THE MANY PARAMOURS OF ZEUS HIMSELF)...
...WHICH LED TO A HIGH LEVEL POSITION AT THE GATEWAY CITY MUSEUM OF CULTURAL ANTIQUITIES (THE HIGHEST ANYONE AS YOUNG AS SHE HAD EVER ACHIEVED).
YET AMONG HER MANY DISTINCTIONS, THE ONE SHE IS THE PROUDEST OF IS ***MOTHER...***

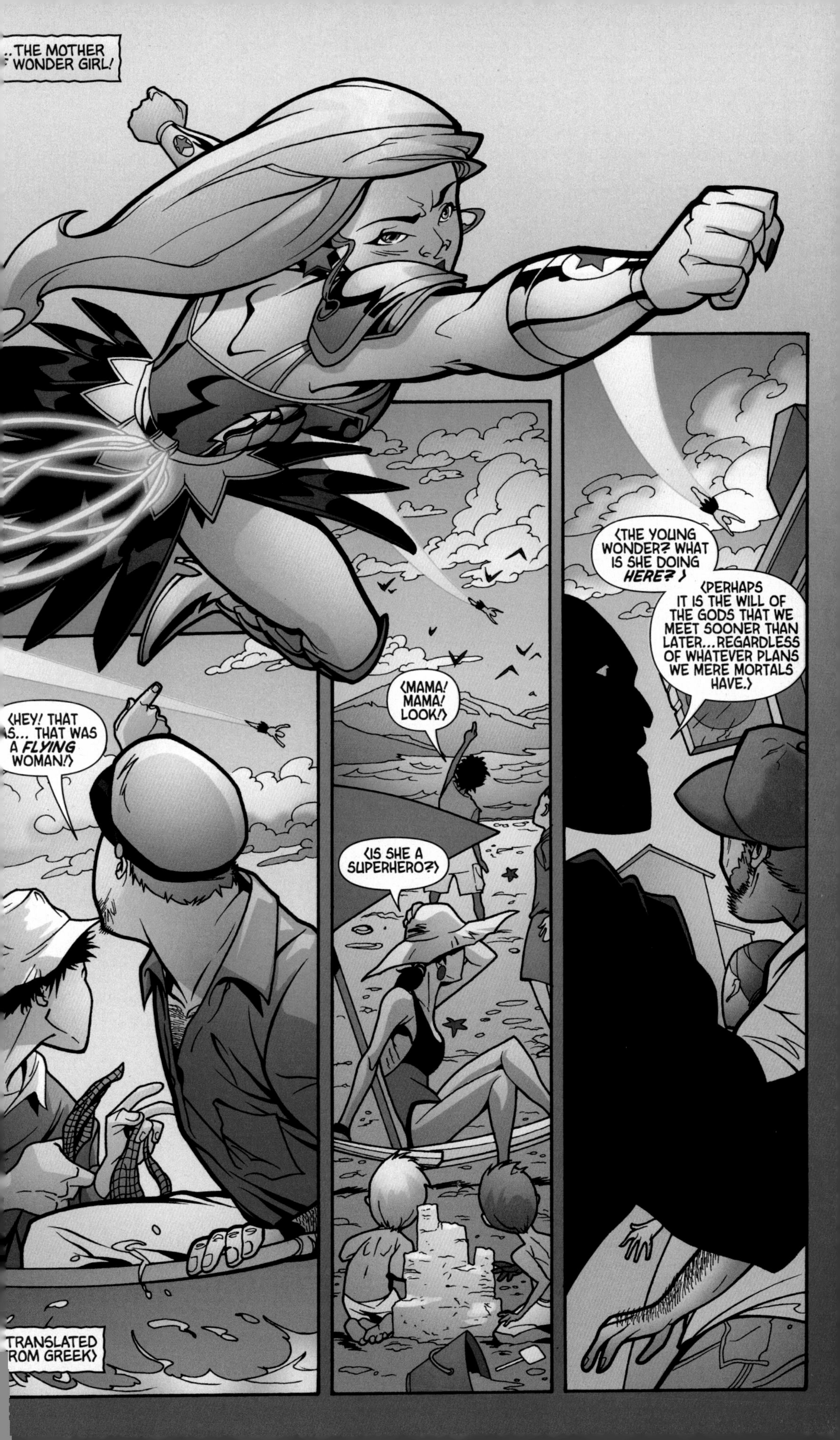
..THE MOTHER
F WONDER GIRL!
‹HEY! THAT
AS... THAT WAS
A FLYING
WOMAN!›
TRANSLATED
ROM GREEK›
‹MAMA!
MAMA!
LOOK!›
‹IS SHE A
SUPERHERO?›
‹THE YOUNG
WONDER? WHAT
IS SHE DOING
HERE? ›
‹PERHAPS
IT IS THE WILL OF
THE GODS THAT WE
MEET SOONER THAN
LATER...REGARDLESS
OF WHATEVER PLANS
WE MERE MORTALS
HAVE.›

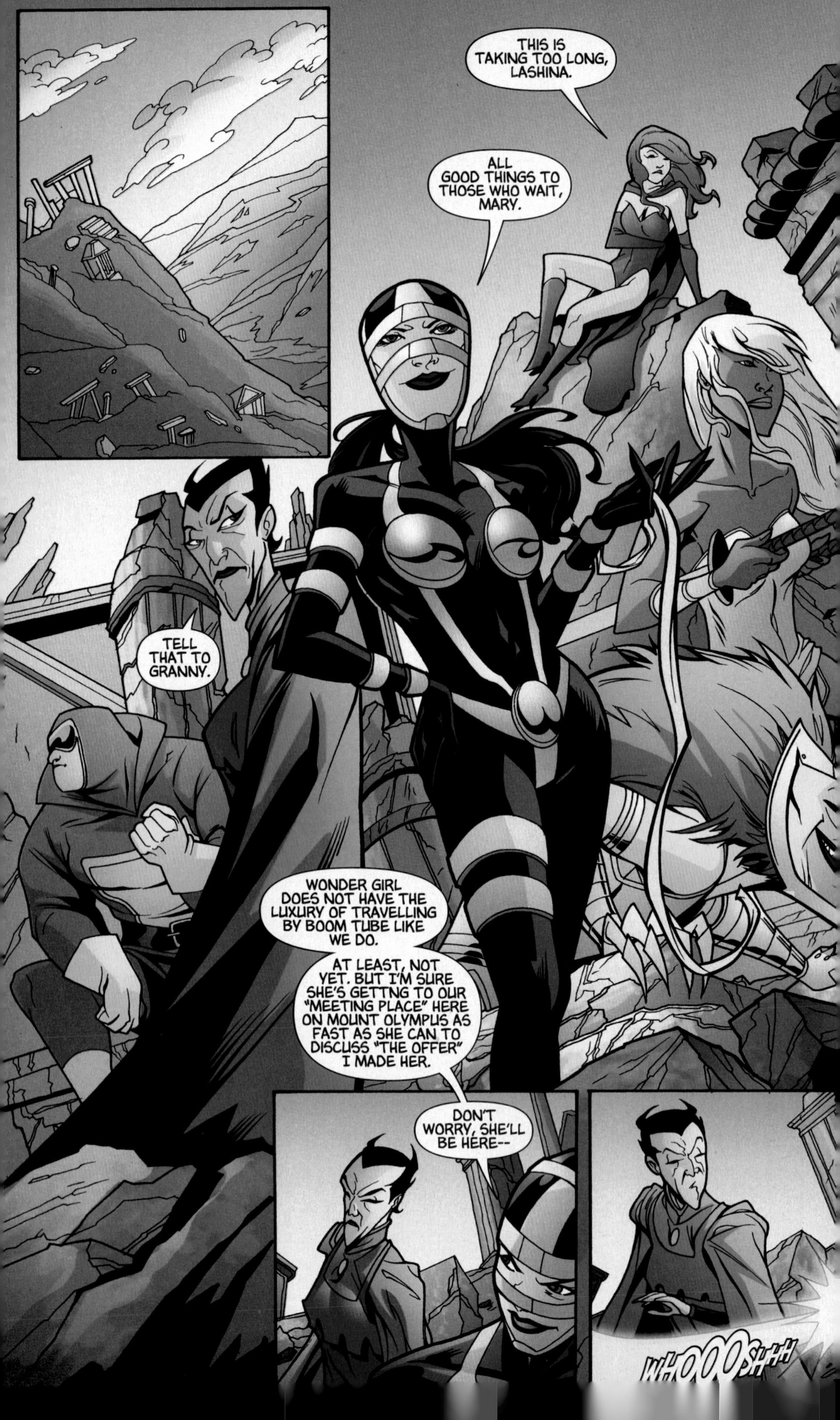
THIS IS TAKING TOO LONG, LASHINA.
ALL GOOD THINGS TO THOSE WHO WAIT, MARY.
TELL THAT TO GRANNY.
WONDER GIRL DOES NOT HAVE THE LUXURY OF TRAVELLING BY BOOM TUBE LIKE WE DO.
AT LEAST, NOT YET. BUT I'M SURE SHE'S GETTNG TO OUR "MEETING PLACE" HERE ON MOUNT OLYMPUS AS FAST AS SHE CAN TO DISCUSS "THE OFFER" I MADE HER.
DON'T WORRY, SHE'LL BE HERE--
WHOOOSHHH

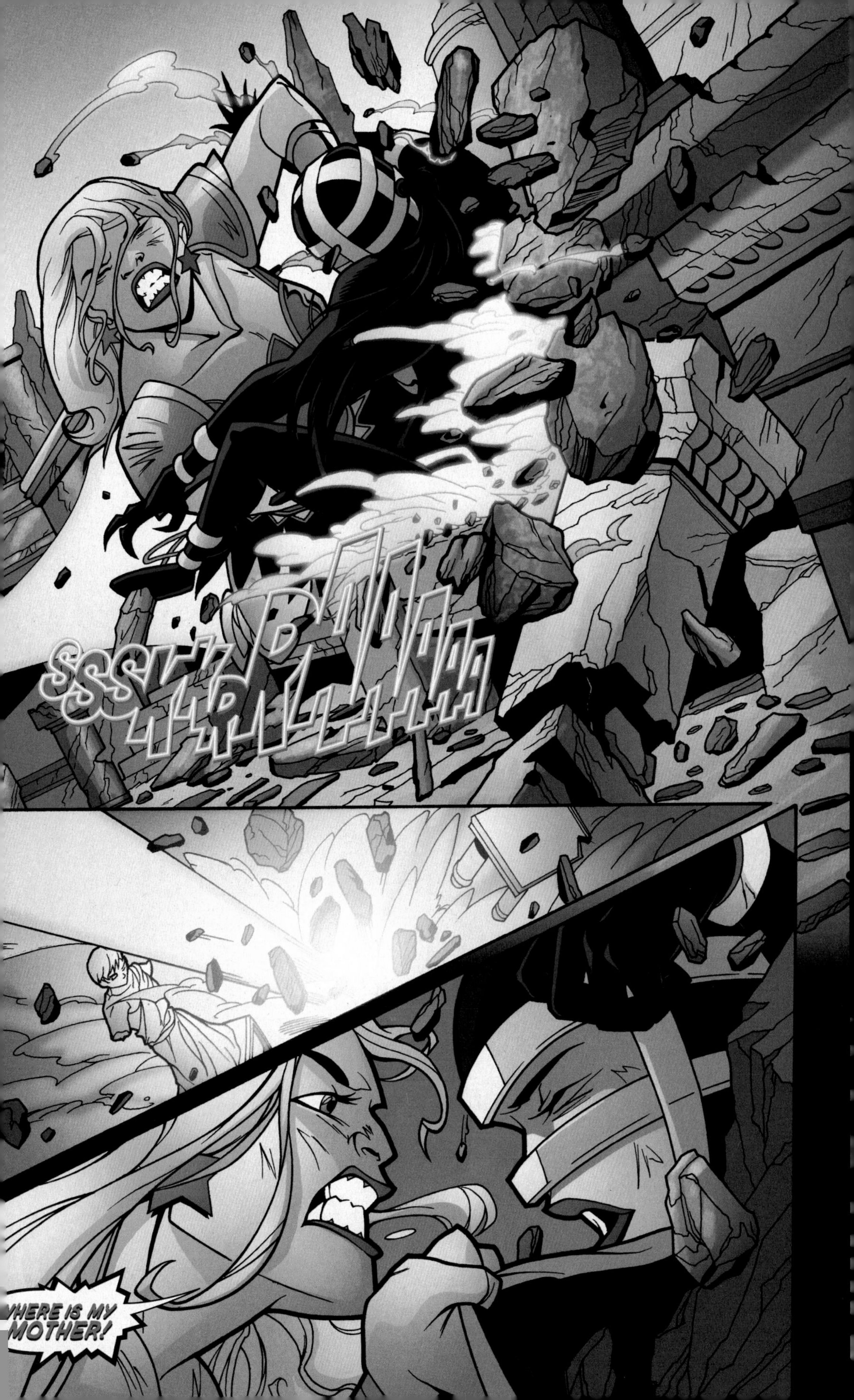
WHERE IS MY MOTHER!

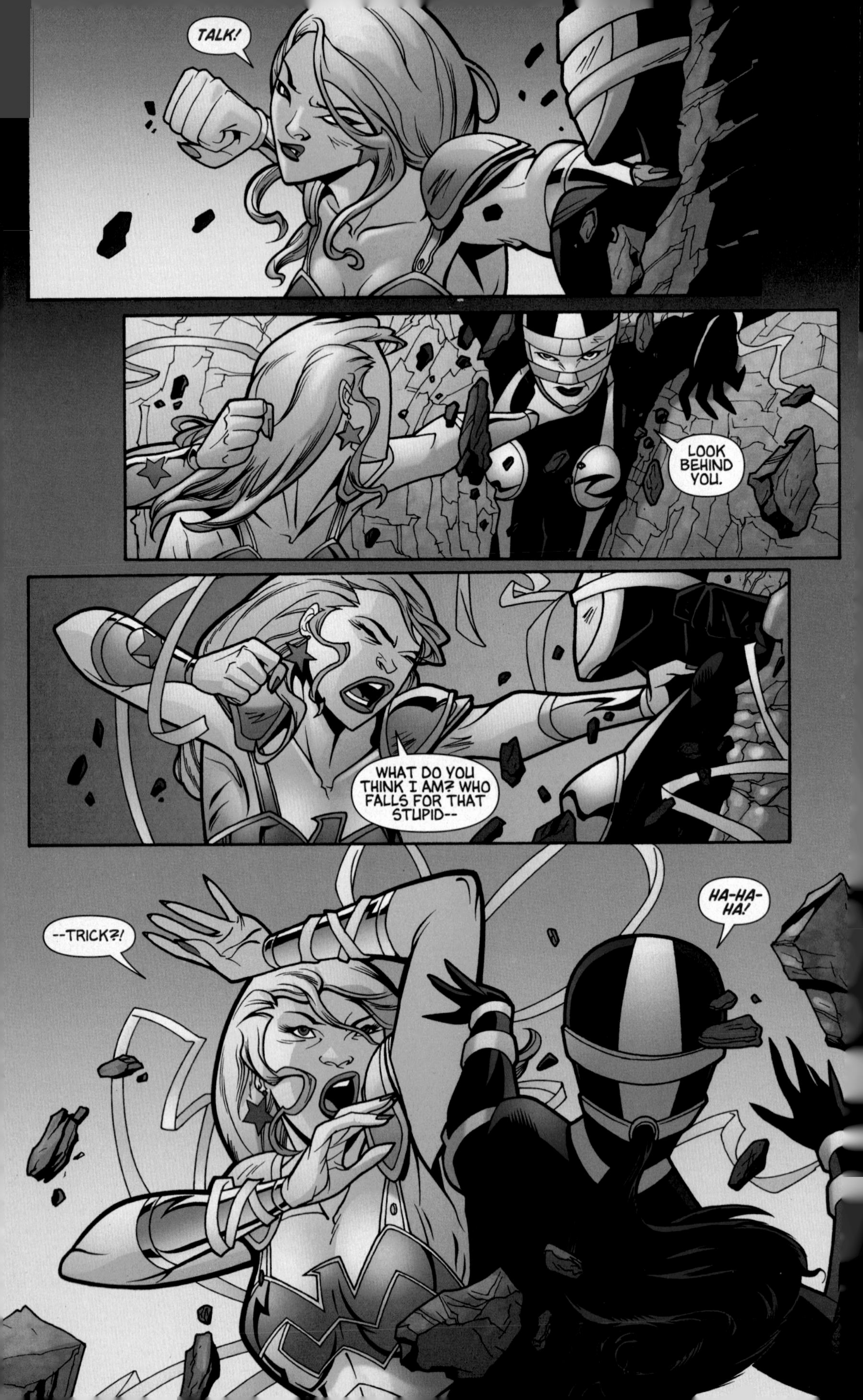
TALK!
LOOK BEHIND YOU.
WHAT DO YOU THINK I AM? WHO FALLS FOR THAT STUPID--
--TRICK?!
HA-HA-HA!

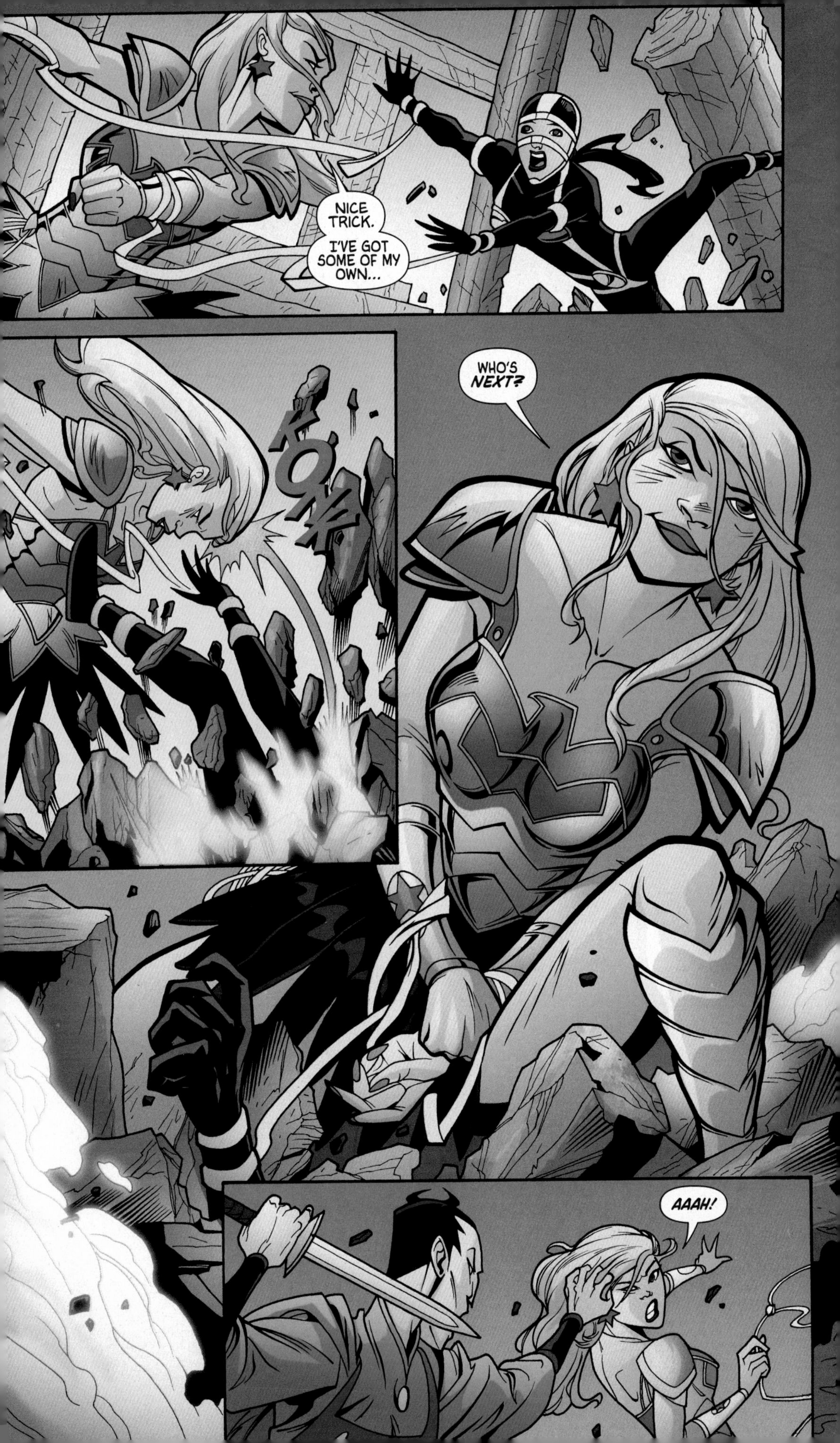
NICE TRICK.
I'VE GOT SOME OF MY OWN...
KONK
WHO'S NEXT?
AAAH!

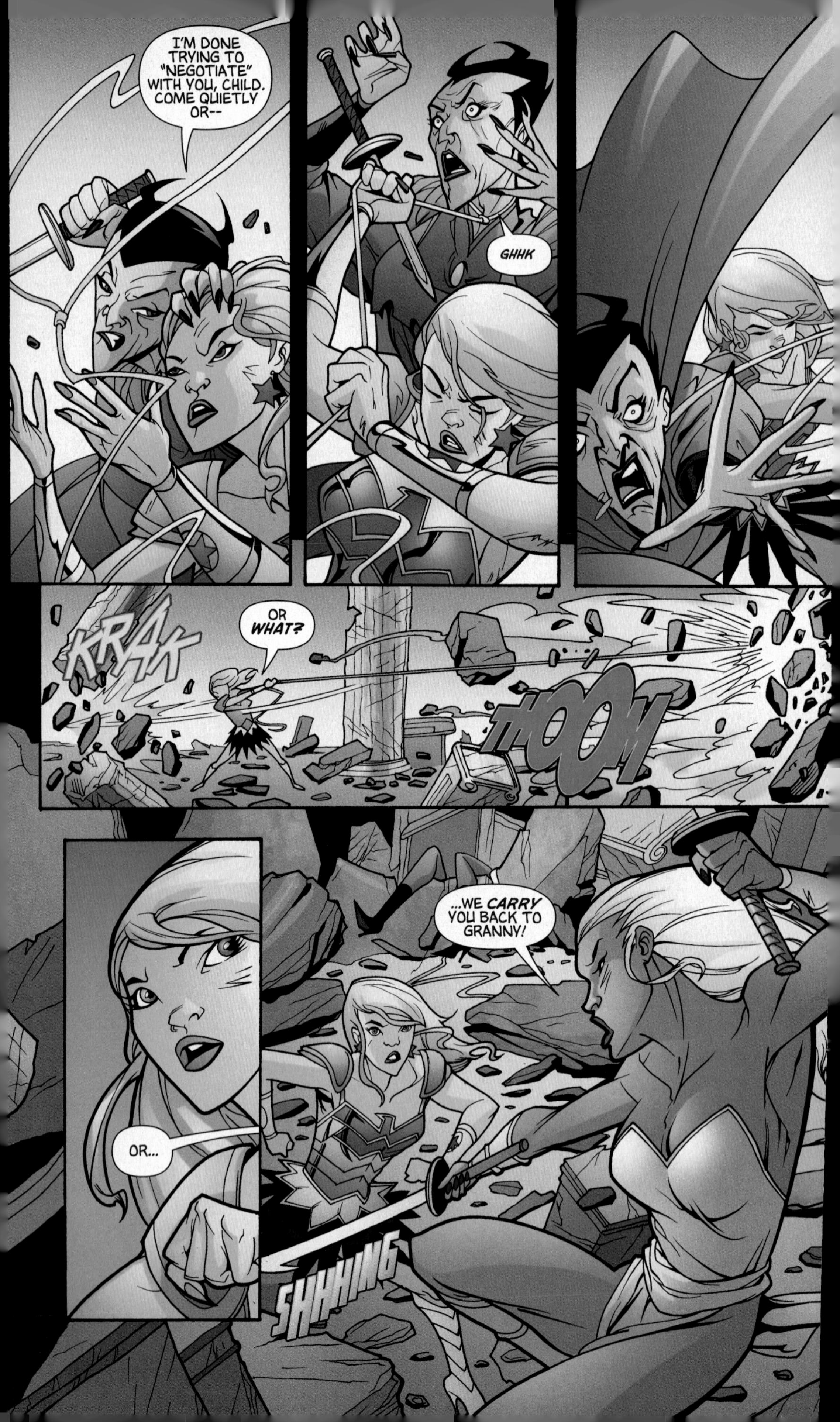
I'M DONE TRYING TO "NEGOTIATE" WITH YOU, CHILD. COME QUIETLY OR--
GHHK
KRAK
OR WHAT?
THOOM
...WE CARRY YOU BACK TO GRANNY!
OR...
SHHHING

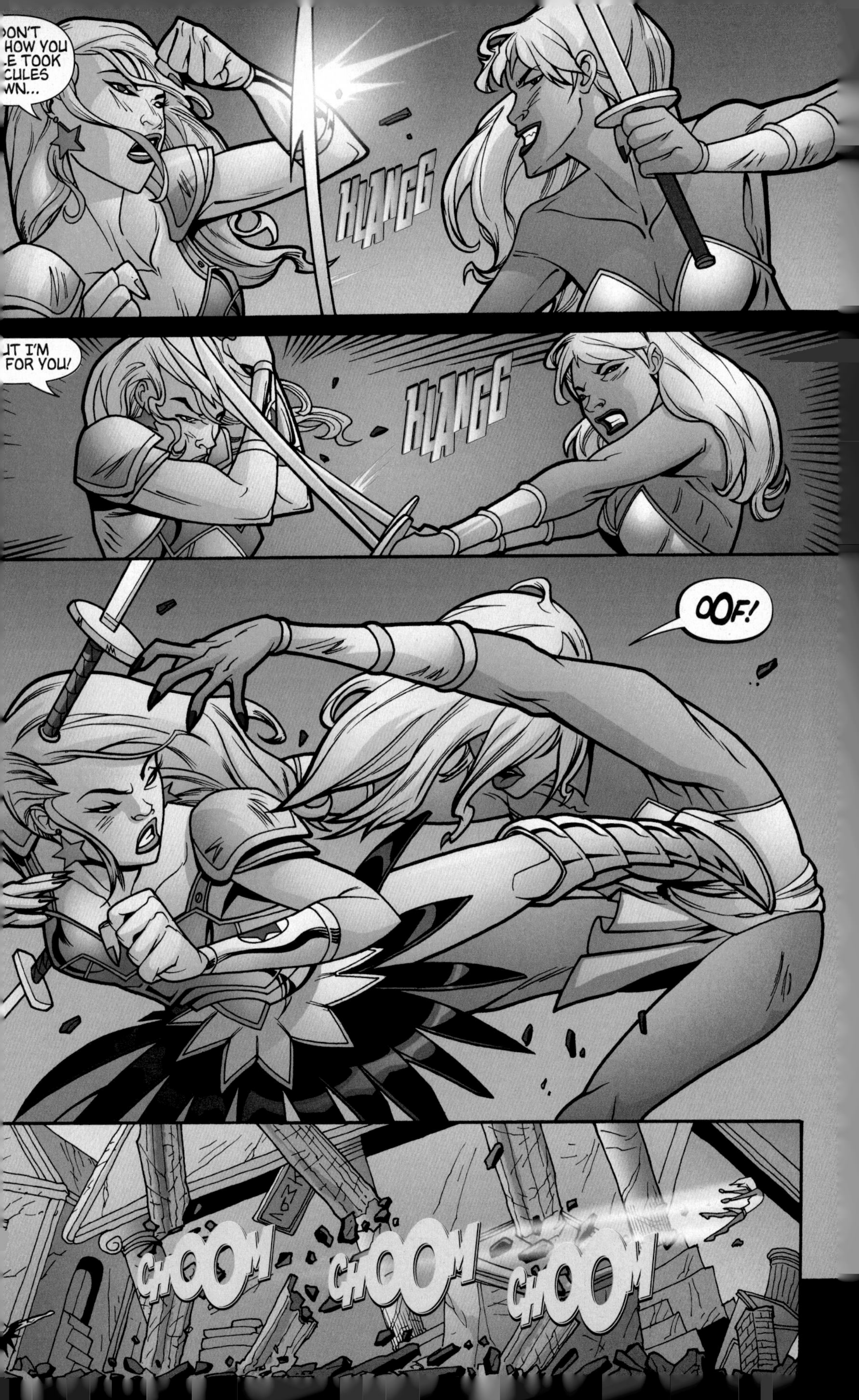

ON'T HOW YOU E TOOK CULES WN...
KLANGG
T I'M FOR YOU!
KLANGG
OOF!
CHOOOM
CHOOOM
CHOOOM

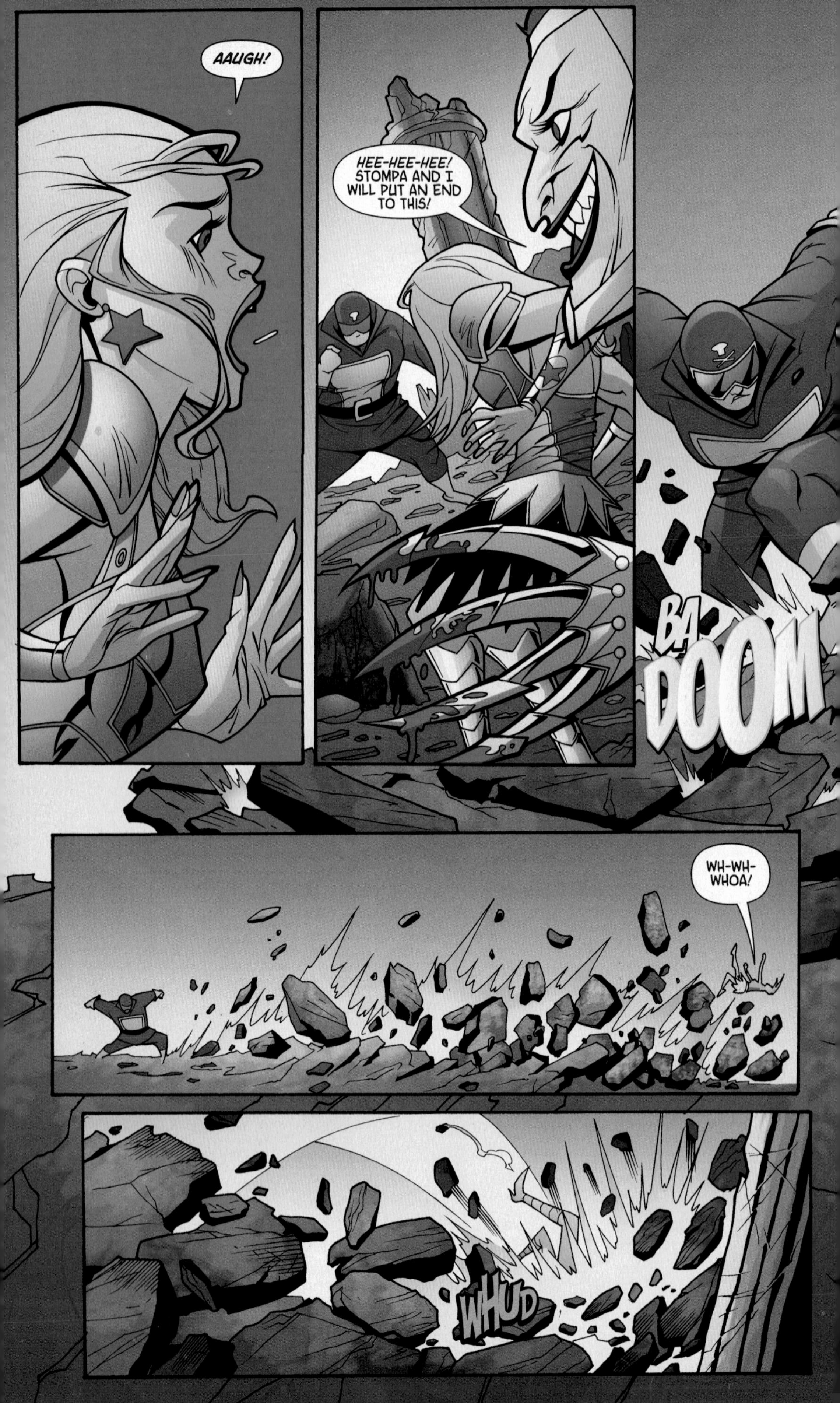
AAUGH!
HEE-HEE-HEE! STOMPA AND I WILL PUT AN END TO THIS!
BA DOOM
WH-WH-WHOA!
WHUD

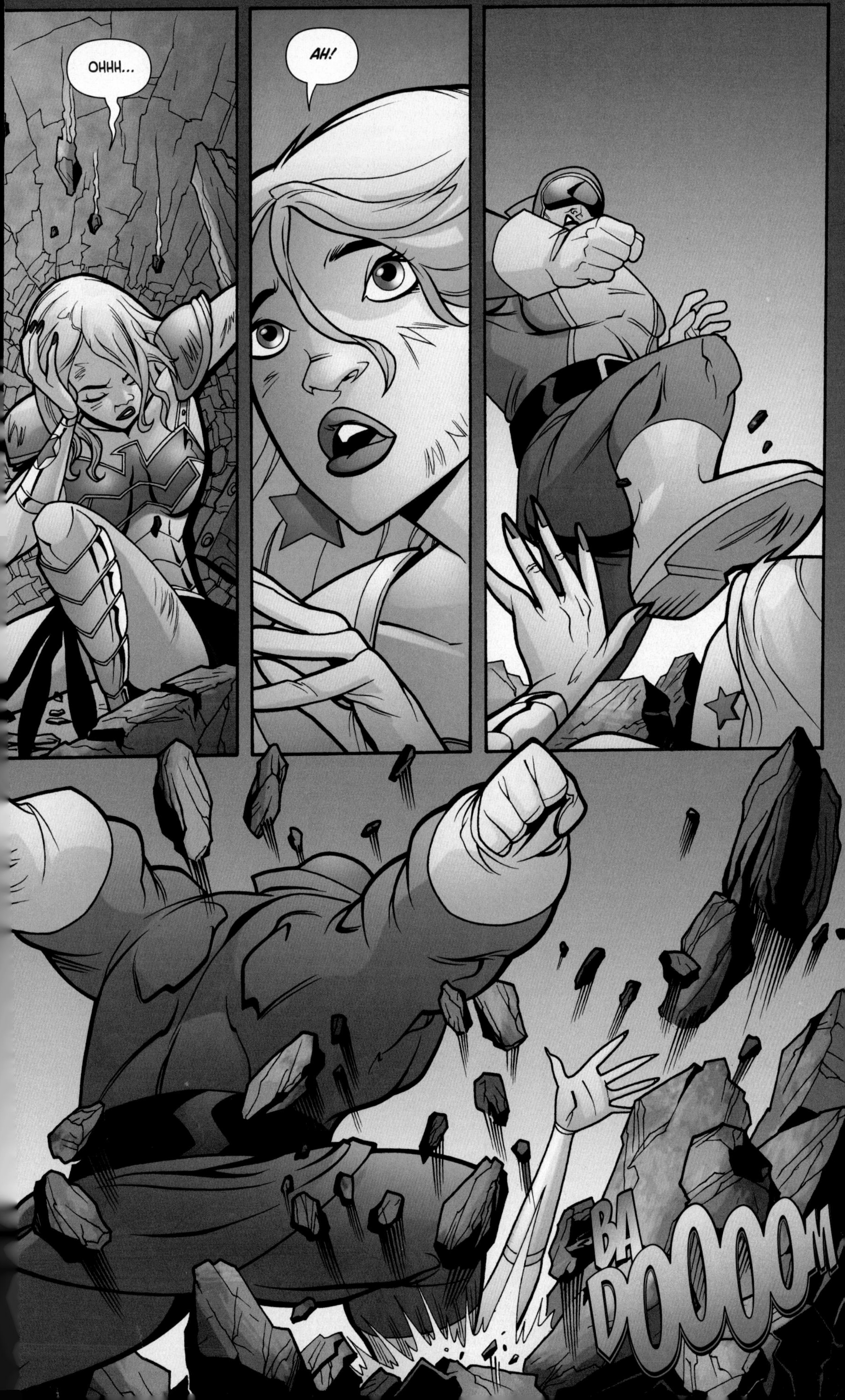
OHHH...
AH!
BA
DOOOOM

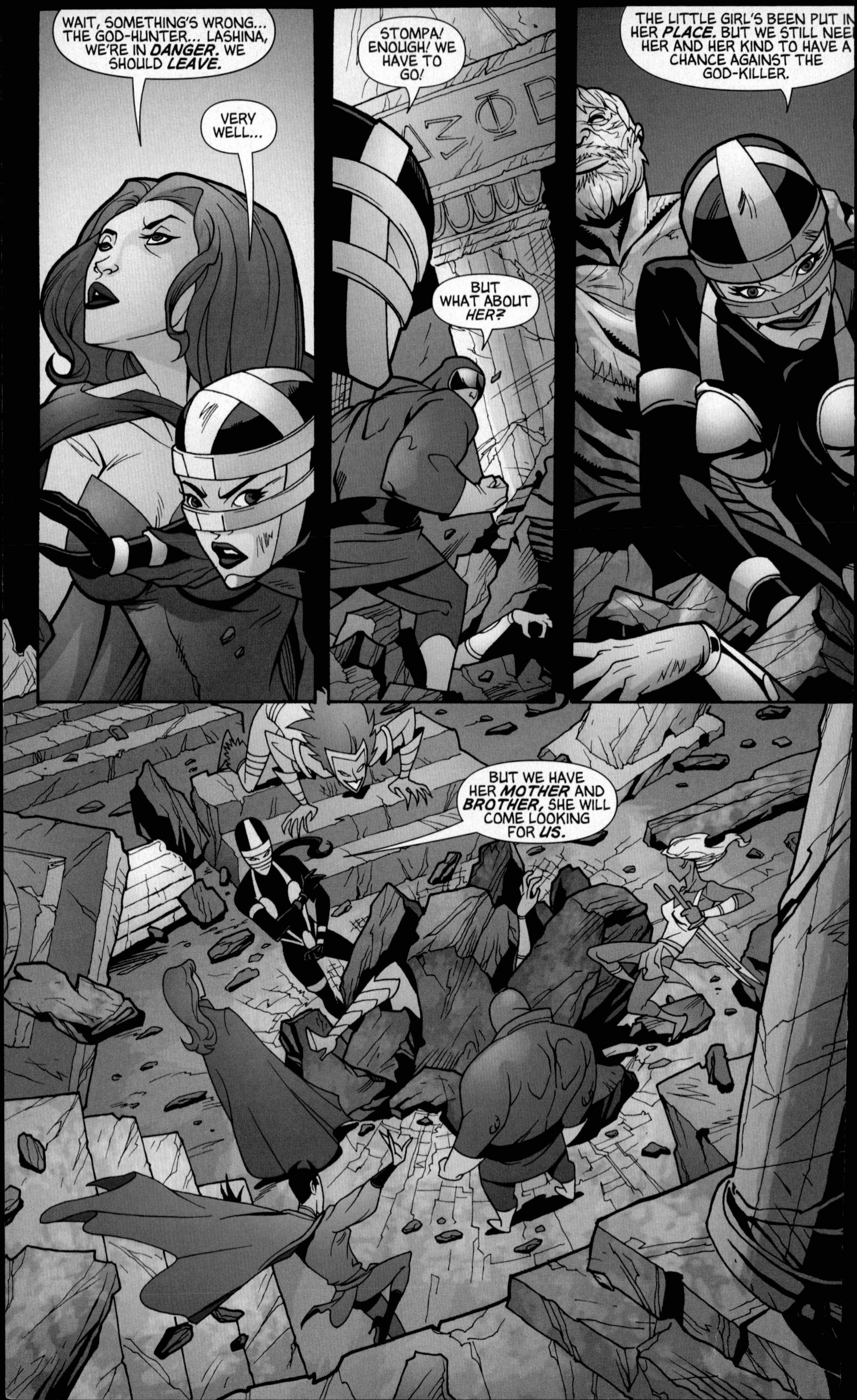
WAIT, SOMETHING'S WRONG... THE GOD-HUNTER... LASHINA, WE'RE IN DANGER. WE SHOULD LEAVE.
VERY WELL...
STOMPA! ENOUGH! WE HAVE TO GO!
BUT WHAT ABOUT HER?
THE LITTLE GIRL'S BEEN PUT IN HER PLACE. BUT WE STILL NEED HER AND HER KIND TO HAVE A CHANCE AGAINST THE GOD-KILLER.
BUT WE HAVE HER MOTHER AND BROTHER, SHE WILL COME LOOKING FOR US.

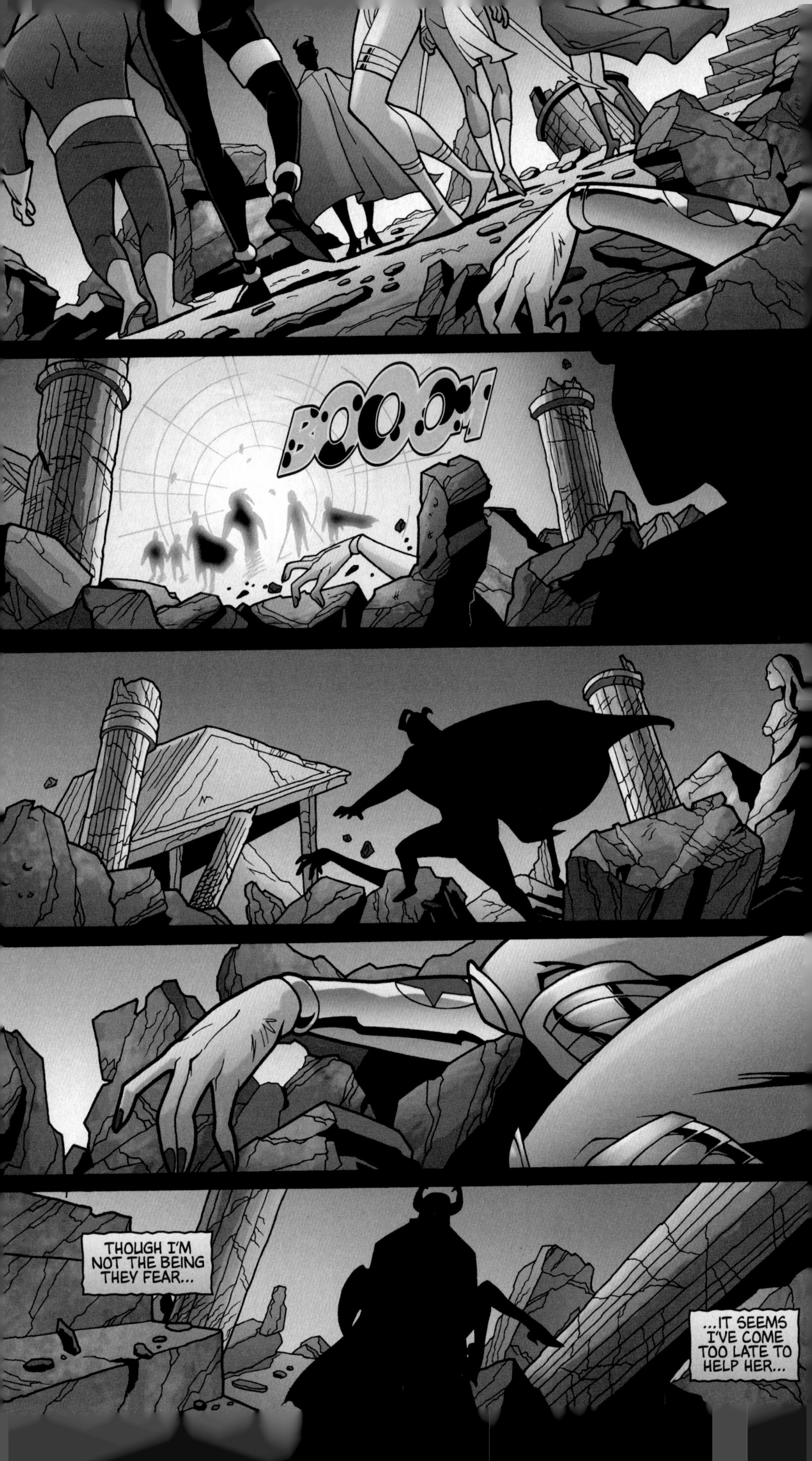
BOOOM
THOUGH I'M NOT THE BEING THEY FEAR...
...IT SEEMS I'VE COME TOO LATE TO HELP HER...

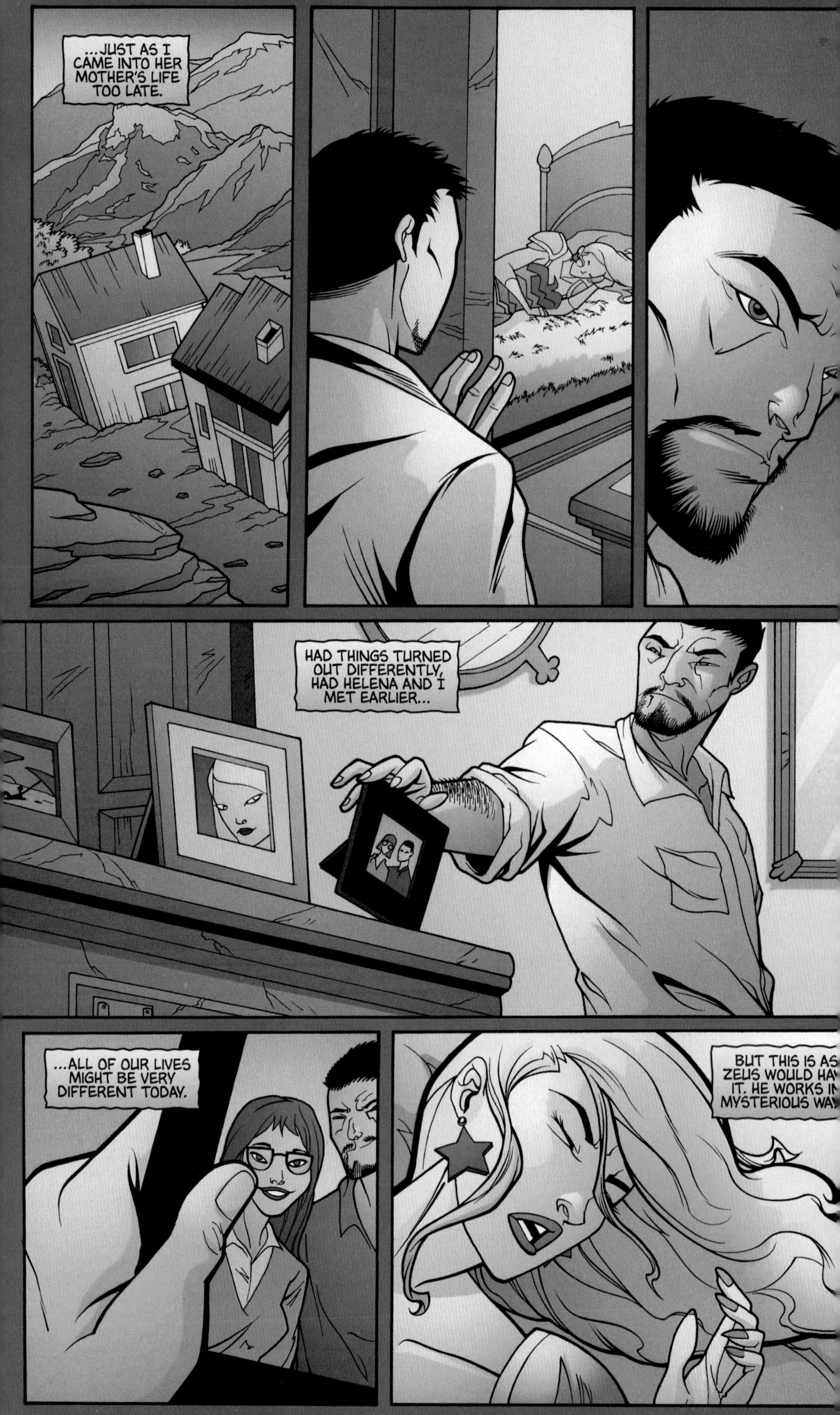

...JUST AS I CAME INTO HER MOTHER'S LIFE TOO LATE.
HAD THINGS TURNED OUT DIFFERENTLY, HAD HELENA AND I MET EARLIER...
...ALL OF OUR LIVES MIGHT BE VERY DIFFERENT TODAY.
BUT THIS IS AS ZEUS WOULD HAV IT. HE WORKS IN MYSTERIOUS WAY

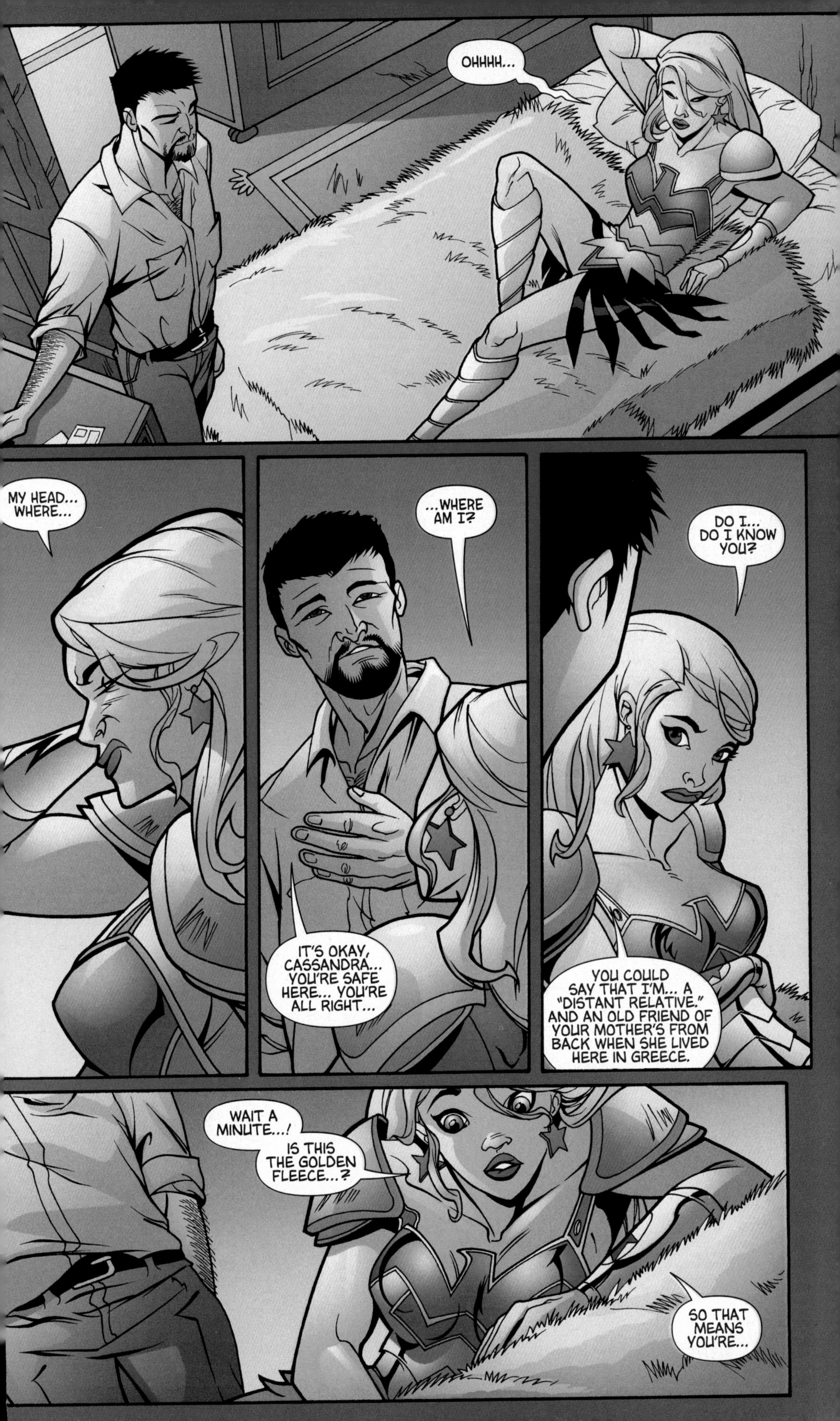
OHHHH...
MY HEAD... WHERE...
...WHERE AM I?
IT'S OKAY, CASSANDRA... YOU'RE SAFE HERE... YOU'RE ALL RIGHT...
DO I... DO I KNOW YOU?
YOU COULD SAY THAT I'M... A "DISTANT RELATIVE." AND AN OLD FRIEND OF YOUR MOTHER'S FROM BACK WHEN SHE LIVED HERE IN GREECE.
WAIT A MINUTE...!
IS THIS THE GOLDEN FLEECE...?
SO THAT MEANS YOU'RE...

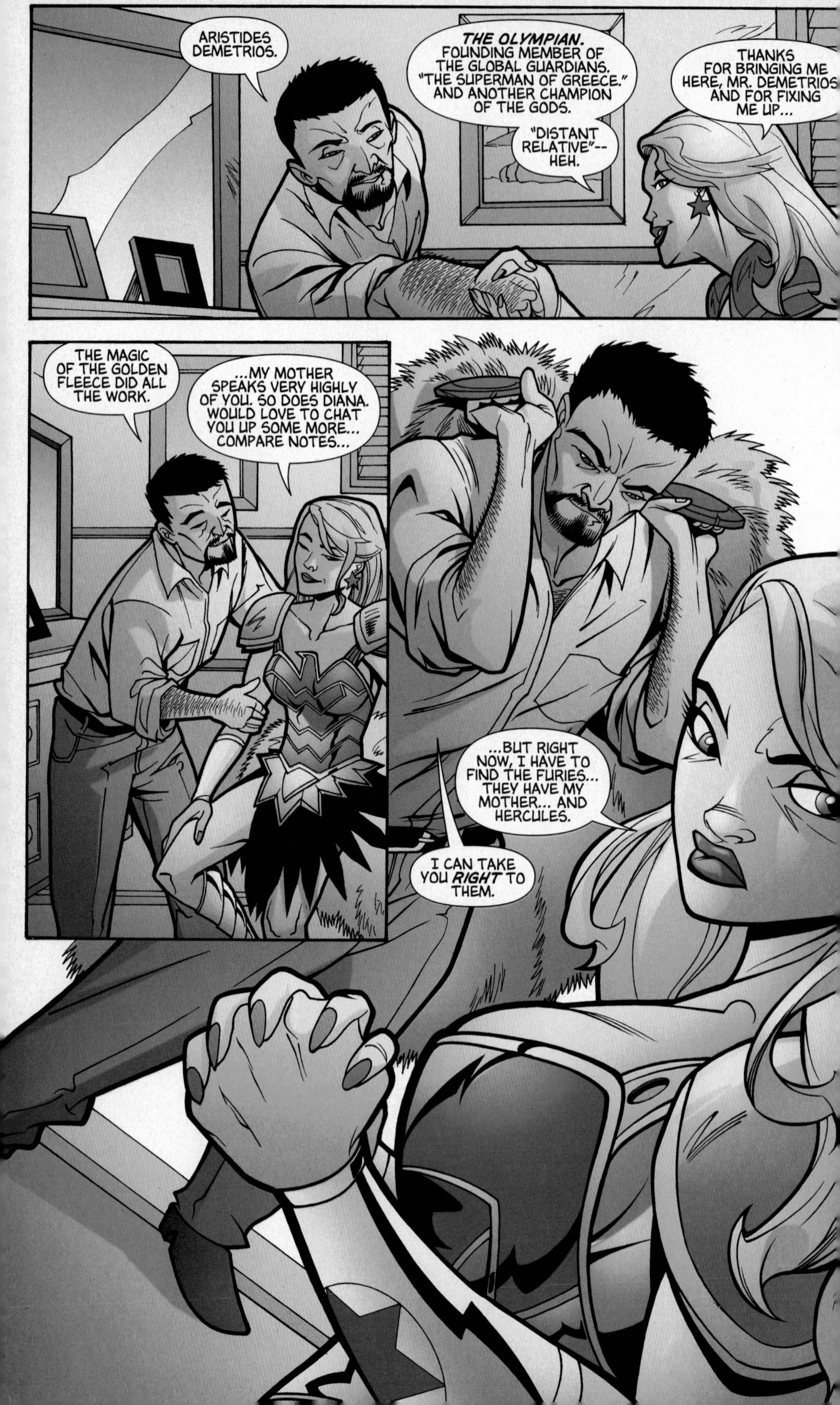
ARISTIDES DEMETRIOS.
THE OLYMPIAN. FOUNDING MEMBER OF THE GLOBAL GUARDIANS. "THE SUPERMAN OF GREECE." AND ANOTHER CHAMPION OF THE GODS.
"DISTANT RELATIVE"-- HEH.
THANKS FOR BRINGING ME HERE, MR. DEMETRIOS AND FOR FIXING ME UP...
THE MAGIC OF THE GOLDEN FLEECE DID ALL THE WORK.
...MY MOTHER SPEAKS VERY HIGHLY OF YOU. SO DOES DIANA. WOULD LOVE TO CHAT YOU UP SOME MORE... COMPARE NOTES...
...BUT RIGHT NOW, I HAVE TO FIND THE FURIES... THEY HAVE MY MOTHER... AND HERCULES.
I CAN TAKE YOU RIGHT TO THEM.

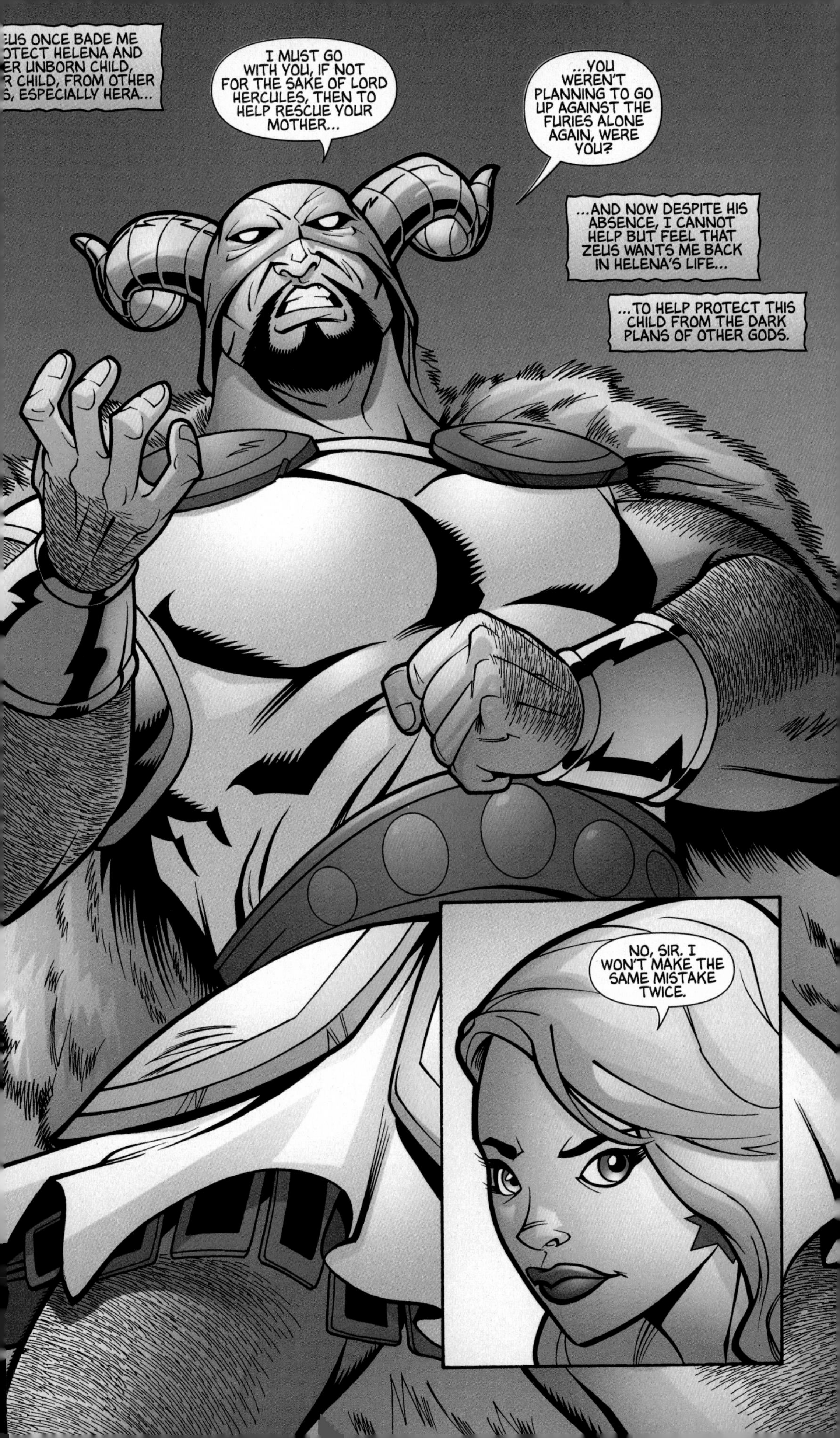
EUS ONCE BADE ME
OTECT HELENA AND
ER UNBORN CHILD,
R CHILD, FROM OTHER
S, ESPECIALLY HERA...
I MUST GO WITH YOU, IF NOT FOR THE SAKE OF LORD HERCULES, THEN TO HELP RESCUE YOUR MOTHER...
...YOU WEREN'T PLANNING TO GO UP AGAINST THE FURIES ALONE AGAIN, WERE YOU?
...AND NOW DESPITE HIS ABSENCE, I CANNOT HELP BUT FEEL THAT ZEUS WANTS ME BACK IN HELENA'S LIFE...
...TO HELP PROTECT THIS CHILD FROM THE DARK PLANS OF OTHER GODS.
NO, SIR. I WON'T MAKE THE SAME MISTAKE TWICE.

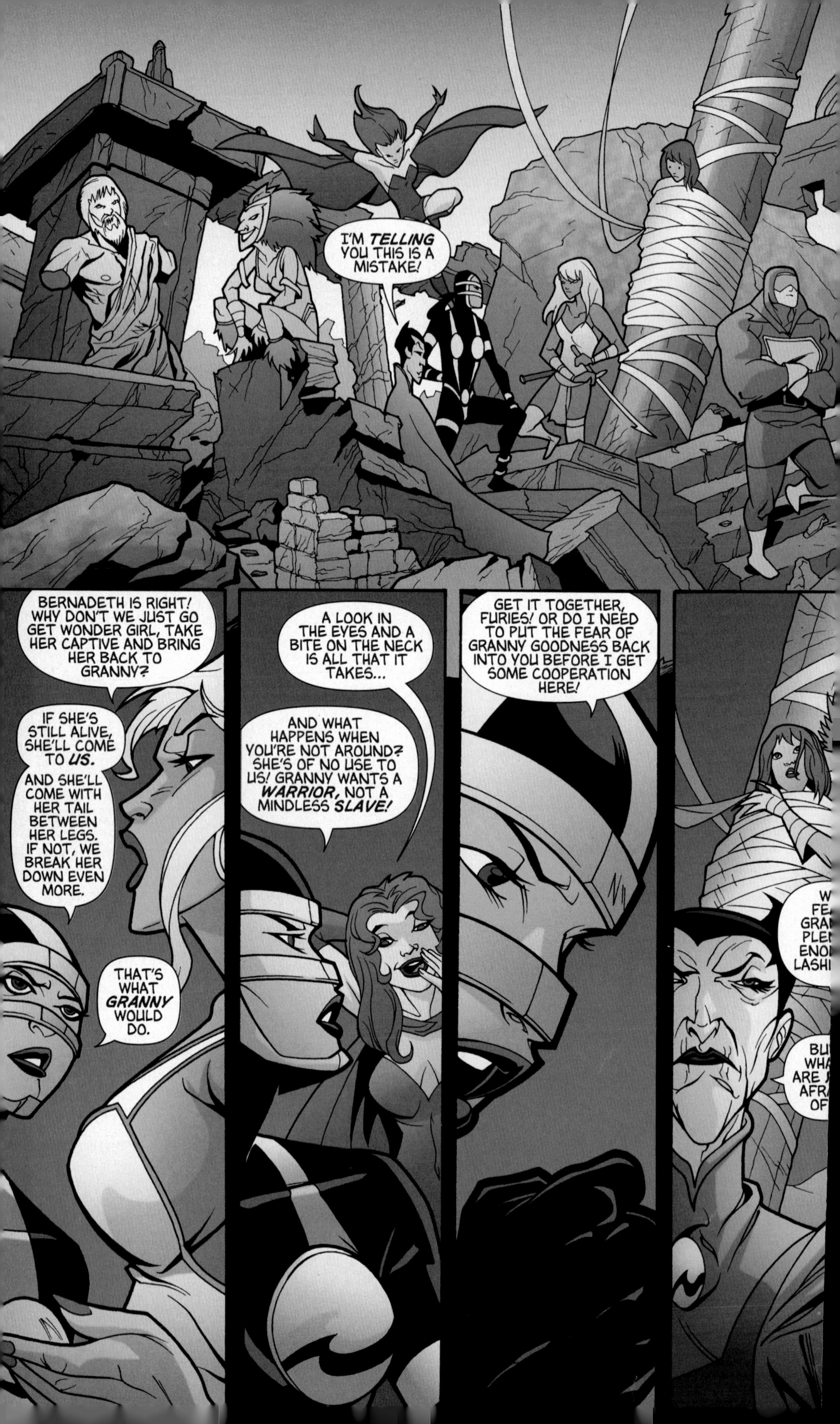
I'M TELLING YOU THIS IS A MISTAKE!
BERNADETH IS RIGHT! WHY DON'T WE JUST GO GET WONDER GIRL, TAKE HER CAPTIVE AND BRING HER BACK TO GRANNY?
IF SHE'S STILL ALIVE, SHE'LL COME TO US.
AND SHE'LL COME WITH HER TAIL BETWEEN HER LEGS. IF NOT, WE BREAK HER DOWN EVEN MORE.
THAT'S WHAT GRANNY WOULD DO.
A LOOK IN THE EYES AND A BITE ON THE NECK IS ALL THAT IT TAKES...
AND WHAT HAPPENS WHEN YOU'RE NOT AROUND? SHE'S OF NO USE TO US! GRANNY WANTS A WARRIOR, NOT A MINDLESS SLAVE!
GET IT TOGETHER, FURIES! OR DO I NEED TO PUT THE FEAR OF GRANNY GOODNESS BACK INTO YOU BEFORE I GET SOME COOPERATION HERE!

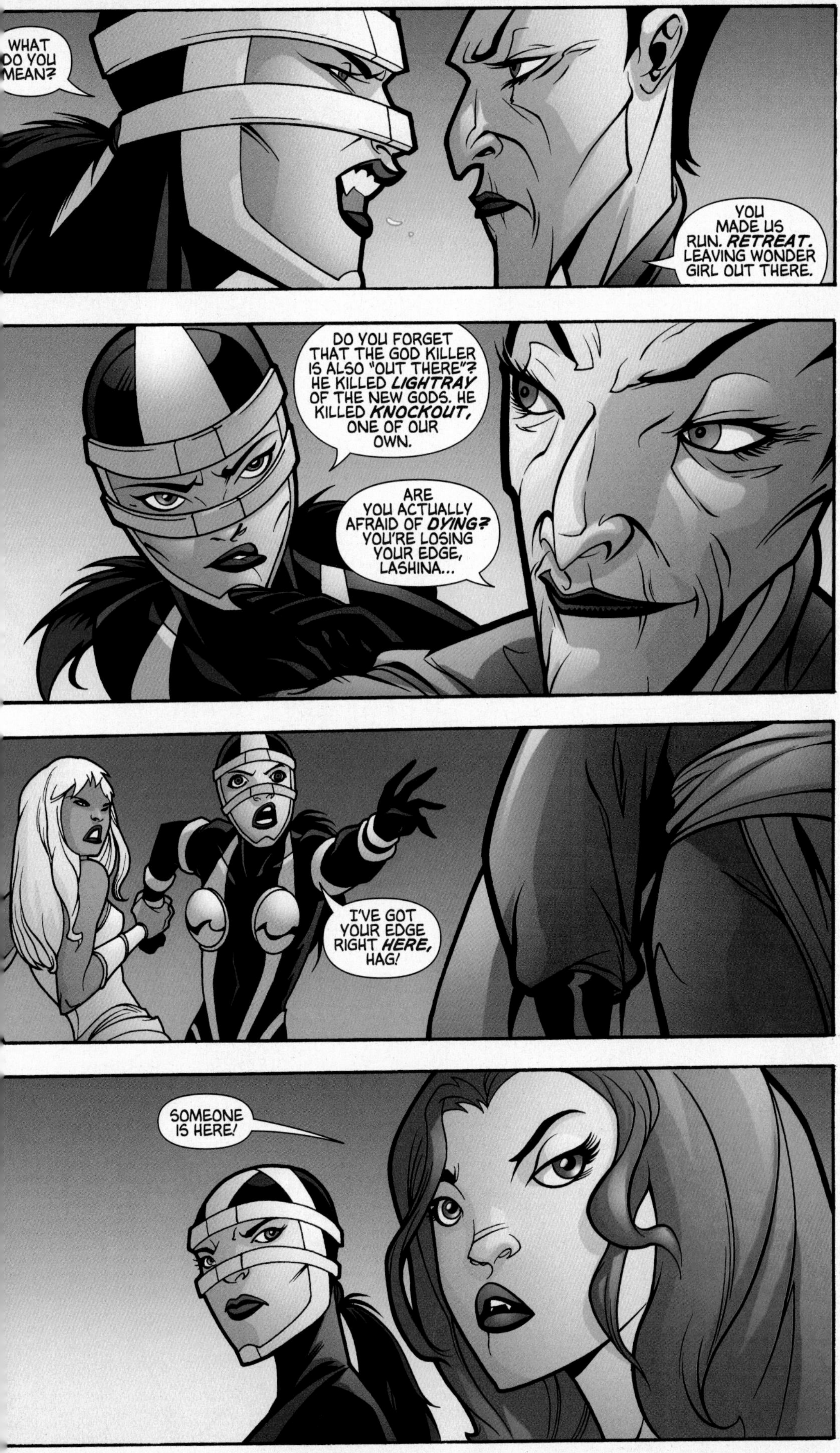
WHAT DO YOU MEAN?
YOU MADE US RUN. RETREAT. LEAVING WONDER GIRL OUT THERE.
DO YOU FORGET THAT THE GOD KILLER IS ALSO "OUT THERE"? HE KILLED LIGHTRAY OF THE NEW GODS. HE KILLED KNOCKOUT, ONE OF OUR OWN.
ARE YOU ACTUALLY AFRAID OF DYING? YOU'RE LOSING YOUR EDGE, LASHINA...
I'VE GOT YOUR EDGE RIGHT HERE, HAG!
SOMEONE IS HERE!

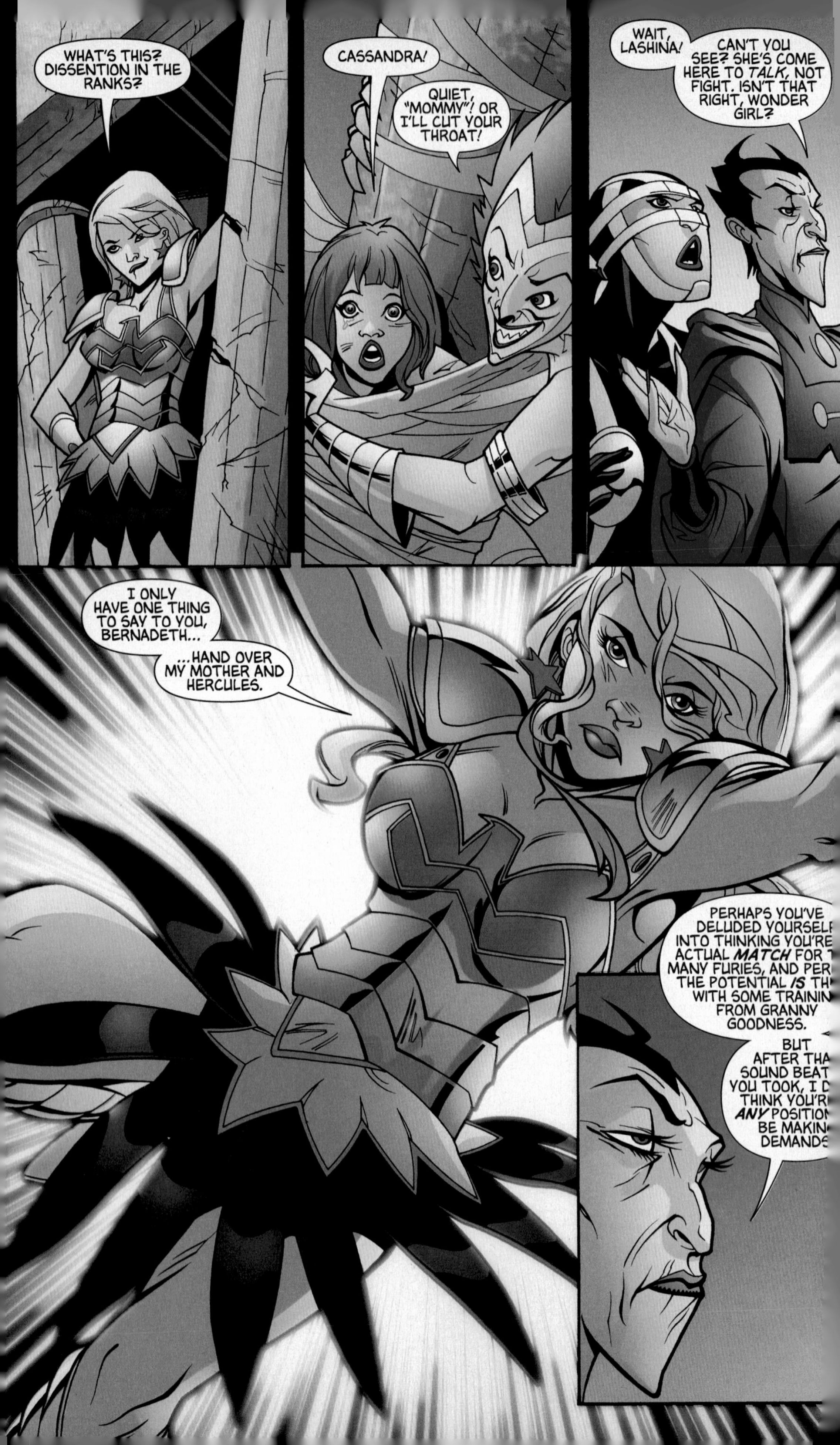
WHAT'S THIS? DISSENTION IN THE RANKS?
CASSANDRA!
QUIET, "MOMMY"! OR I'LL CUT YOUR THROAT!
WAIT, LASHINA!
CAN'T YOU SEE? SHE'S COME HERE TO *TALK*, NOT FIGHT. ISN'T THAT RIGHT, WONDER GIRL?
I ONLY HAVE ONE THING TO SAY TO YOU, BERNADETH...
...HAND OVER MY MOTHER AND HERCULES.
PERHAPS YOU'VE DELUDED YOURSELF INTO THINKING YOU'RE ACTUAL ***MATCH*** FOR T MANY FURIES, AND PER THE POTENTIAL ***IS*** TH WITH SOME TRAININ FROM GRANNY GOODNESS.
BUT AFTER THA SOUND BEAT YOU TOOK, I D THINK YOU'R ***ANY*** POSITION BE MAKIN DEMANDS

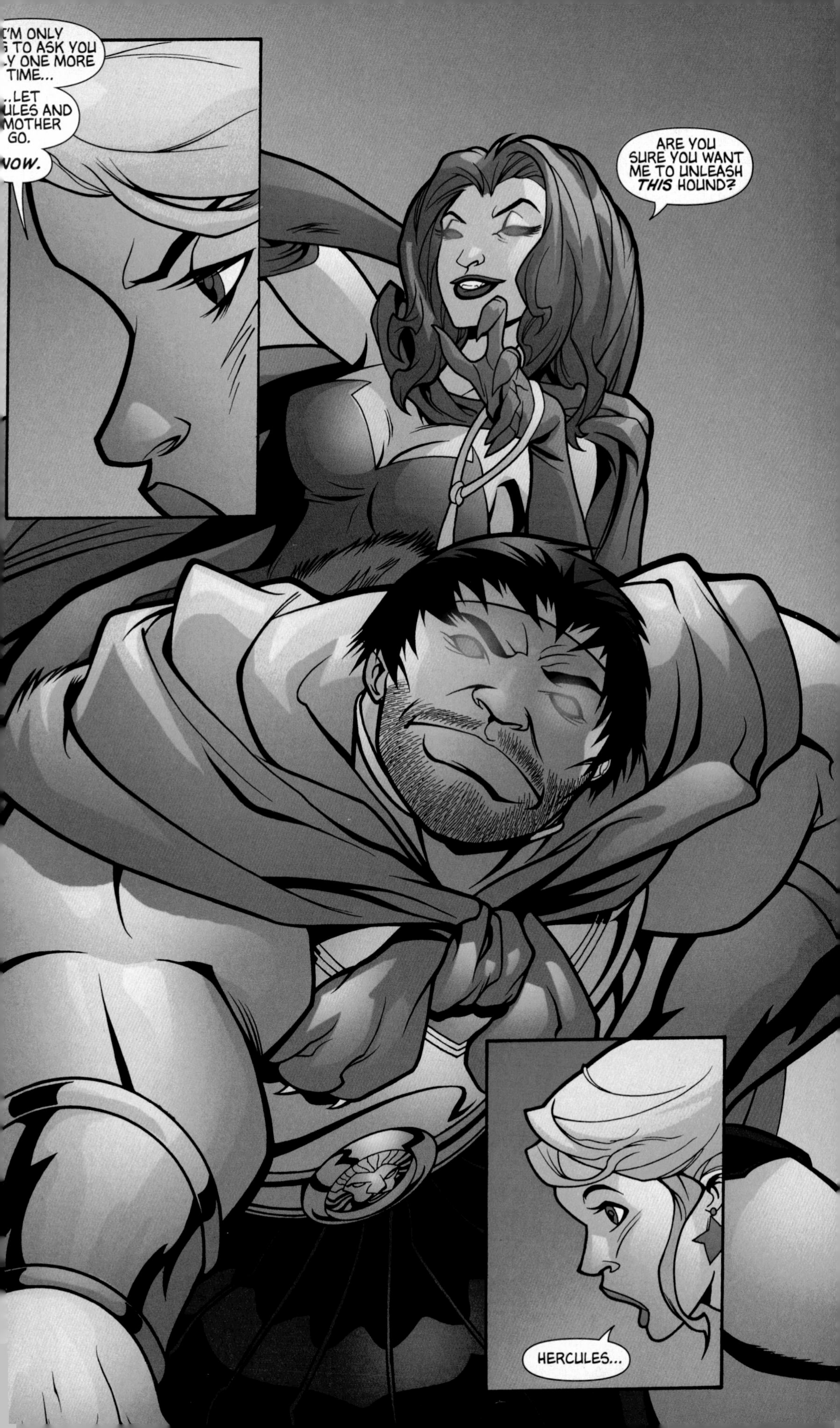
I'M ONLY
G TO ASK YOU
Y ONE MORE
TIME...
...LET
ULES AND
MOTHER
GO.
NOW.
ARE YOU SURE YOU WANT ME TO UNLEASH THIS HOUND?
HERCULES...

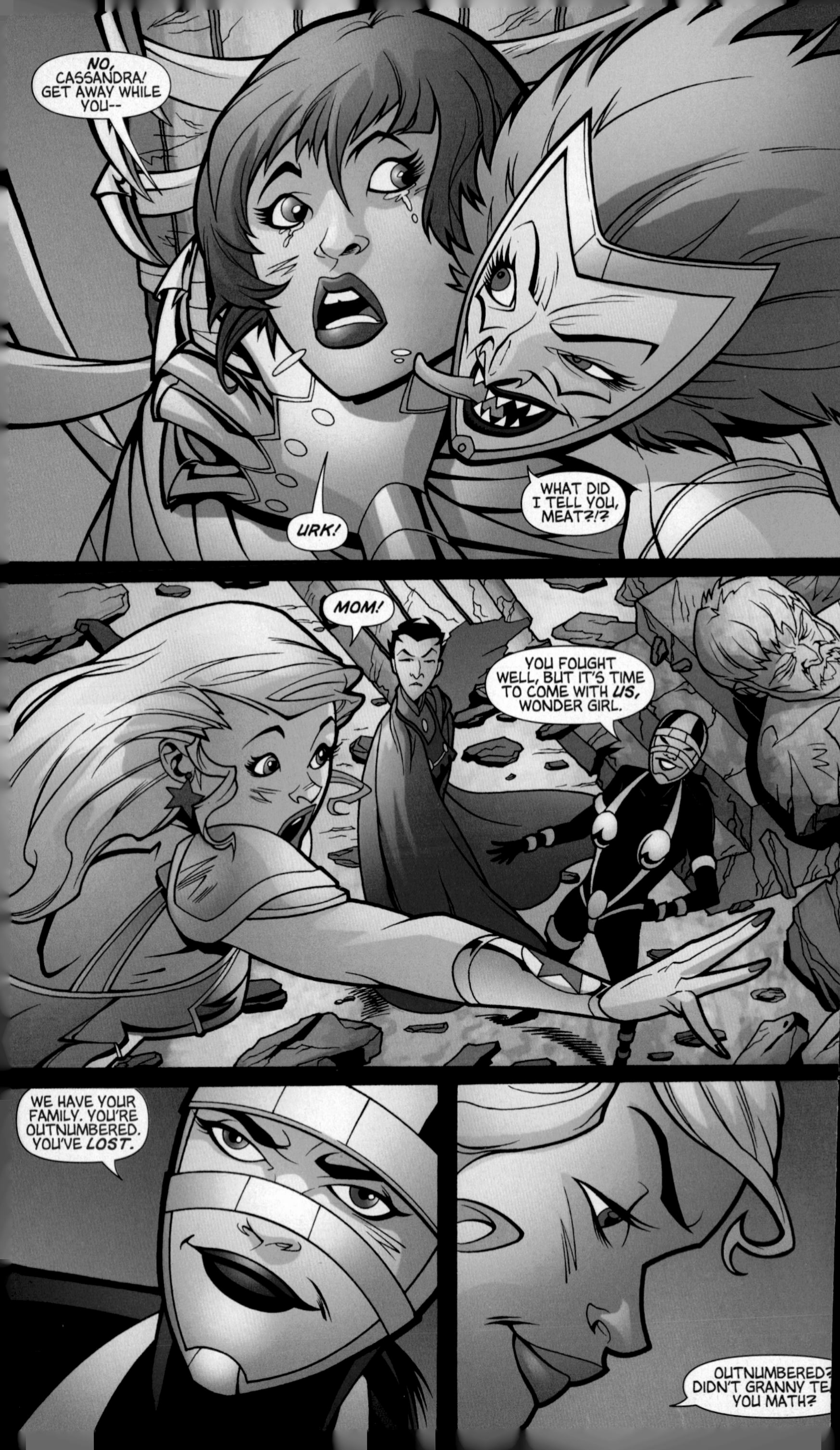
NO, CASSANDRA! GET AWAY WHILE YOU--
URK!
WHAT DID I TELL YOU, MEAT?!?
MOM!
YOU FOUGHT WELL, BUT IT'S TIME TO COME WITH US, WONDER GIRL.
WE HAVE YOUR FAMILY. YOU'RE OUTNUMBERED. YOU'VE LOST.
OUTNUMBERED? DIDN'T GRANNY TE
YOU MATH?

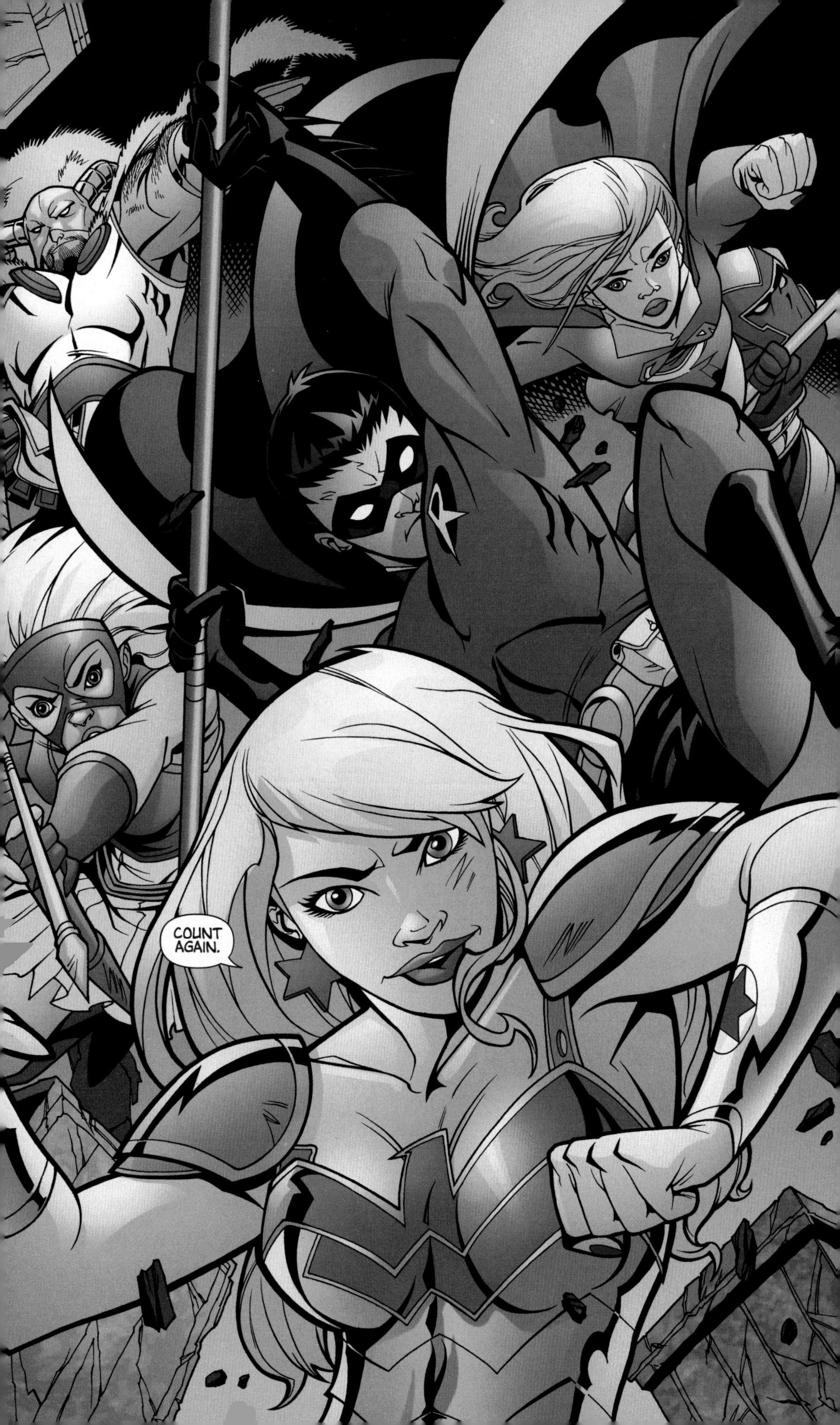
COUNT AGAIN.

Part 5: Clash of the Titans

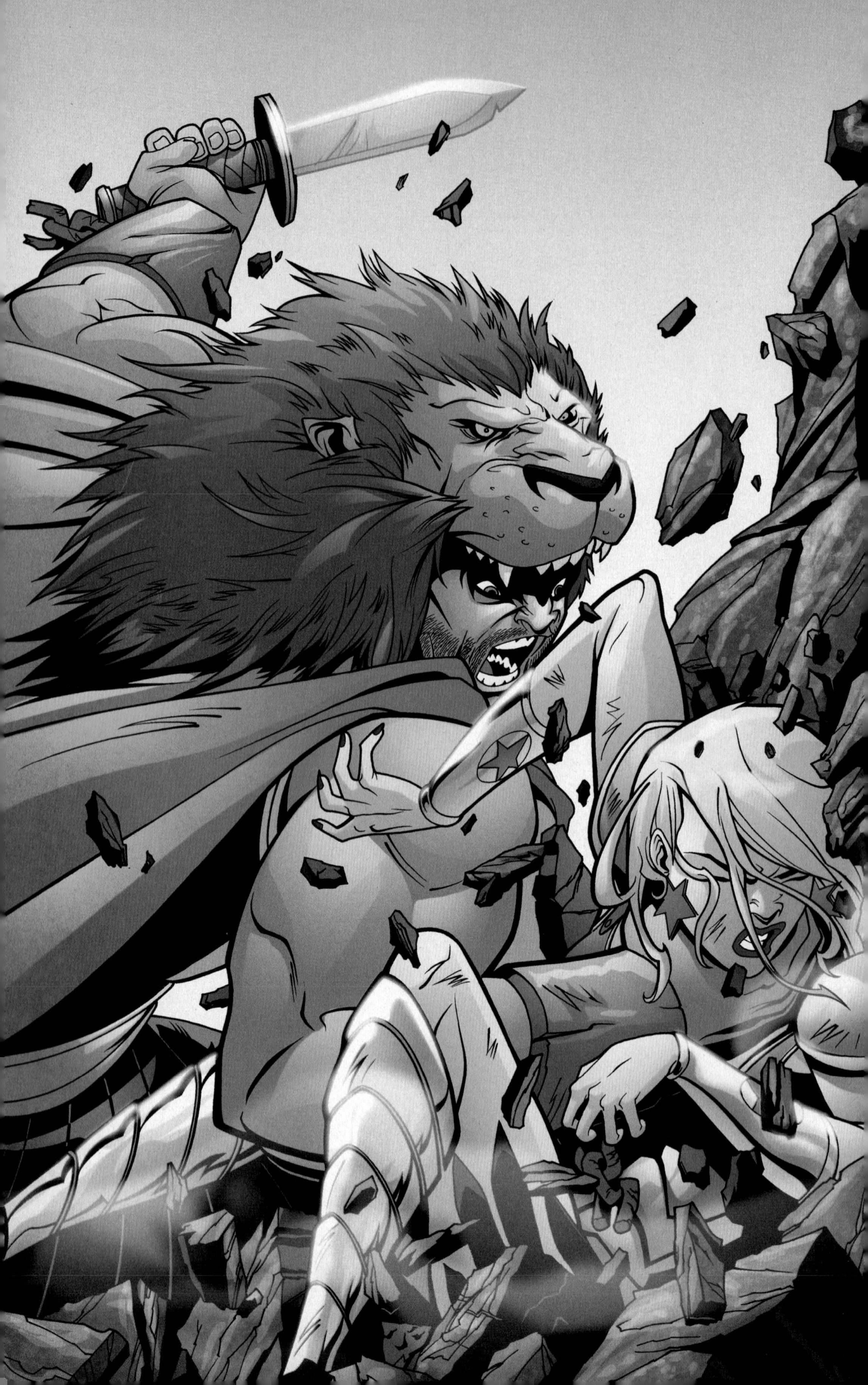

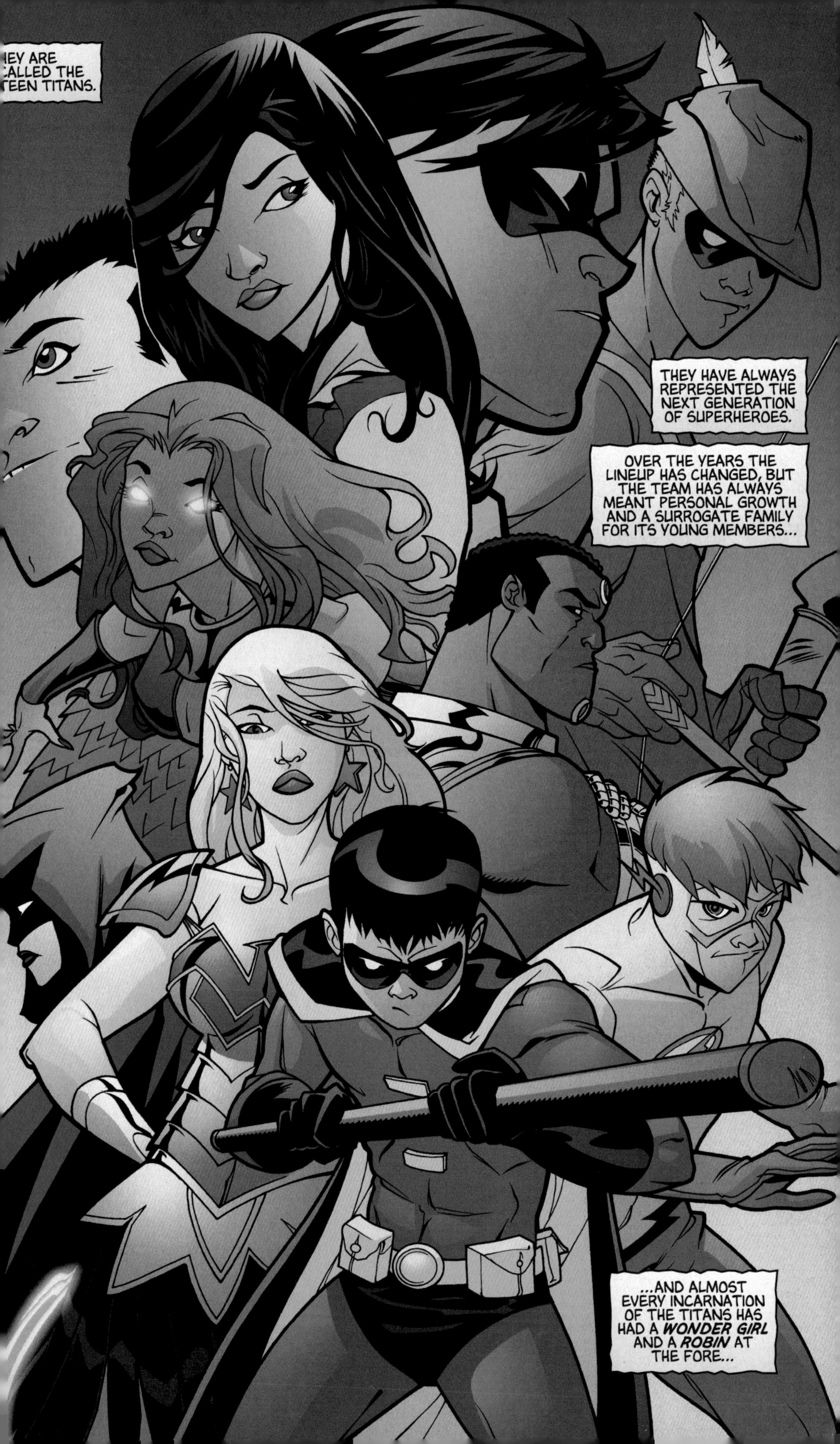

HEY ARE CALLED THE TEEN TITANS.
THEY HAVE ALWAYS REPRESENTED THE NEXT GENERATION OF SUPERHEROES.
OVER THE YEARS THE LINEUP HAS CHANGED, BUT THE TEAM HAS ALWAYS MEANT PERSONAL GROWTH AND A SURROGATE FAMILY FOR ITS YOUNG MEMBERS...
...AND ALMOST EVERY INCARNATION OF THE TITANS HAS HAD A *WONDER GIRL* AND A *ROBIN* AT THE FORE...

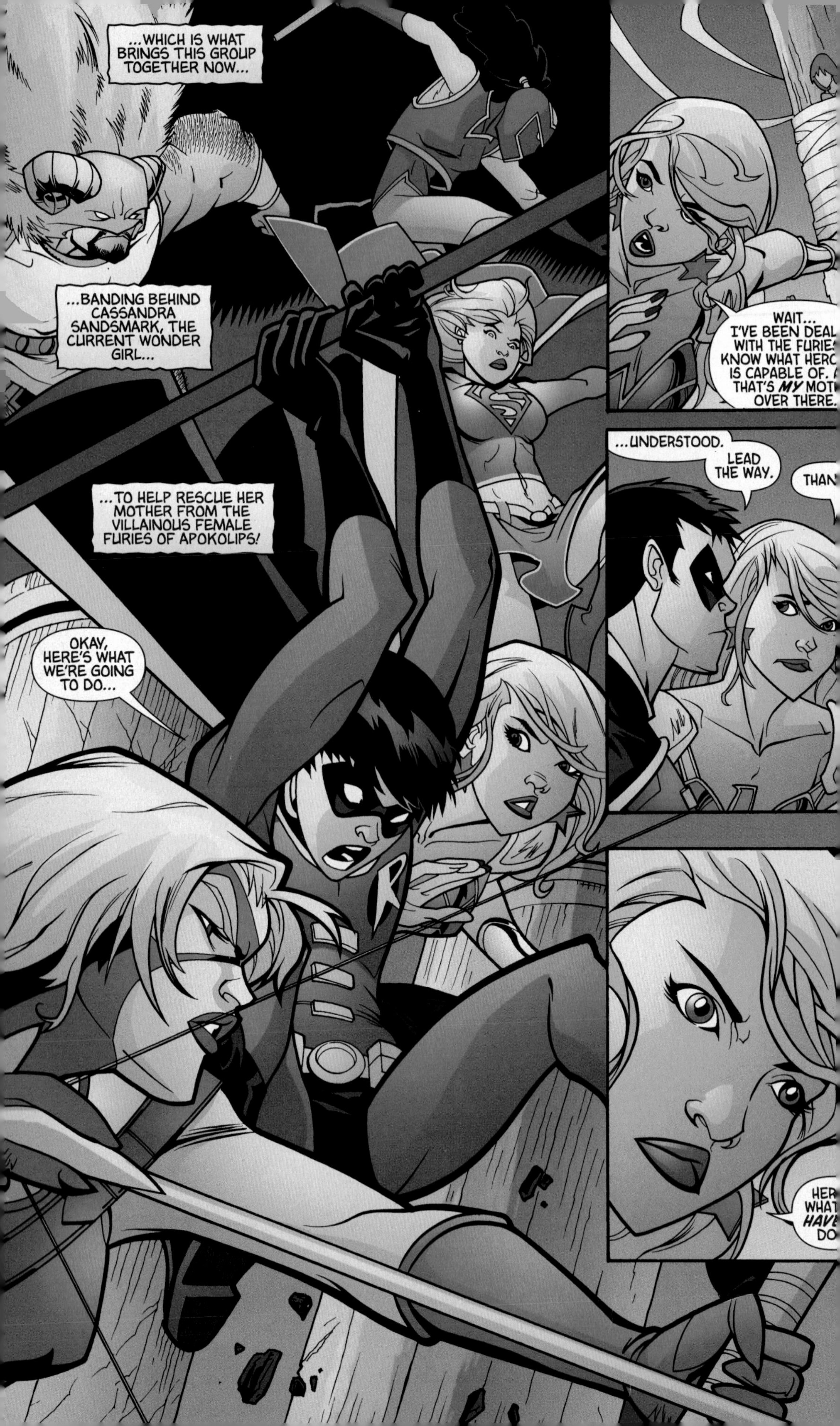
...WHICH IS WHAT BRINGS THIS GROUP TOGETHER NOW...
...BANDING BEHIND CASSANDRA SANDSMARK, THE CURRENT WONDER GIRL...
...TO HELP RESCUE HER MOTHER FROM THE VILLAINOUS FEMALE FURIES OF APOKOLIPS!
OKAY, HERE'S WHAT WE'RE GOING TO DO...
WAIT... I'VE BEEN DEAL WITH THE FURIES KNOW WHAT HERC IS CAPABLE OF. THAT'S MY MOT OVER THERE.
...UNDERSTOOD.
LEAD THE WAY.
THAN
HER WHAT HAVE DO

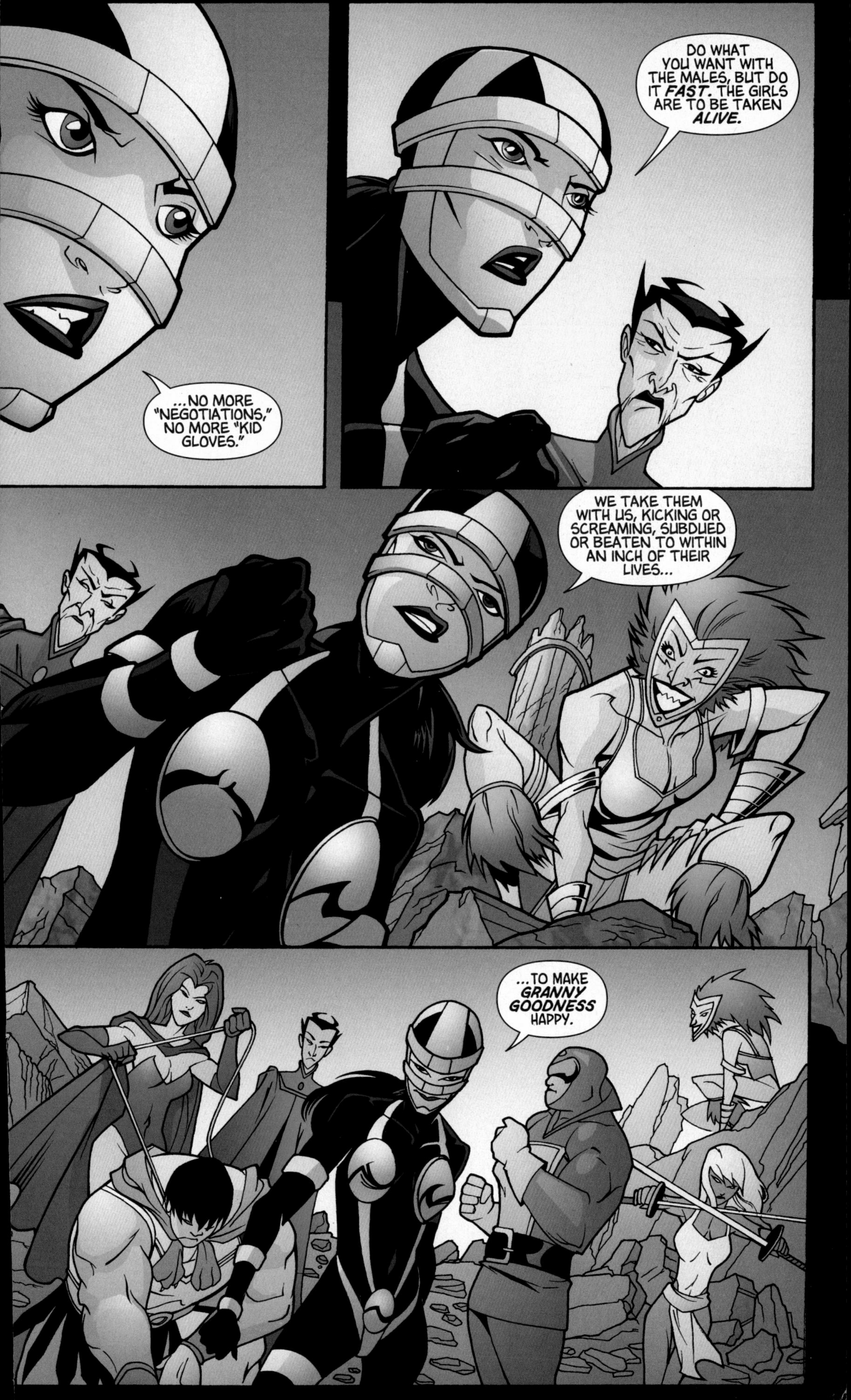
...NO MORE "NEGOTIATIONS," NO MORE "KID GLOVES."
DO WHAT YOU WANT WITH THE MALES, BUT DO IT *FAST*. THE GIRLS ARE TO BE TAKEN *ALIVE*.
WE TAKE THEM WITH US, KICKING OR SCREAMING, SUBDUED OR BEATEN TO WITHIN AN INCH OF THEIR LIVES...
...TO MAKE *GRANNY GOODNESS* HAPPY.

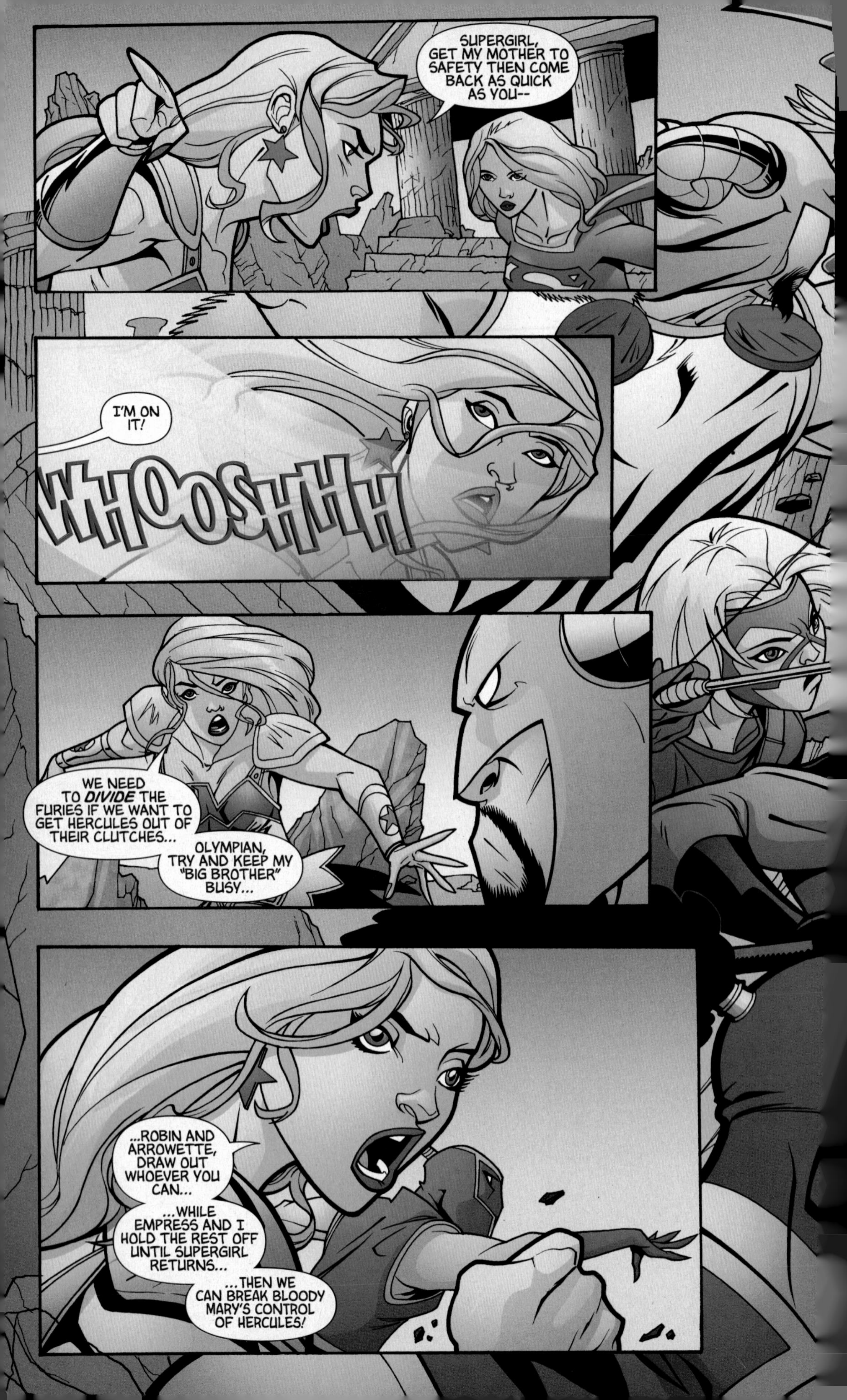
SUPERGIRL, GET MY MOTHER TO SAFETY THEN COME BACK AS QUICK AS YOU--
I'M ON IT!
WHOOSHHH
WE NEED TO *DIVIDE* THE FURIES IF WE WANT TO GET HERCULES OUT OF THEIR CLUTCHES...
OLYMPIAN, TRY AND KEEP MY "BIG BROTHER" BUSY...
...ROBIN AND ARROWETTE, DRAW OUT WHOEVER YOU CAN...
...WHILE EMPRESS AND I HOLD THE REST OFF UNTIL SUPERGIRL RETURNS...
...THEN WE CAN BREAK BLOODY MARY'S CONTROL OF HERCULES!

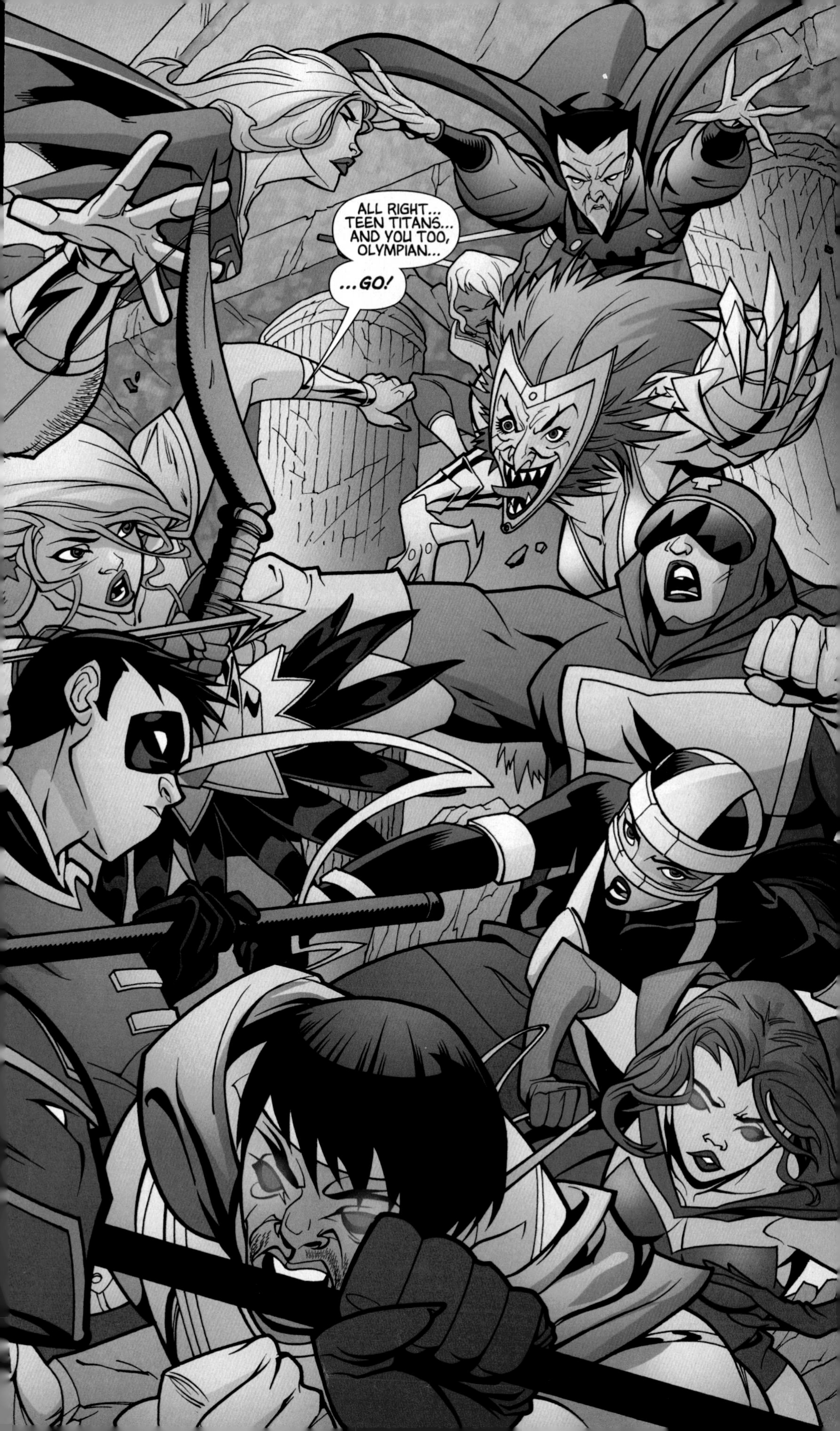
ALL RIGHT... TEEN TITANS... AND YOU TOO, OLYMPIAN...
...GO!

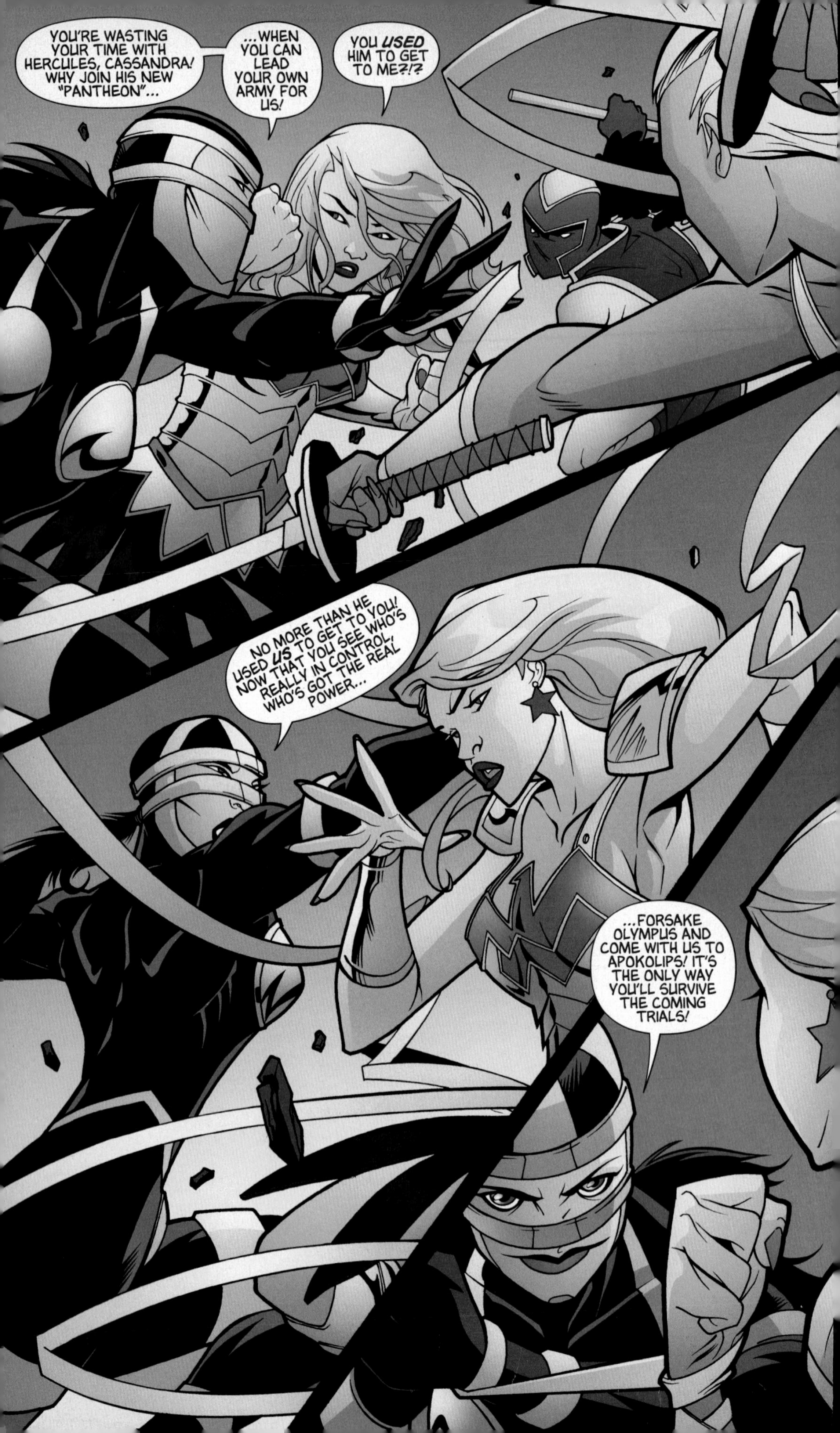
YOU'RE WASTING YOUR TIME WITH HERCULES, CASSANDRA! WHY JOIN HIS NEW "PANTHEON"...
...WHEN YOU CAN LEAD YOUR OWN ARMY FOR US!
YOU USED HIM TO GET TO ME?!?
NO MORE THAN HE USED US TO GET TO YOU! NOW THAT YOU SEE WHO'S REALLY IN CONTROL, WHO'S GOT THE REAL POWER...
...FORSAKE OLYMPUS AND COME WITH US TO APOKOLIPS! IT'S THE ONLY WAY YOU'LL SURVIVE THE COMING TRIALS!

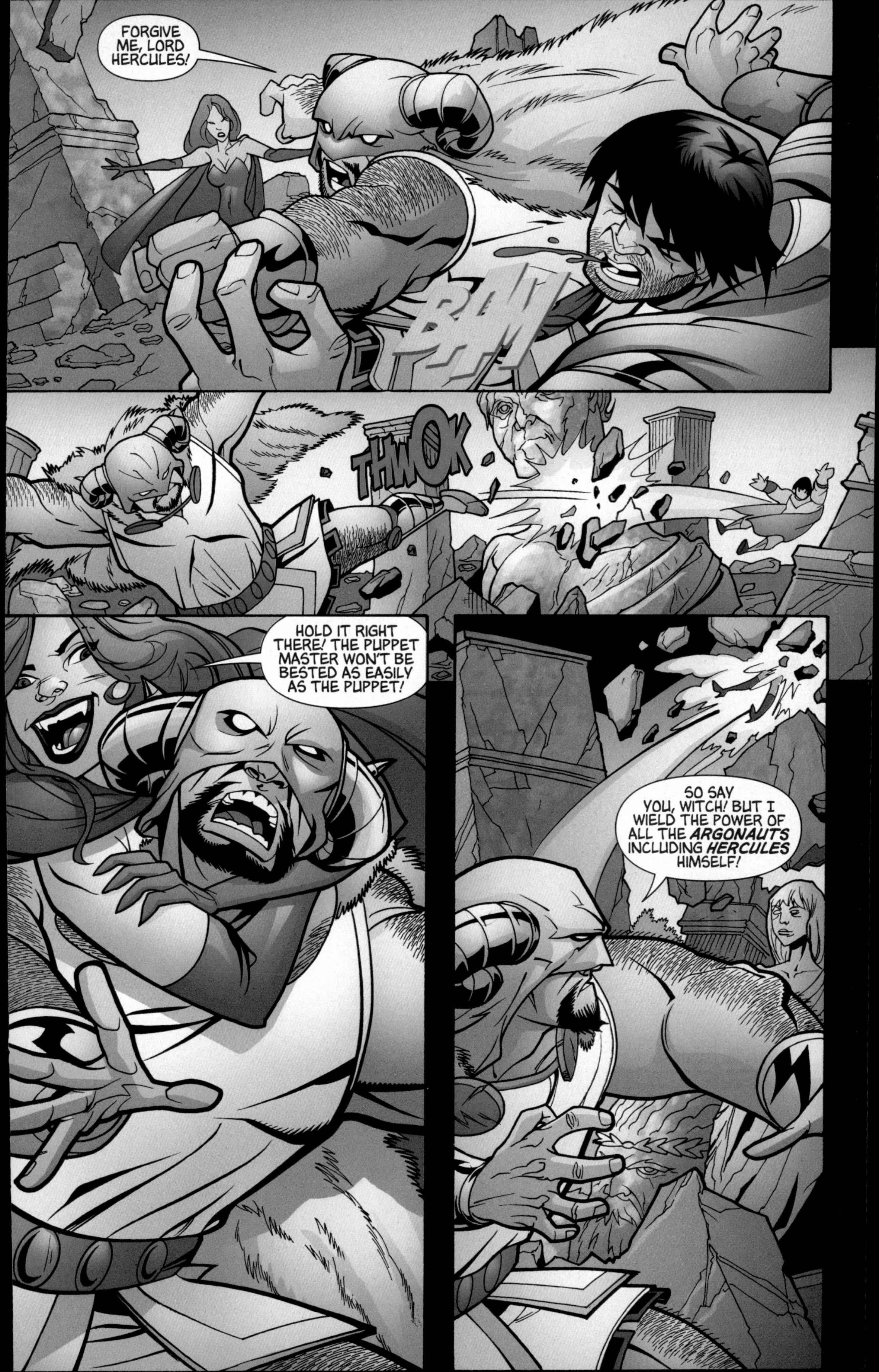
FORGIVE ME, LORD HERCULES!
BAM
THWOK
HOLD IT RIGHT THERE! THE PUPPET MASTER WON'T BE BESTED AS EASILY AS THE PUPPET!
SO SAY YOU, WITCH! BUT I WIELD THE POWER OF ALL THE *ARGONAUTS* INCLUDING *HERCULES* HIMSELF!

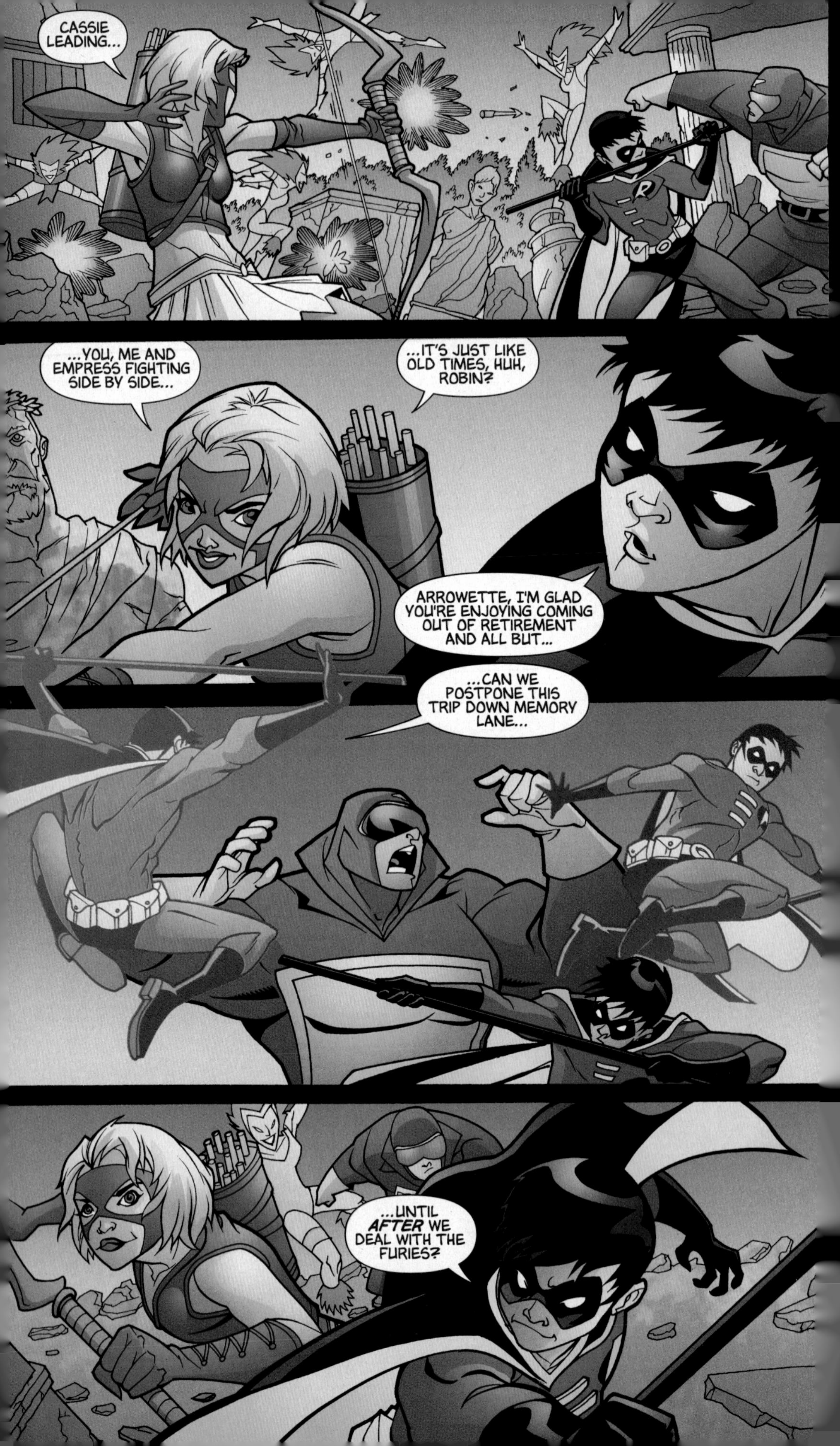
CASSIE LEADING...
...YOU, ME AND EMPRESS FIGHTING SIDE BY SIDE...
...IT'S JUST LIKE OLD TIMES, HUH, ROBIN?
ARROWETTE, I'M GLAD YOU'RE ENJOYING COMING OUT OF RETIREMENT AND ALL BUT...
...CAN WE POSTPONE THIS TRIP DOWN MEMORY LANE...
...UNTIL *AFTER* WE DEAL WITH THE FURIES?

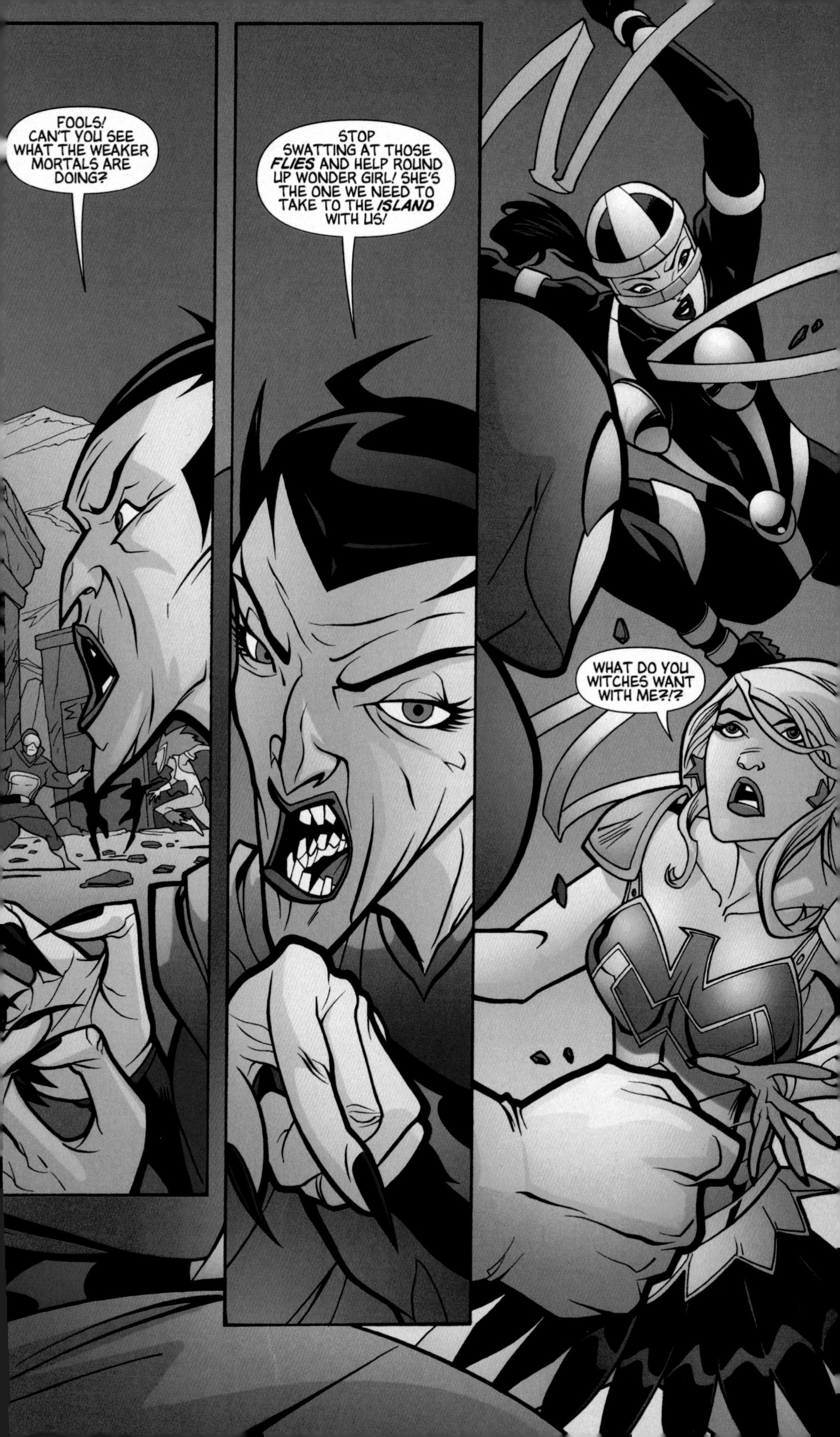
FOOLS! CAN'T YOU SEE WHAT THE WEAKER MORTALS ARE DOING?
STOP SWATTING AT THOSE FLIES AND HELP ROUND UP WONDER GIRL! SHE'S THE ONE WE NEED TO TAKE TO THE ISLAND WITH US!
WHAT DO YOU WITCHES WANT WITH ME?!?

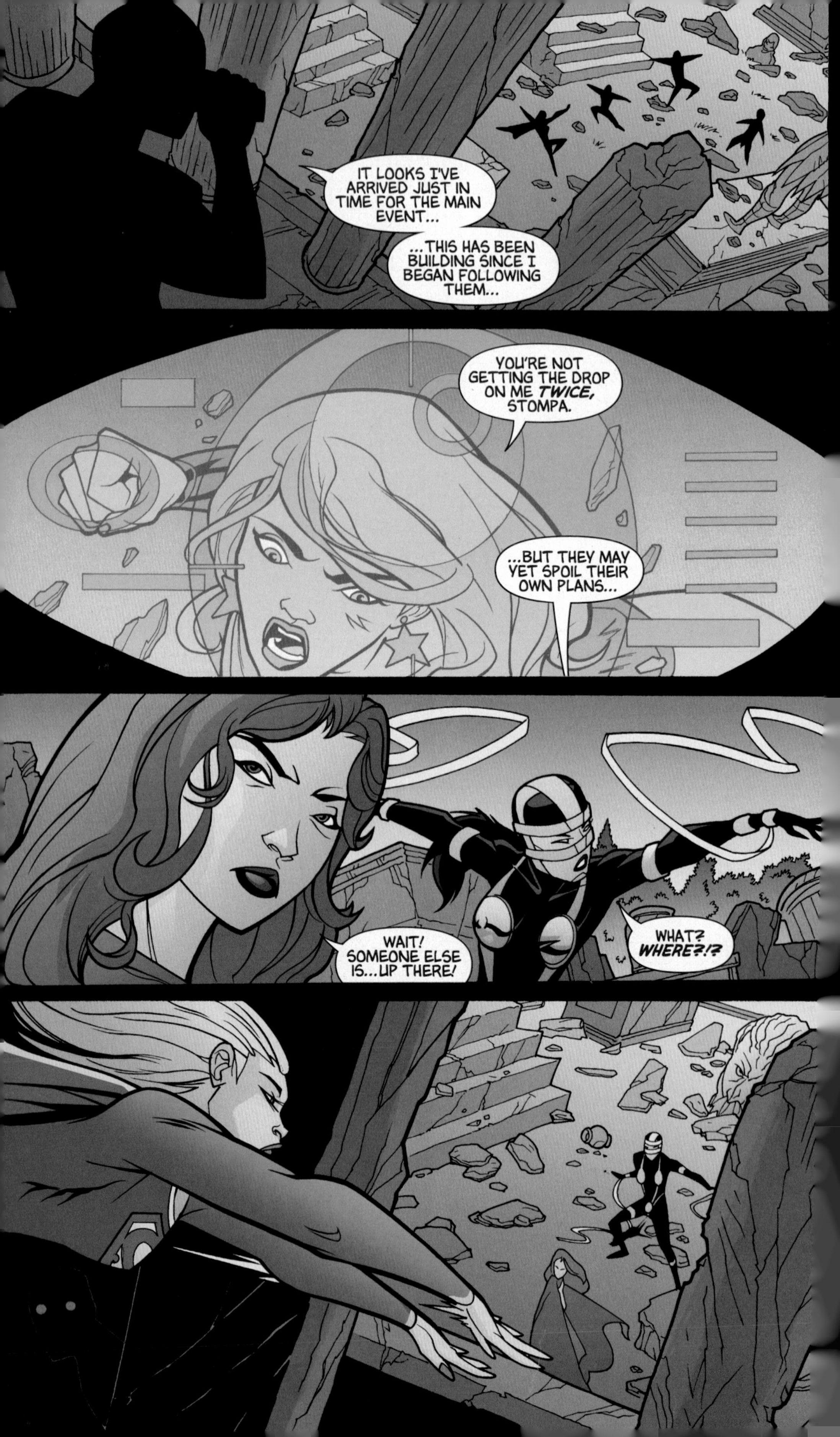
IT LOOKS I'VE ARRIVED JUST IN TIME FOR THE MAIN EVENT...
...THIS HAS BEEN BUILDING SINCE I BEGAN FOLLOWING THEM...
YOU'RE NOT GETTING THE DROP ON ME *TWICE,* STOMPA.
...BUT THEY MAY YET SPOIL THEIR OWN PLANS...
WAIT! SOMEONE ELSE IS...UP THERE!
WHAT? *WHERE?!?*

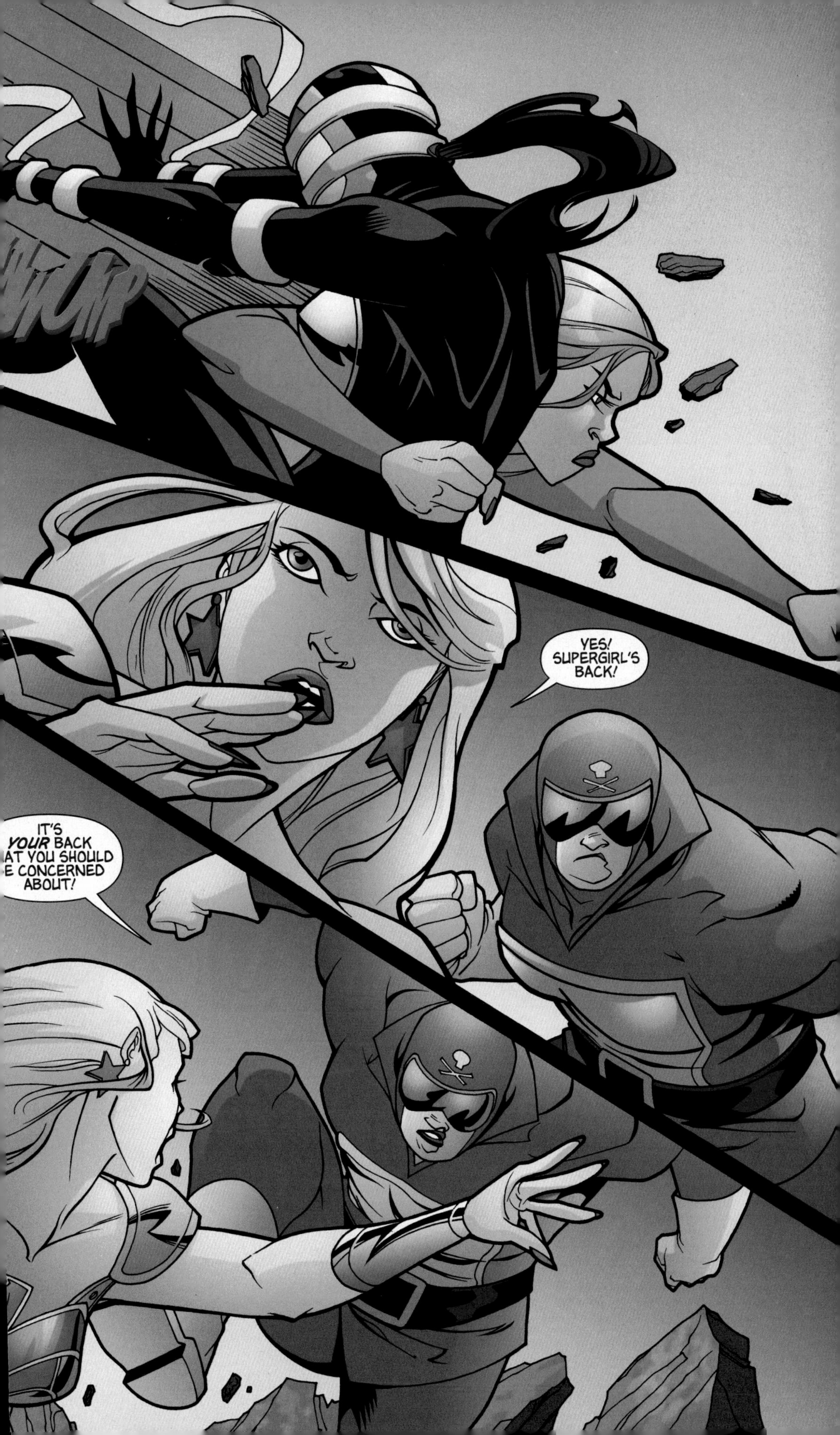
YES! SUPERGIRL'S BACK!
IT'S *YOUR* BACK AT YOU SHOULD E CONCERNED ABOUT!

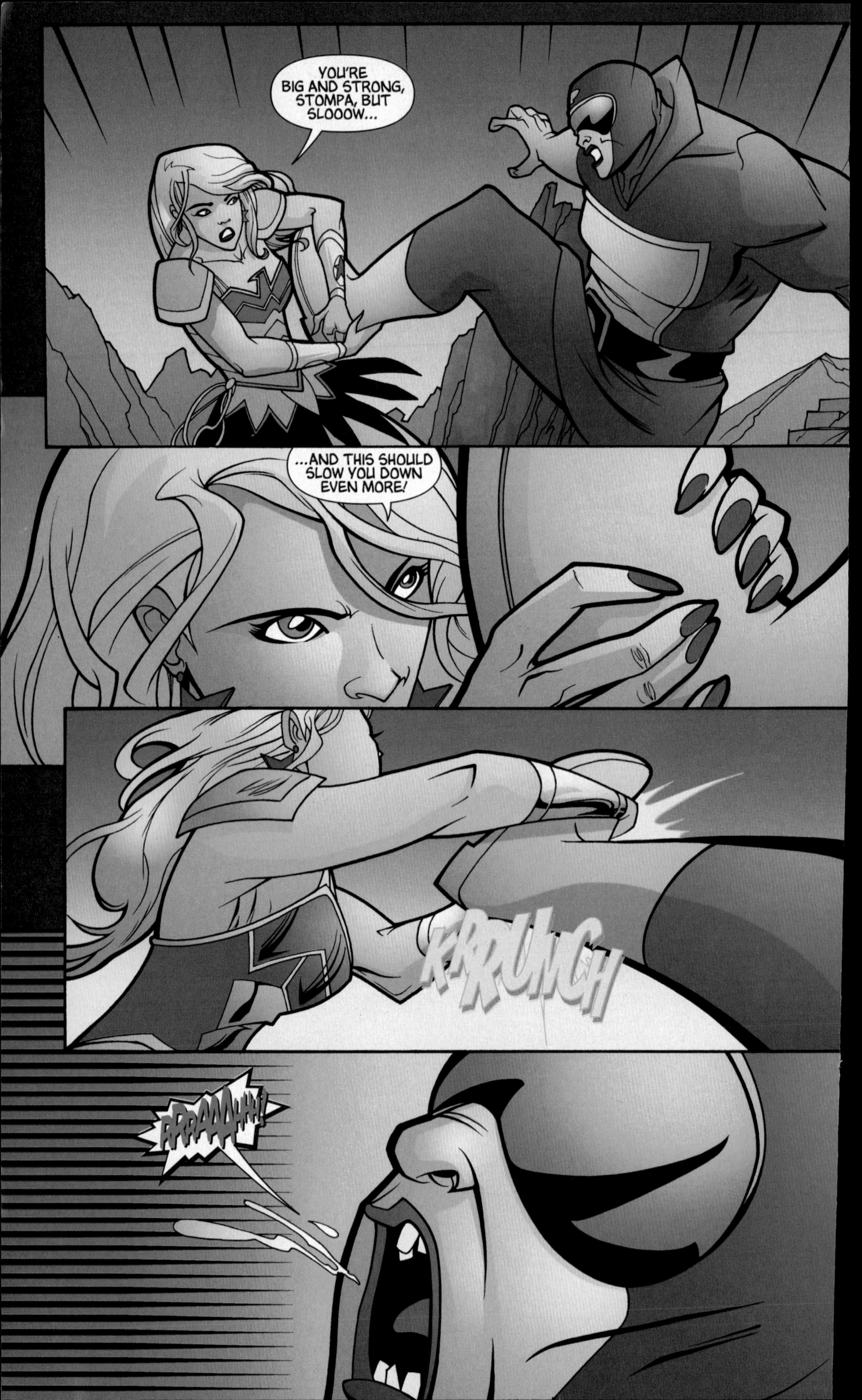
YOU'RE BIG AND STRONG, STOMPA, BUT SLOOOW...
...AND THIS SHOULD SLOW YOU DOWN EVEN MORE!
K-RRUNCH
RRRAAAHHH!

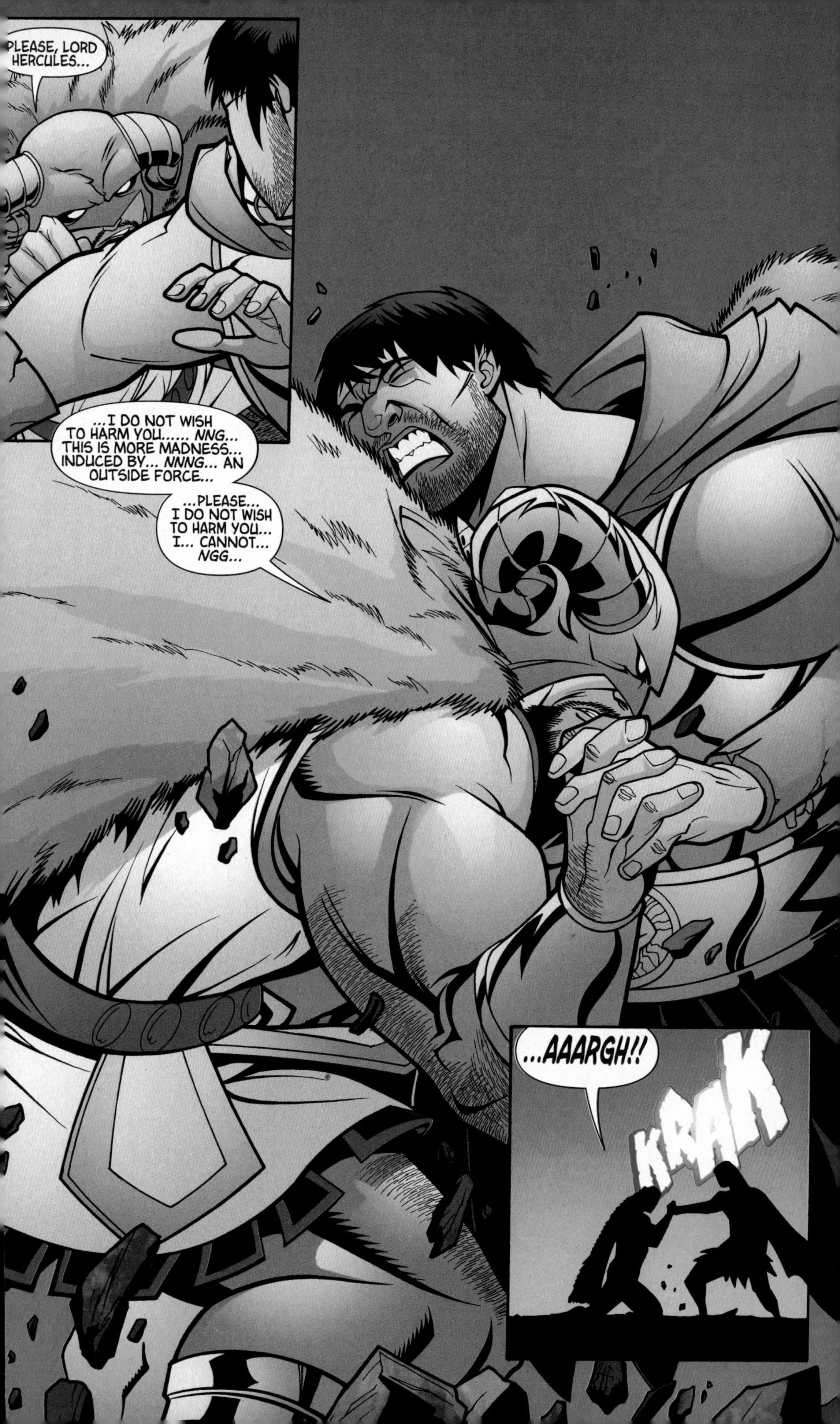
PLEASE, LORD HERCULES...
...I DO NOT WISH TO HARM YOU...... NNG... THIS IS MORE MADNESS... INDUCED BY... NNNG... AN OUTSIDE FORCE...
...PLEASE... I DO NOT WISH TO HARM YOU... I... CANNOT... NGG...
...AAARGH!!
KRAK

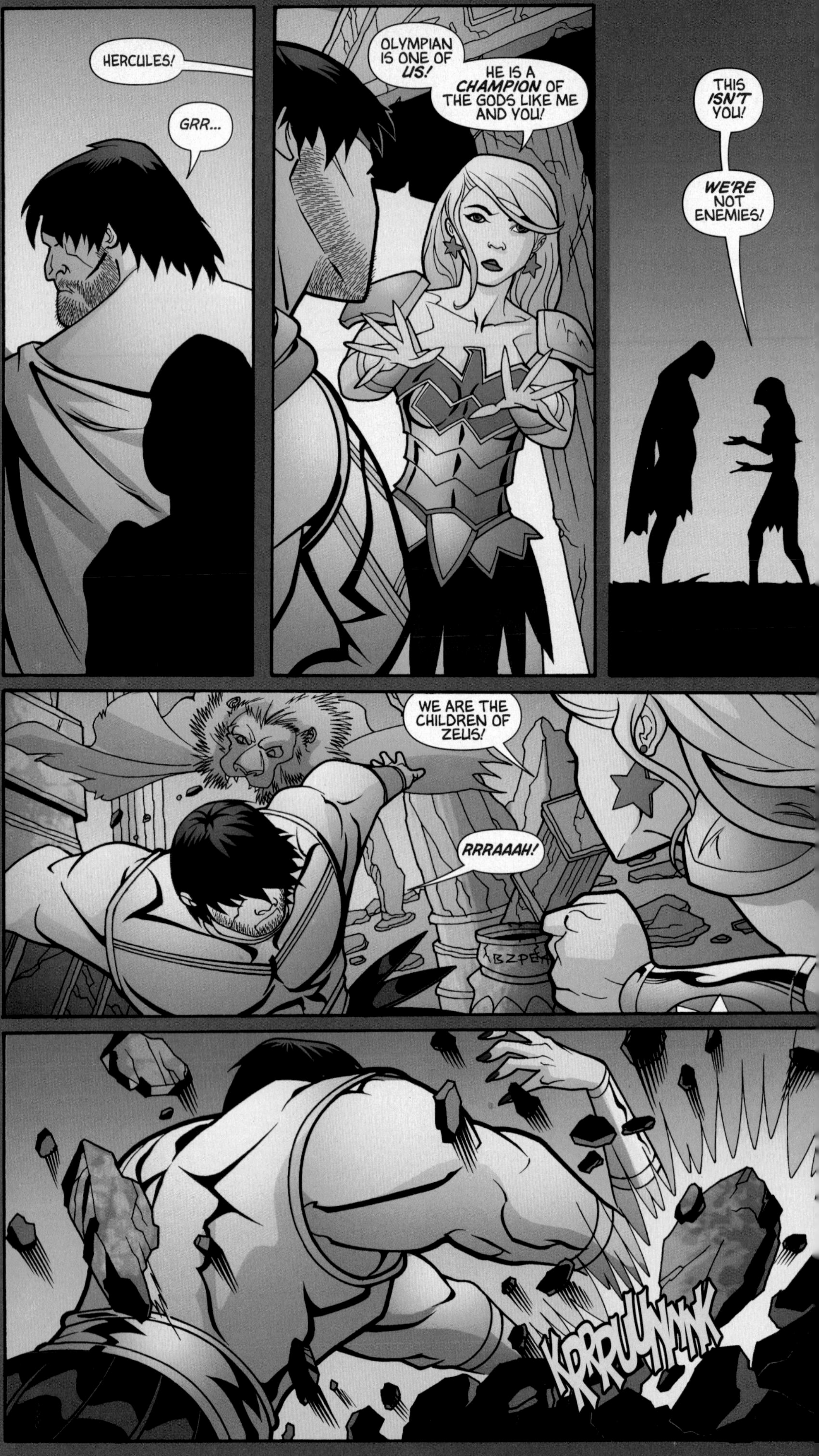
HERCULES!
GRR...
OLYMPIAN IS ONE OF US!
HE IS A CHAMPION OF THE GODS LIKE ME AND YOU!
THIS ISN'T YOU!
WE'RE NOT ENEMIES!
WE ARE THE CHILDREN OF ZEUS!
RRRAAAH!
KRRRUUNNNK

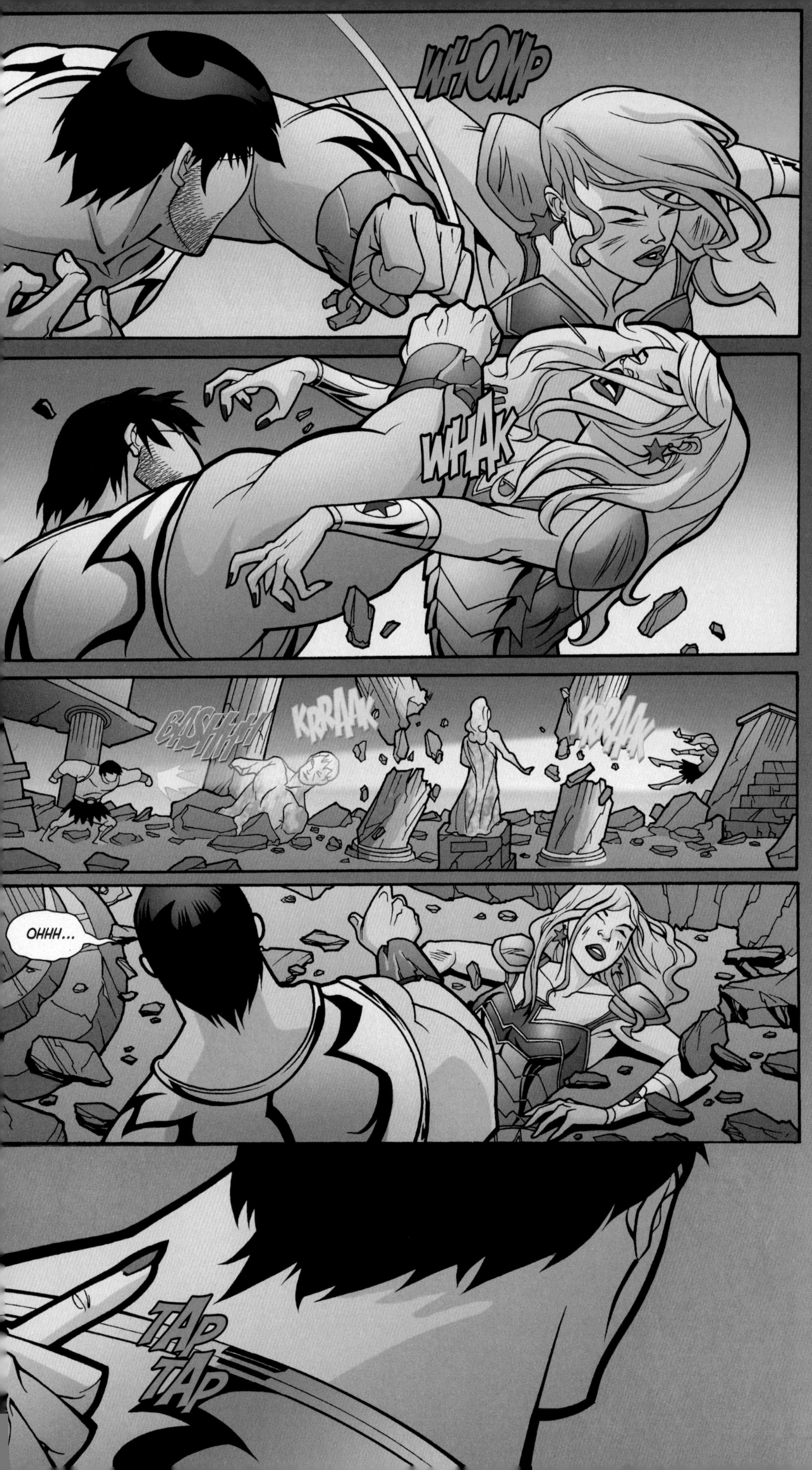
WHOMP
WHAK
BASHHH
KRRAAAK
KRRAAK
OHHH...
TAP
TAP

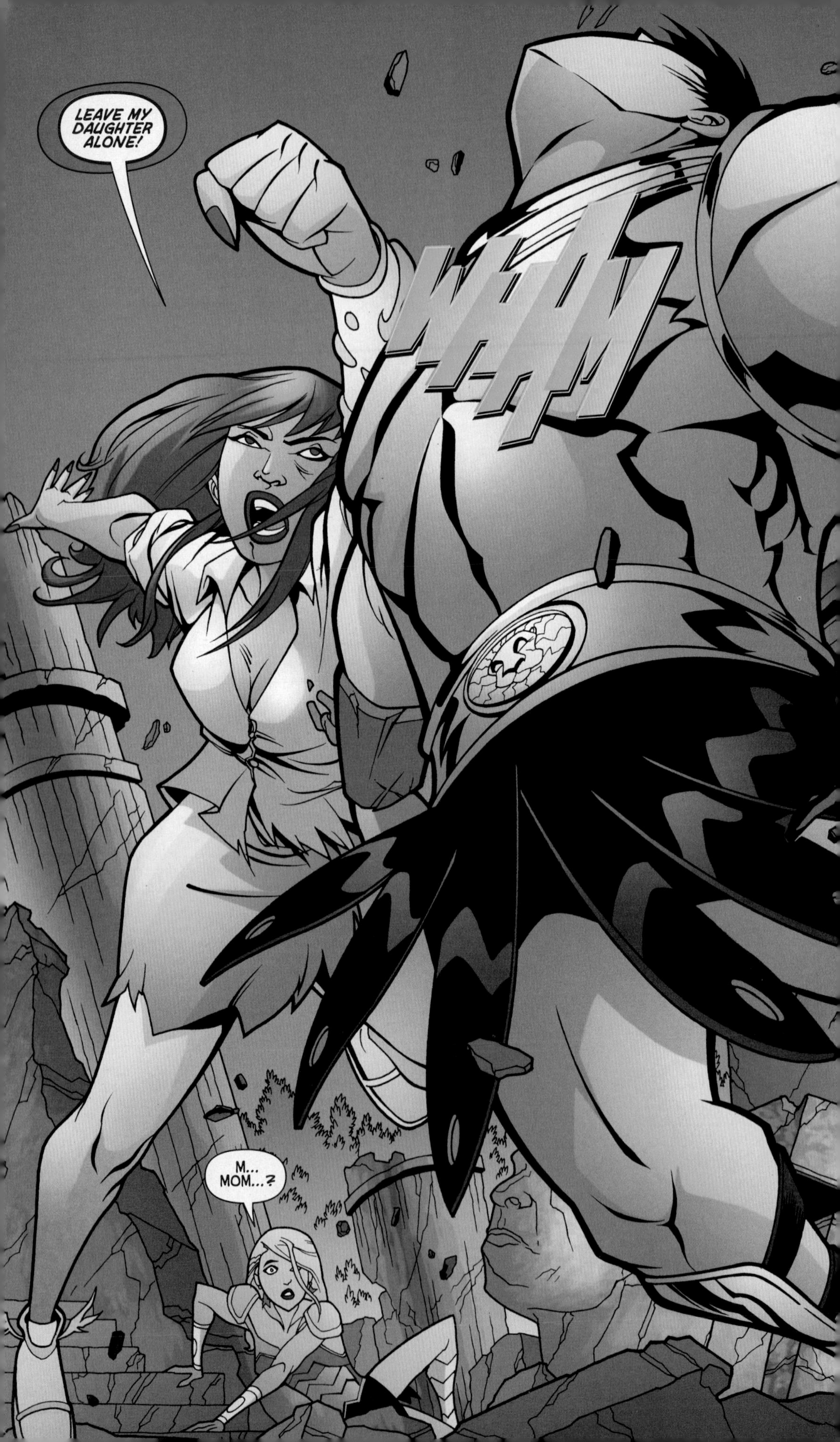
LEAVE MY DAUGHTER ALONE!
WHAM
M... MOM...?

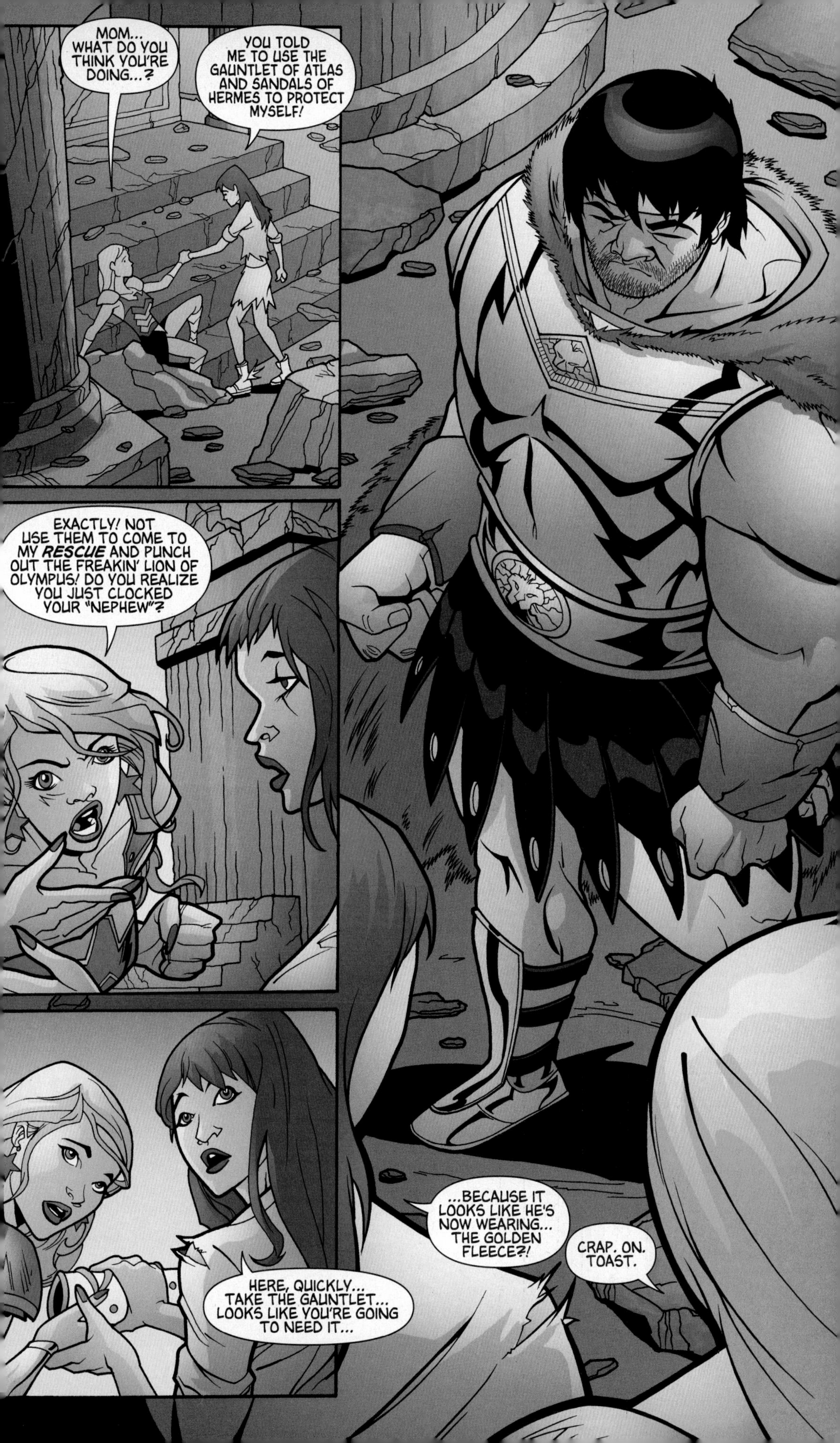
MOM... WHAT DO YOU THINK YOU'RE DOING...?
YOU TOLD ME TO USE THE GAUNTLET OF ATLAS AND SANDALS OF HERMES TO PROTECT MYSELF!
EXACTLY! NOT USE THEM TO COME TO MY *RESCUE* AND PUNCH OUT THE FREAKIN' LION OF OLYMPUS! DO YOU REALIZE YOU JUST CLOCKED YOUR "NEPHEW"?
HERE, QUICKLY... TAKE THE GAUNTLET... LOOKS LIKE YOU'RE GOING TO NEED IT...
...BECAUSE IT LOOKS LIKE HE'S NOW WEARING... THE GOLDEN FLEECE?!
CRAP. ON. TOAST.

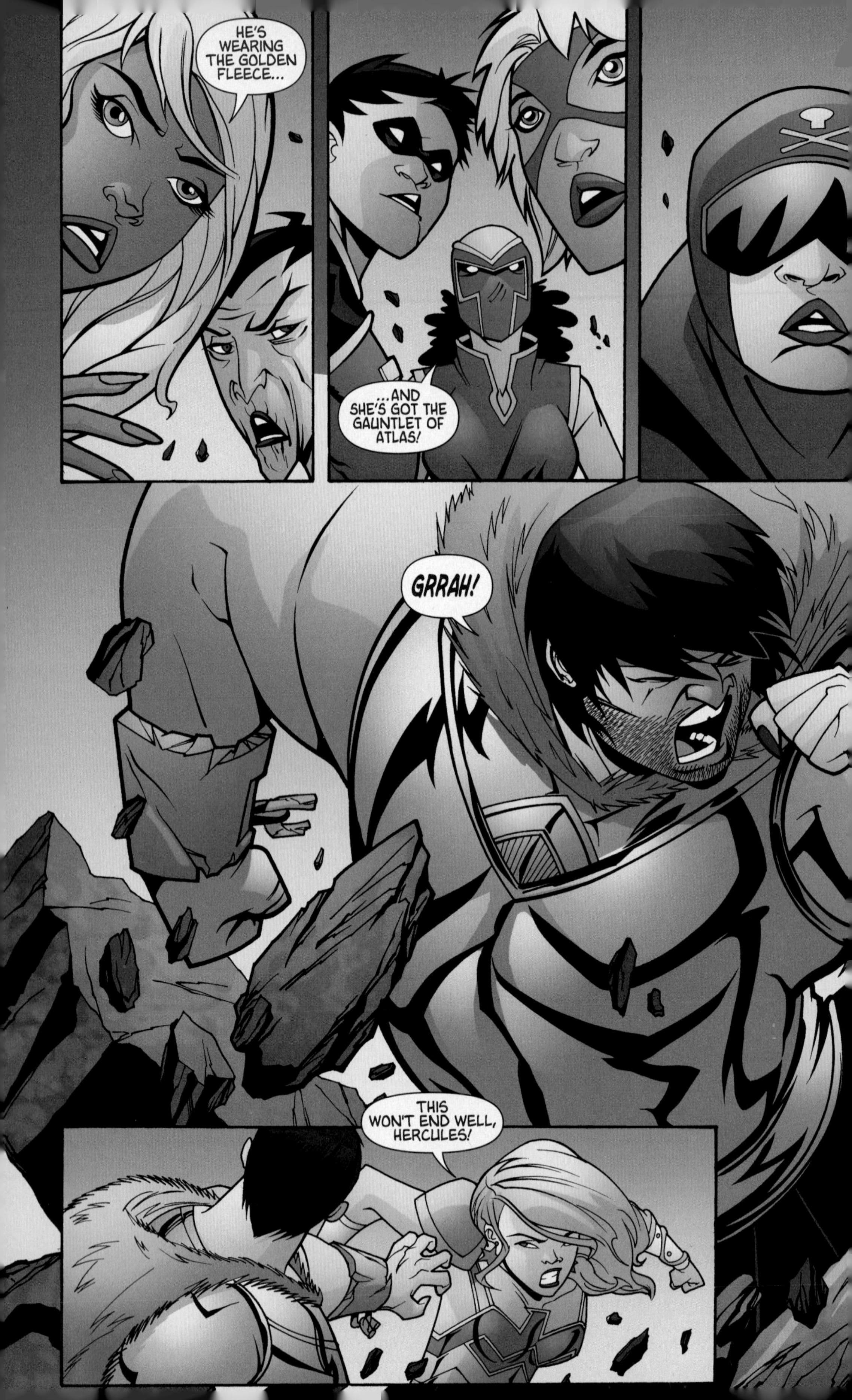
HE'S WEARING THE GOLDEN FLEECE...
...AND SHE'S GOT THE GAUNTLET OF ATLAS!
GRRAH!
THIS WON'T END WELL, HERCULES!

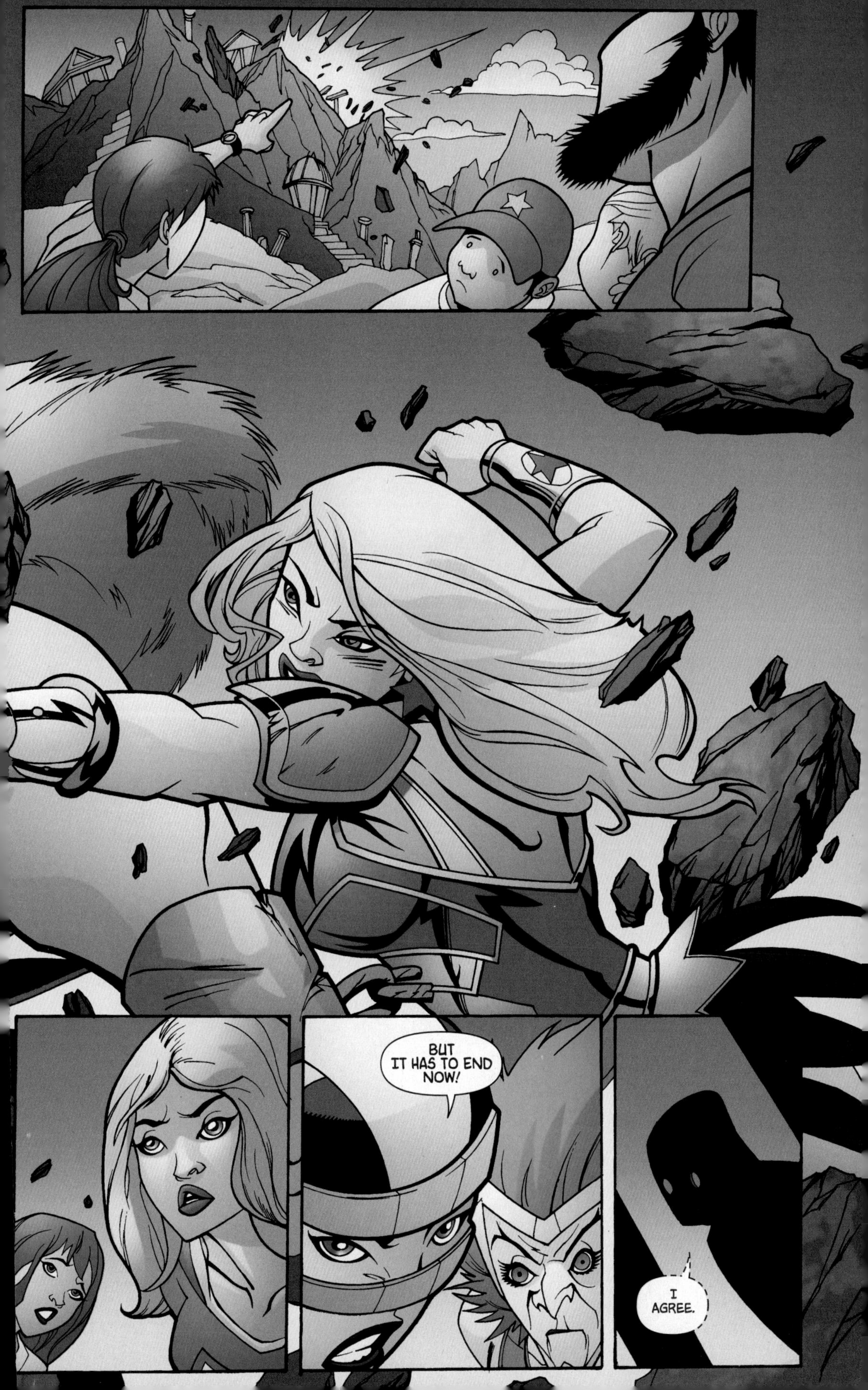
BUT IT HAS TO END NOW!
I AGREE.

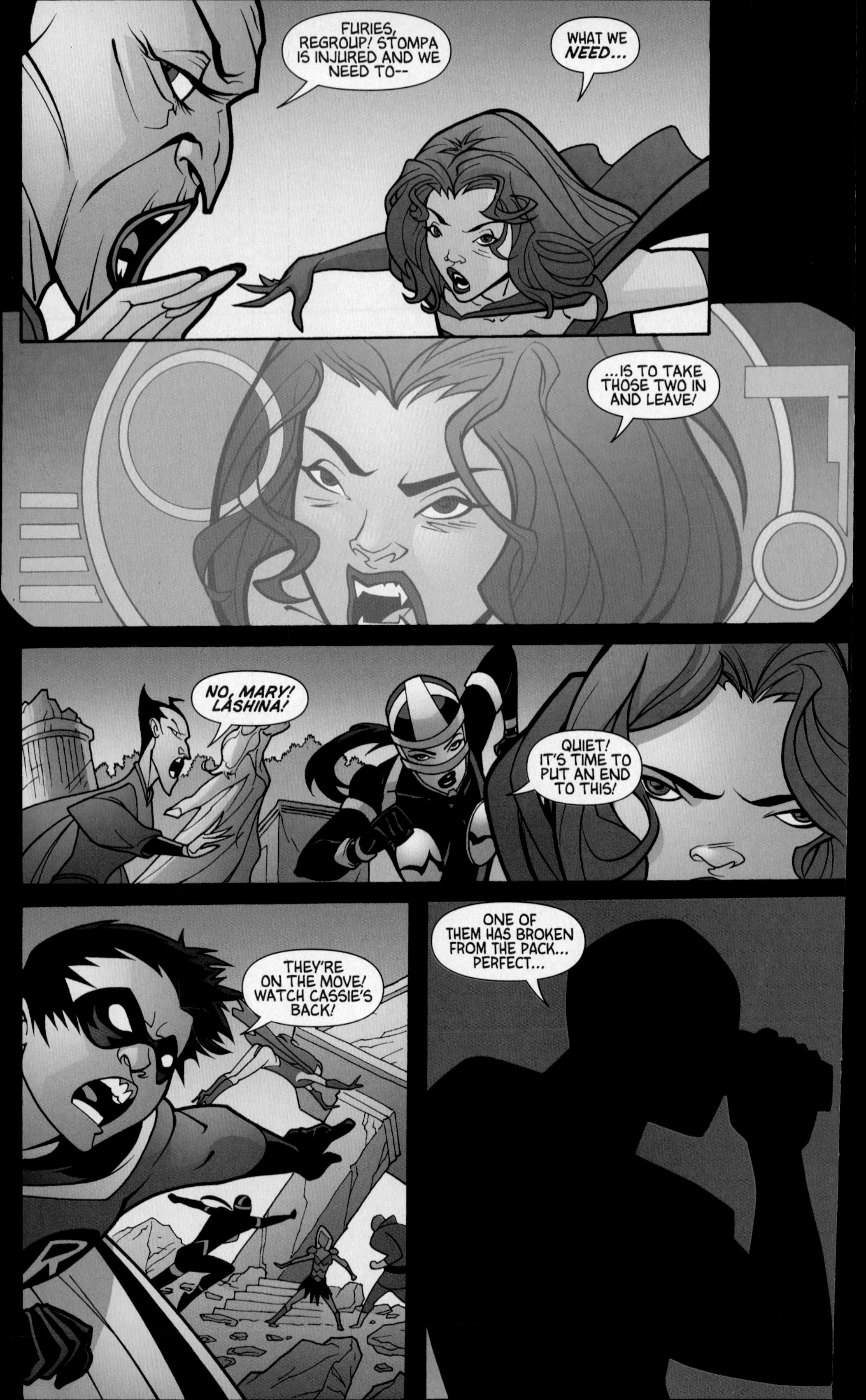
FURIES, REGROUP! STOMPA IS INJURED AND WE NEED TO--
WHAT WE *NEED*...
...IS TO TAKE THOSE TWO IN AND LEAVE!
NO, MARY! LASHINA!
QUIET! IT'S TIME TO PUT AN END TO THIS!
THEY'RE ON THE MOVE! WATCH CASSIE'S BACK!
ONE OF THEM HAS BROKEN FROM THE PACK... PERFECT...

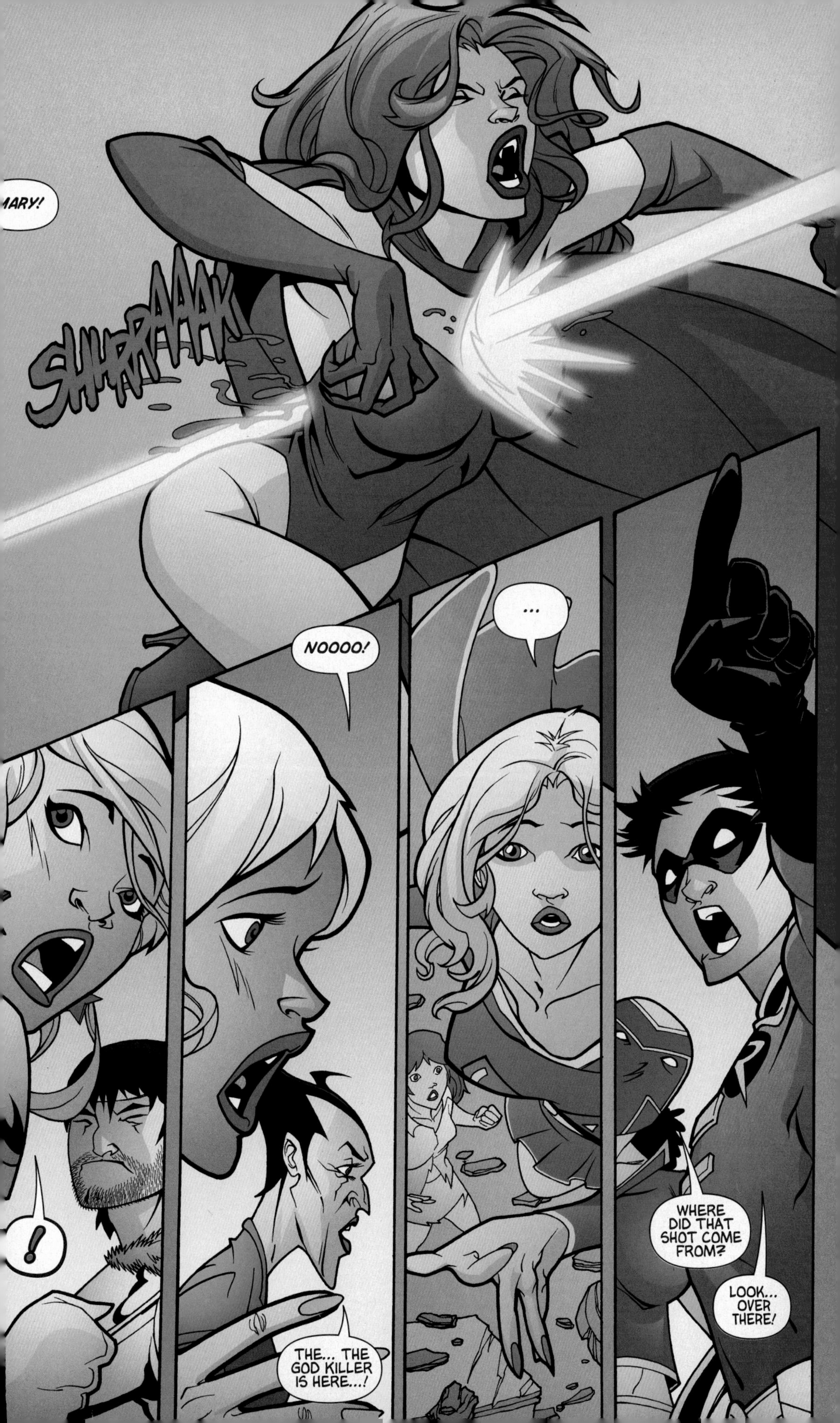
MARY!
SHHRAAAK
!
NOOOO!
THE... THE GOD KILLER IS HERE...!
...
WHERE DID THAT SHOT COME FROM?
LOOK... OVER THERE!

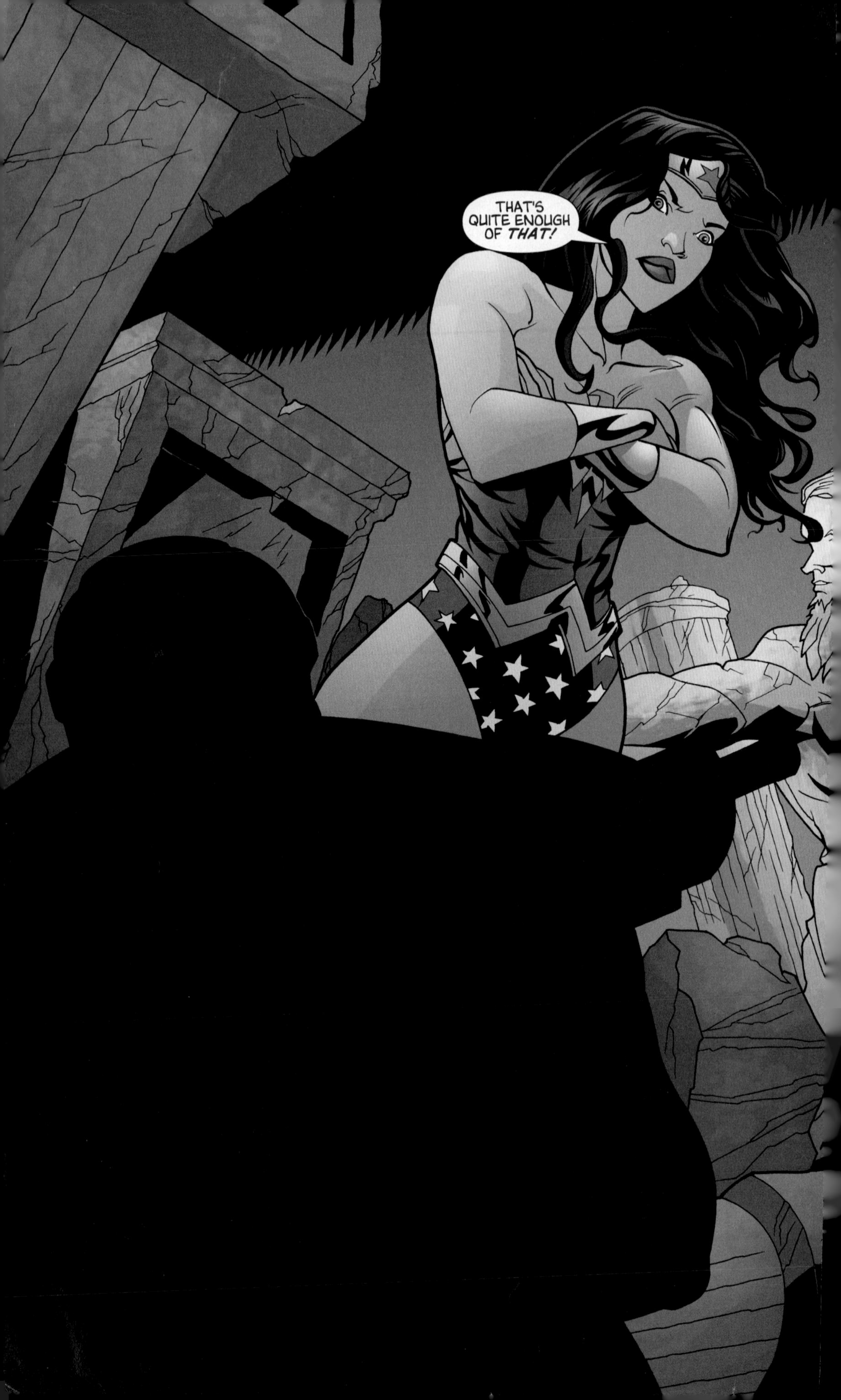
THAT'S QUITE ENOUGH OF *THAT!*

art 6: World of Wonders

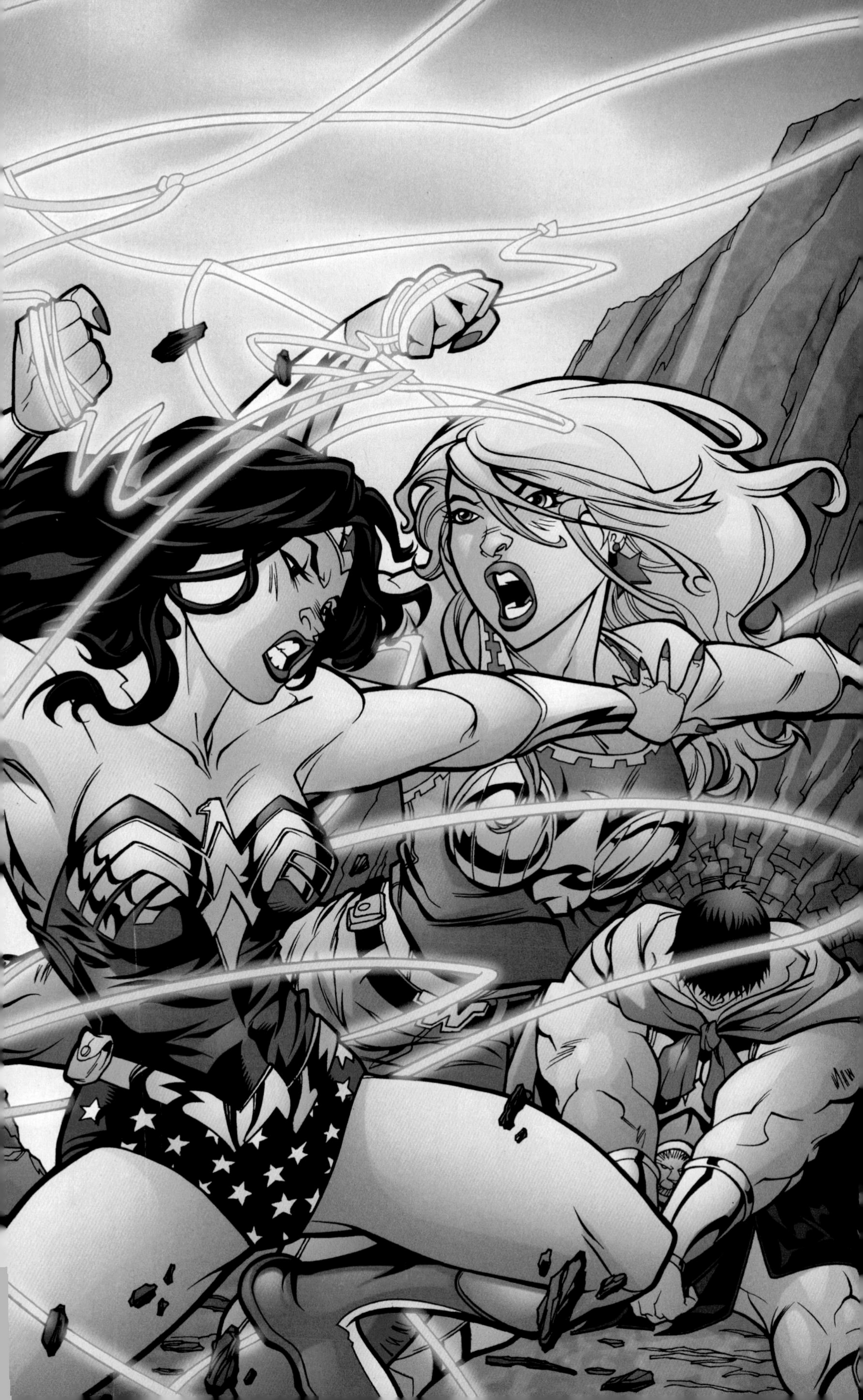

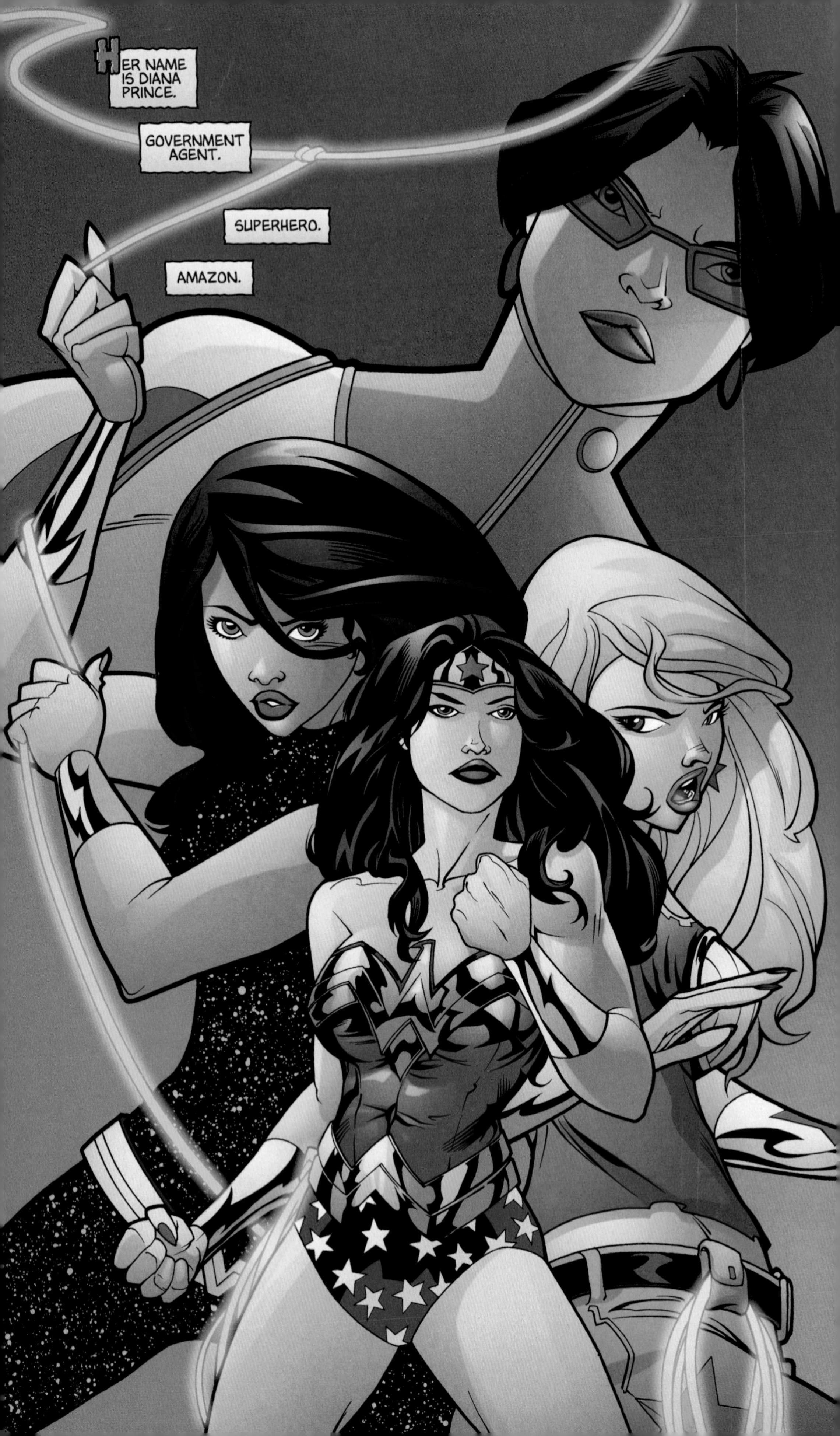
HER NAME IS DIANA PRINCE.
GOVERNMENT AGENT.
SUPERHERO.
AMAZON.

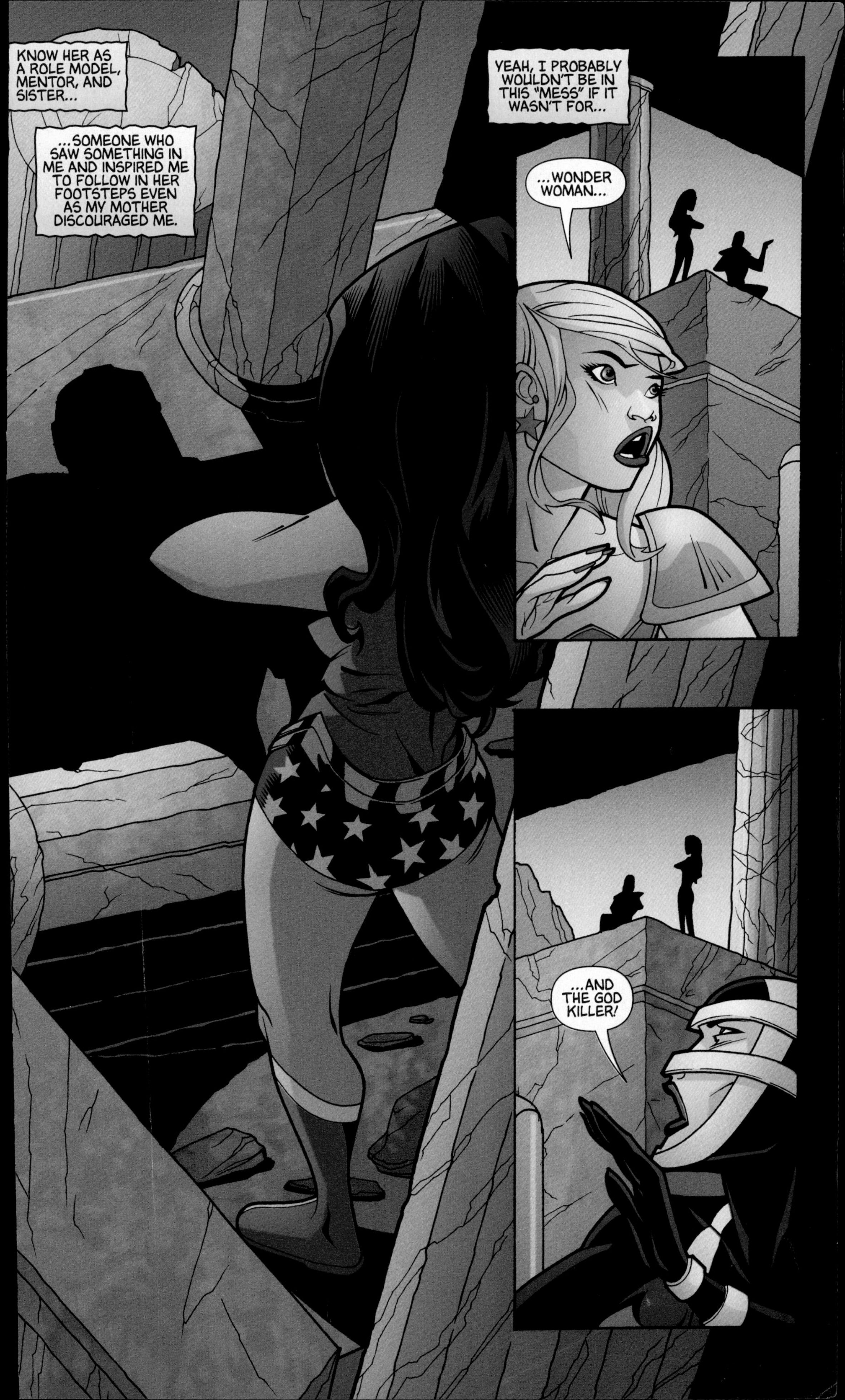
KNOW HER AS A ROLE MODEL, MENTOR, AND SISTER...
...SOMEONE WHO SAW SOMETHING IN ME AND INSPIRED ME TO FOLLOW IN HER FOOTSTEPS EVEN AS MY MOTHER DISCOURAGED ME.
YEAH, I PROBABLY WOULDN'T BE IN THIS "MESS" IF IT WASN'T FOR...
...WONDER WOMAN...
...AND THE GOD KILLER!

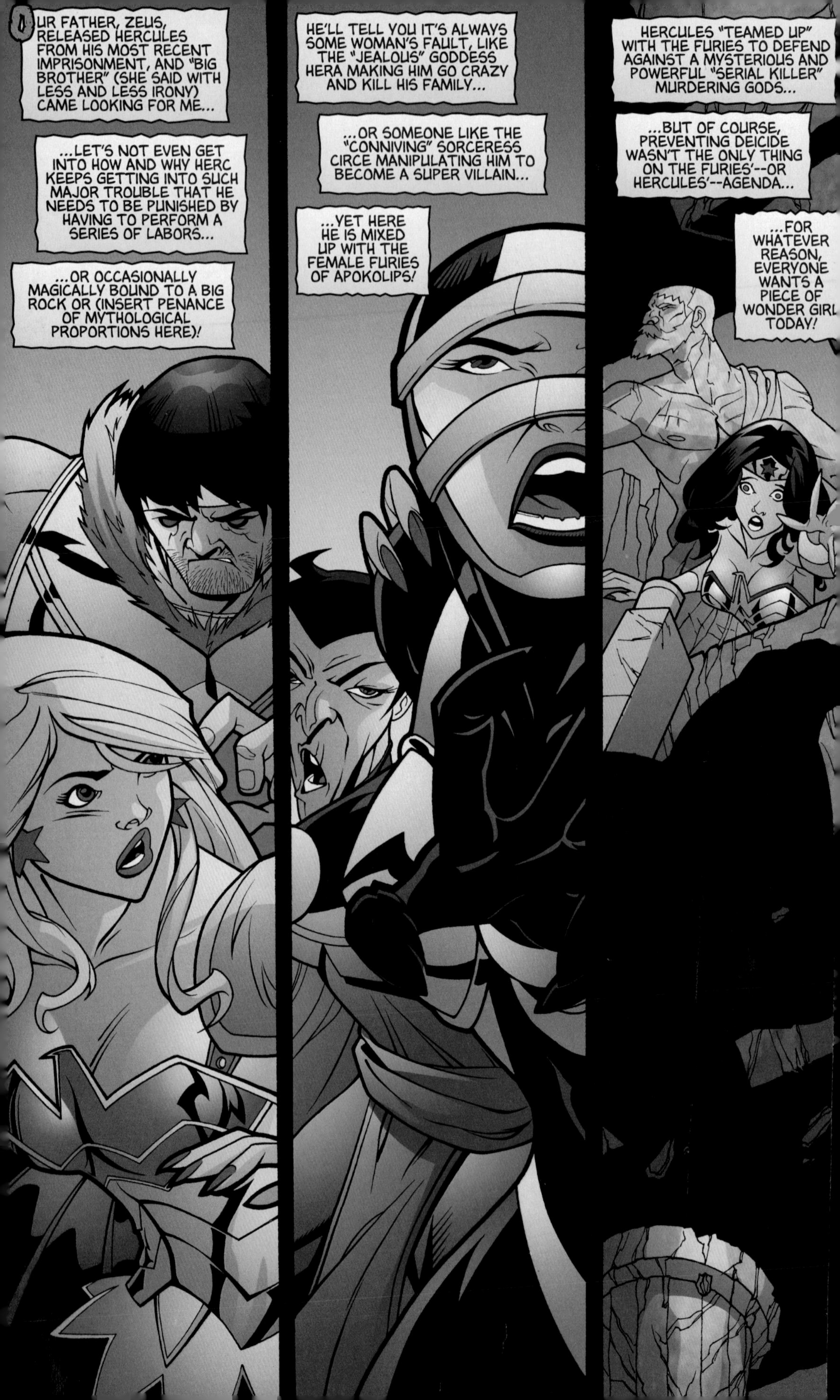
OUR FATHER, ZEUS, RELEASED HERCULES FROM HIS MOST RECENT IMPRISONMENT, AND "BIG BROTHER" (SHE SAID WITH LESS AND LESS IRONY) CAME LOOKING FOR ME...
...LET'S NOT EVEN GET INTO HOW AND WHY HERC KEEPS GETTING INTO SUCH MAJOR TROUBLE THAT HE NEEDS TO BE PUNISHED BY HAVING TO PERFORM A SERIES OF LABORS...
...OR OCCASIONALLY MAGICALLY BOUND TO A BIG ROCK OR (INSERT PENANCE OF MYTHOLOGICAL PROPORTIONS HERE)!
HE'LL TELL YOU IT'S ALWAYS SOME WOMAN'S FAULT, LIKE THE "JEALOUS" GODDESS HERA MAKING HIM GO CRAZY AND KILL HIS FAMILY...
...OR SOMEONE LIKE THE "CONNIVING" SORCERESS CIRCE MANIPULATING HIM TO BECOME A SUPER VILLAIN...
...YET HERE HE IS MIXED UP WITH THE FEMALE FURIES OF APOKOLIPS!
HERCULES "TEAMED UP" WITH THE FURIES TO DEFEND AGAINST A MYSTERIOUS AND POWERFUL "SERIAL KILLER" MURDERING GODS...
...BUT OF COURSE, PREVENTING DEICIDE WASN'T THE ONLY THING ON THE FURIES'--OR HERCULES'--AGENDA...
...FOR WHATEVER REASON, EVERYONE WANTS A PIECE OF WONDER GIRL TODAY!

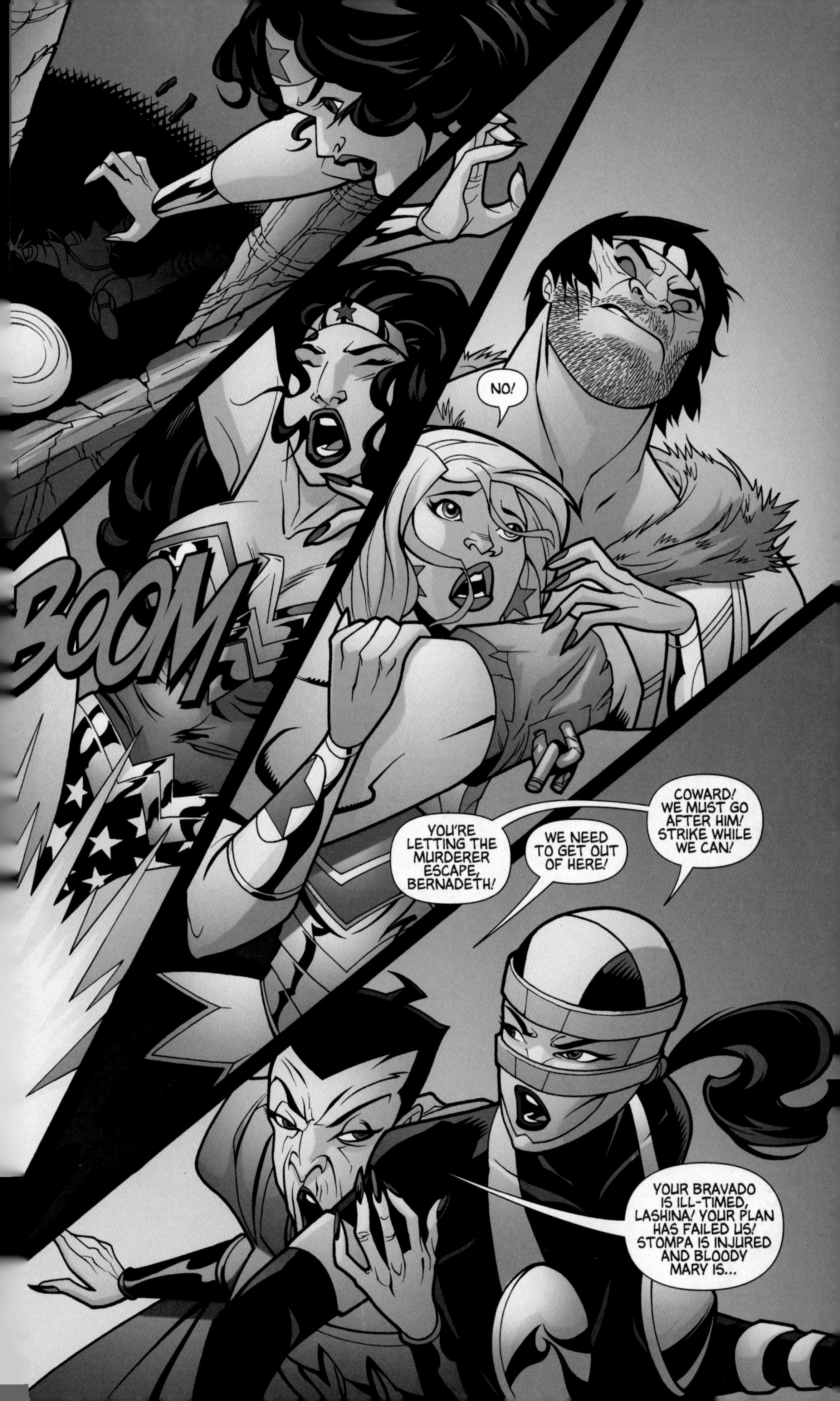
NO!
BOOM
YOU'RE LETTING THE MURDERER ESCAPE, BERNADETH!
WE NEED TO GET OUT OF HERE!
COWARD! WE MUST GO AFTER HIM! STRIKE WHILE WE CAN!
YOUR BRAVADO IS ILL-TIMED, LASHINA! YOUR PLAN HAS FAILED US! STOMPA IS INJURED AND BLOODY MARY IS...

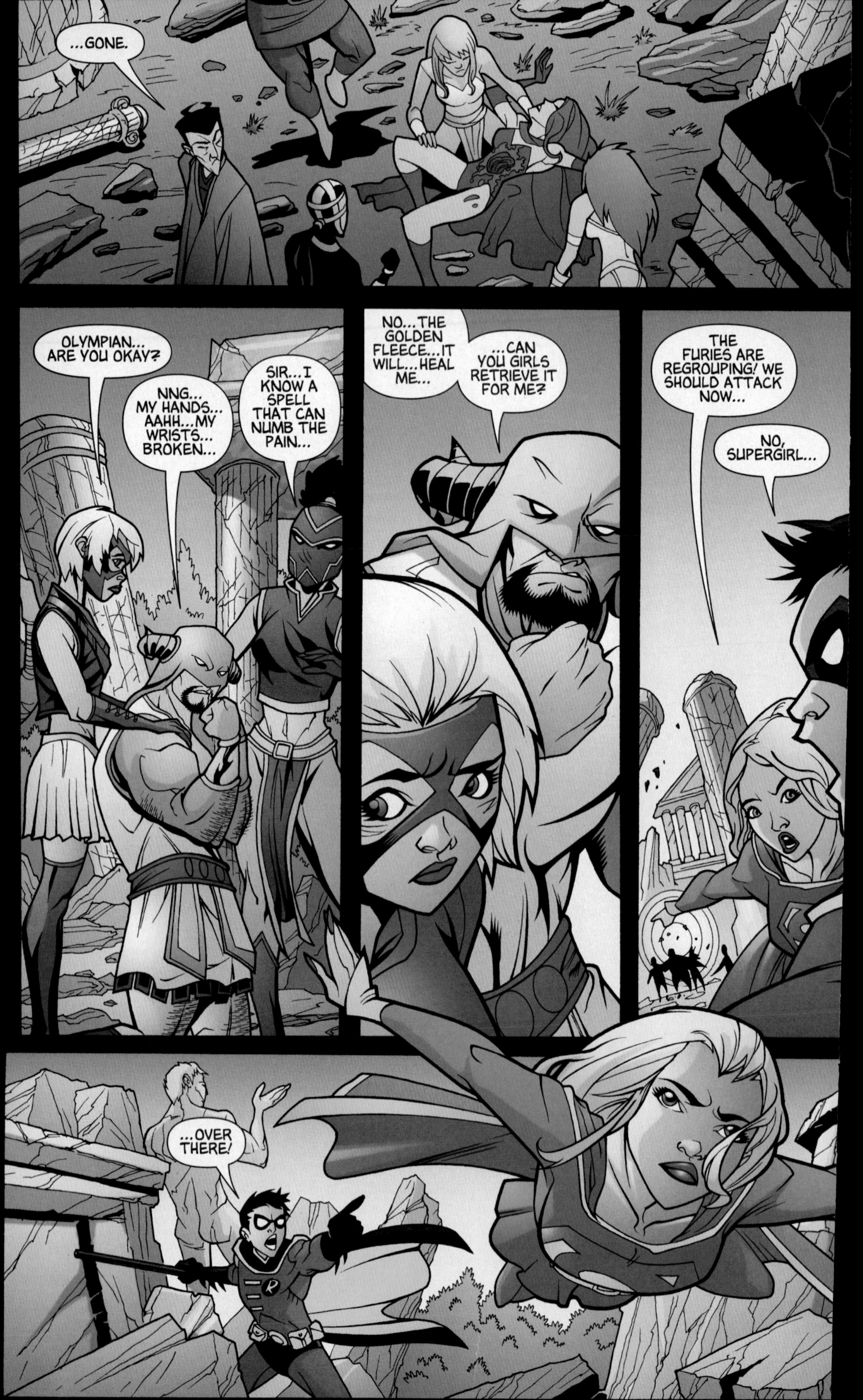
...GONE.
OLYMPIAN... ARE YOU OKAY?
NNG... MY HANDS... AAHH...MY WRISTS... BROKEN...
SIR...I KNOW A SPELL THAT CAN NUMB THE PAIN...
NO...THE GOLDEN FLEECE...IT WILL...HEAL ME...
...CAN YOU GIRLS RETRIEVE IT FOR ME?
THE FURIES ARE REGROUPING! WE SHOULD ATTACK NOW...
NO, SUPERGIRL...
...OVER THERE!

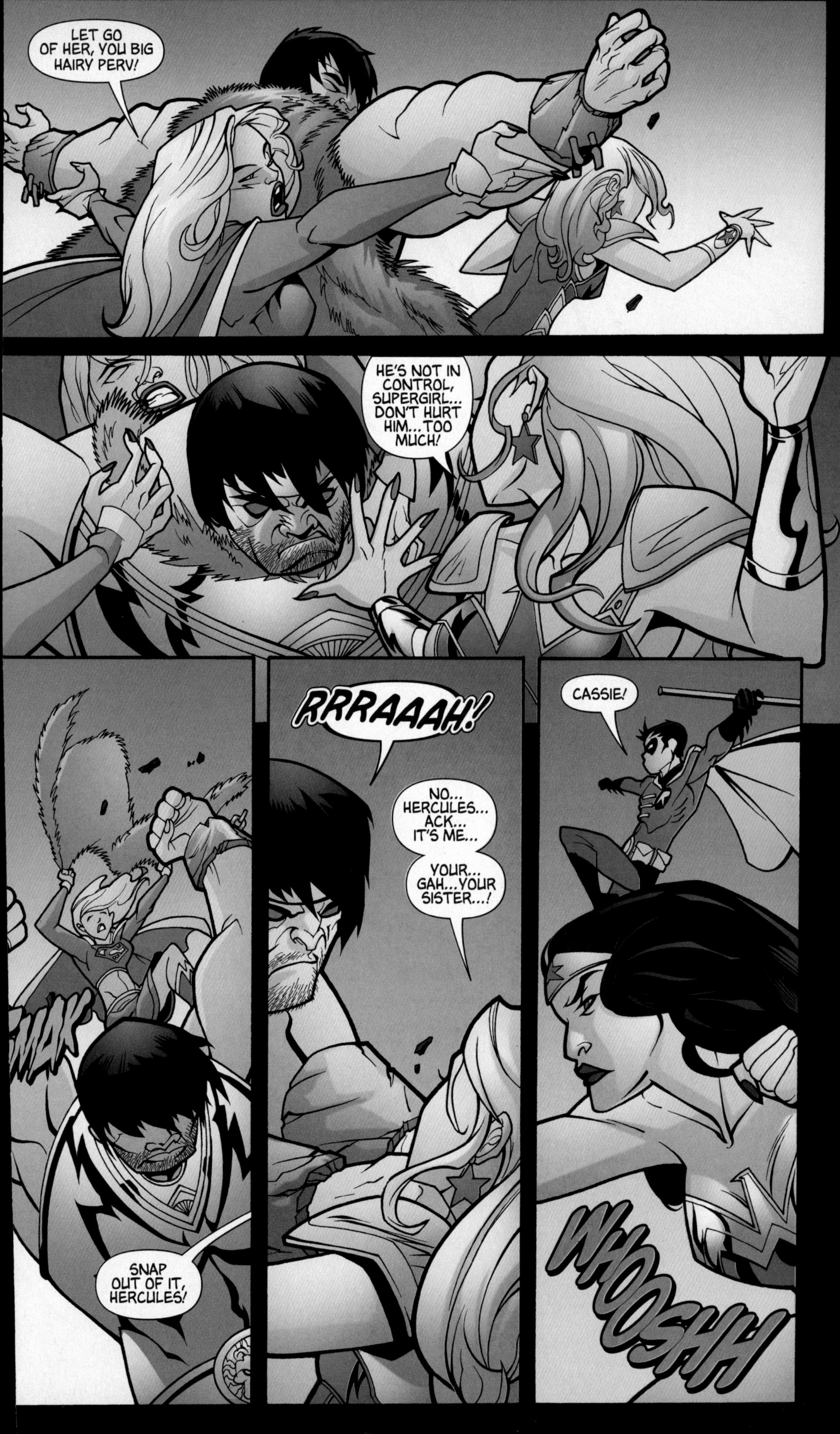
LET GO OF HER, YOU BIG HAIRY PERV!
HE'S NOT IN CONTROL, SUPERGIRL... DON'T HURT HIM...TOO MUCH!
SNAP OUT OF IT, HERCULES!
RRRAAAH!
NO... HERCULES... ACK... IT'S ME...
YOUR... GAH...YOUR SISTER...!
CASSIE!
WHOOSHH

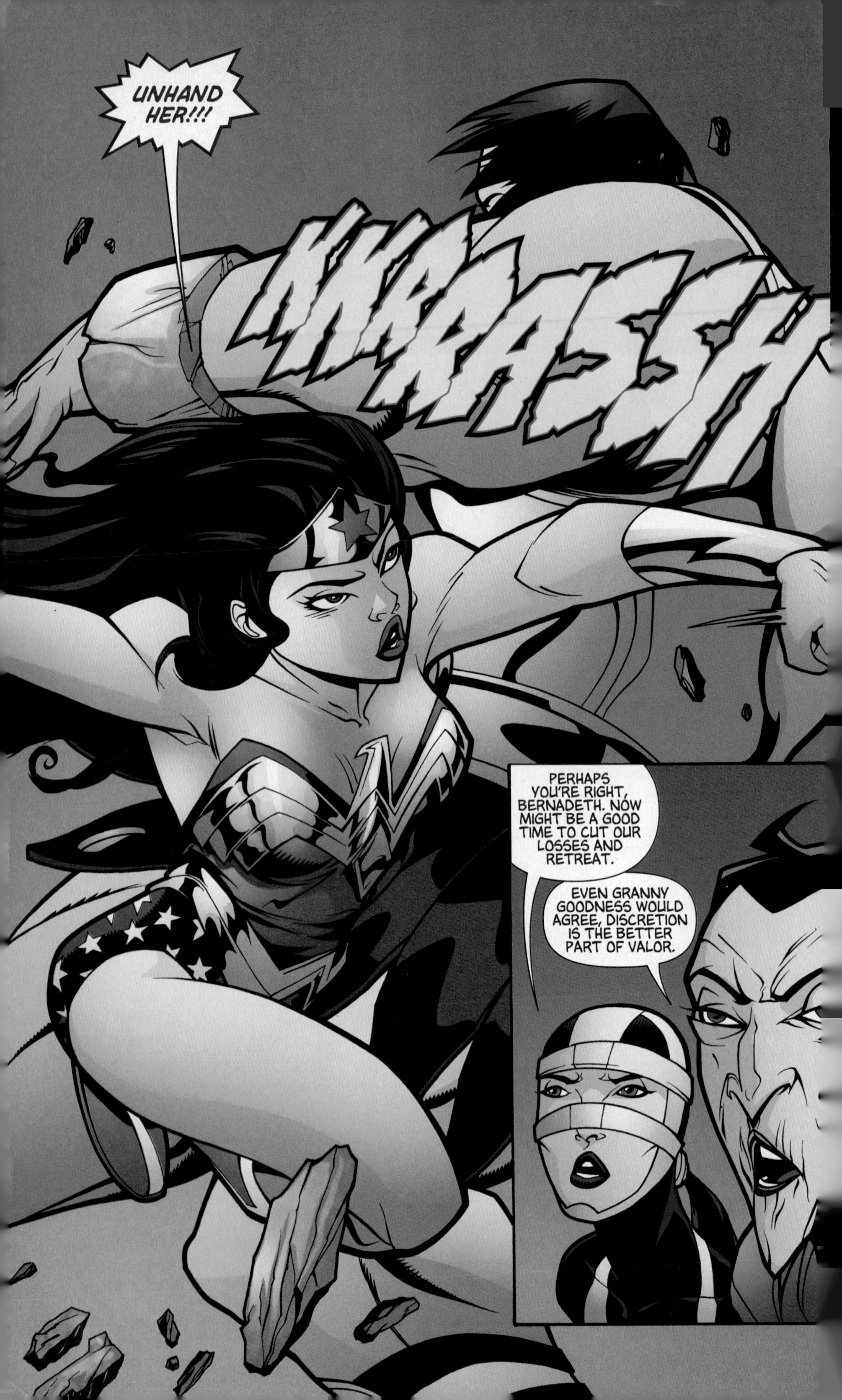

UNHAND HER!!!
KKRASH
PERHAPS YOU'RE RIGHT, BERNADETH. NOW MIGHT BE A GOOD TIME TO CUT OUR LOSSES AND RETREAT.
EVEN GRANNY GOODNESS WOULD AGREE, DISCRETION IS THE BETTER PART OF VALOR.

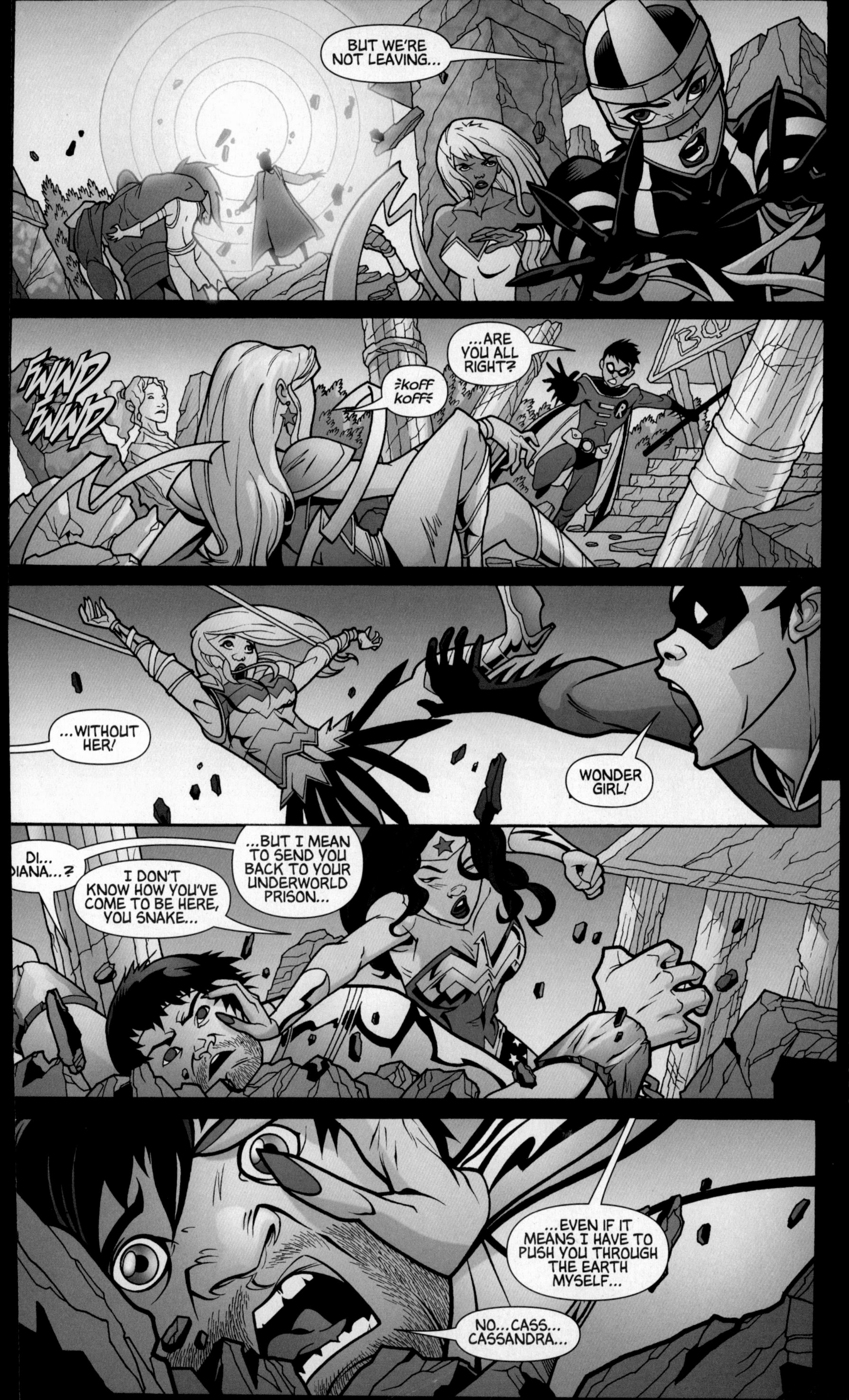
BUT WE'RE NOT LEAVING...
FWND FWND
...ARE YOU ALL RIGHT?
koff koff
...WITHOUT HER!
WONDER GIRL!
DI... DIANA...?
I DON'T KNOW HOW YOU'VE COME TO BE HERE, YOU SNAKE...
...BUT I MEAN TO SEND YOU BACK TO YOUR UNDERWORLD PRISON...
...EVEN IF IT MEANS I HAVE TO PUSH YOU THROUGH THE EARTH MYSELF...
NO...CASS... CASSANDRA...

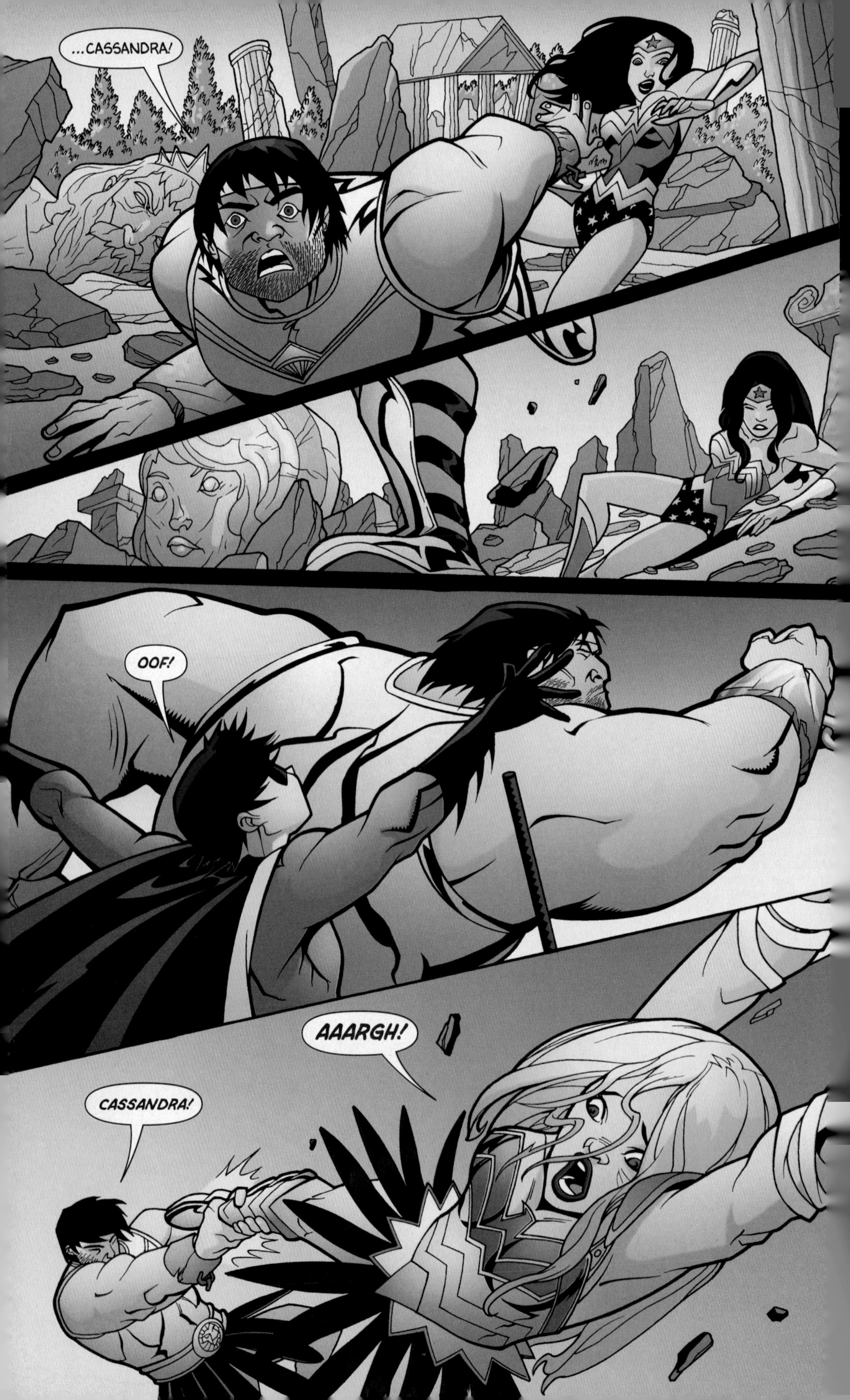
...CASSANDRA!
OOF!
AAARGH!
CASSANDRA!

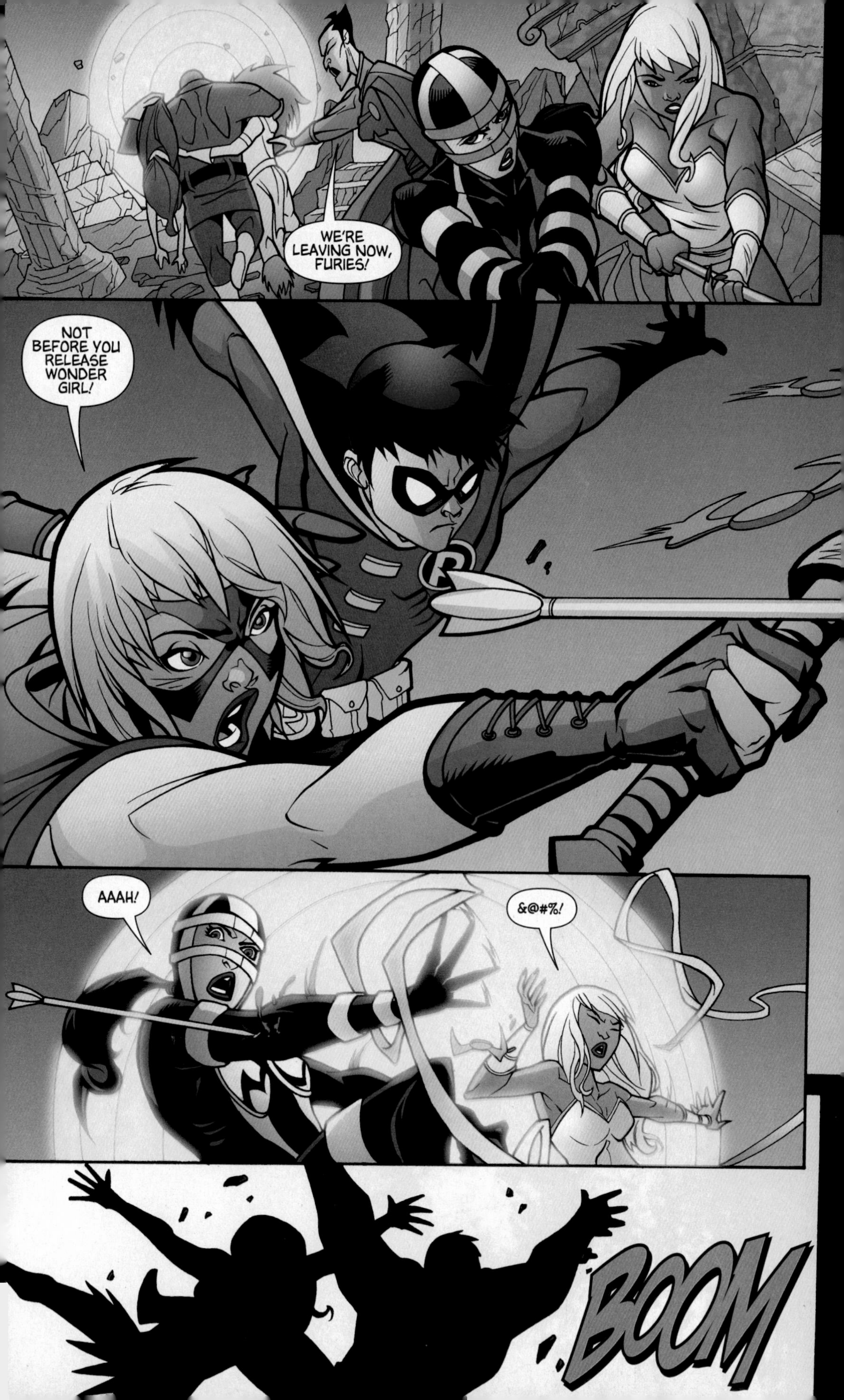
WE'RE LEAVING NOW, FURIES!
NOT BEFORE YOU RELEASE WONDER GIRL!
AAAH!
&@#%!
BOOM

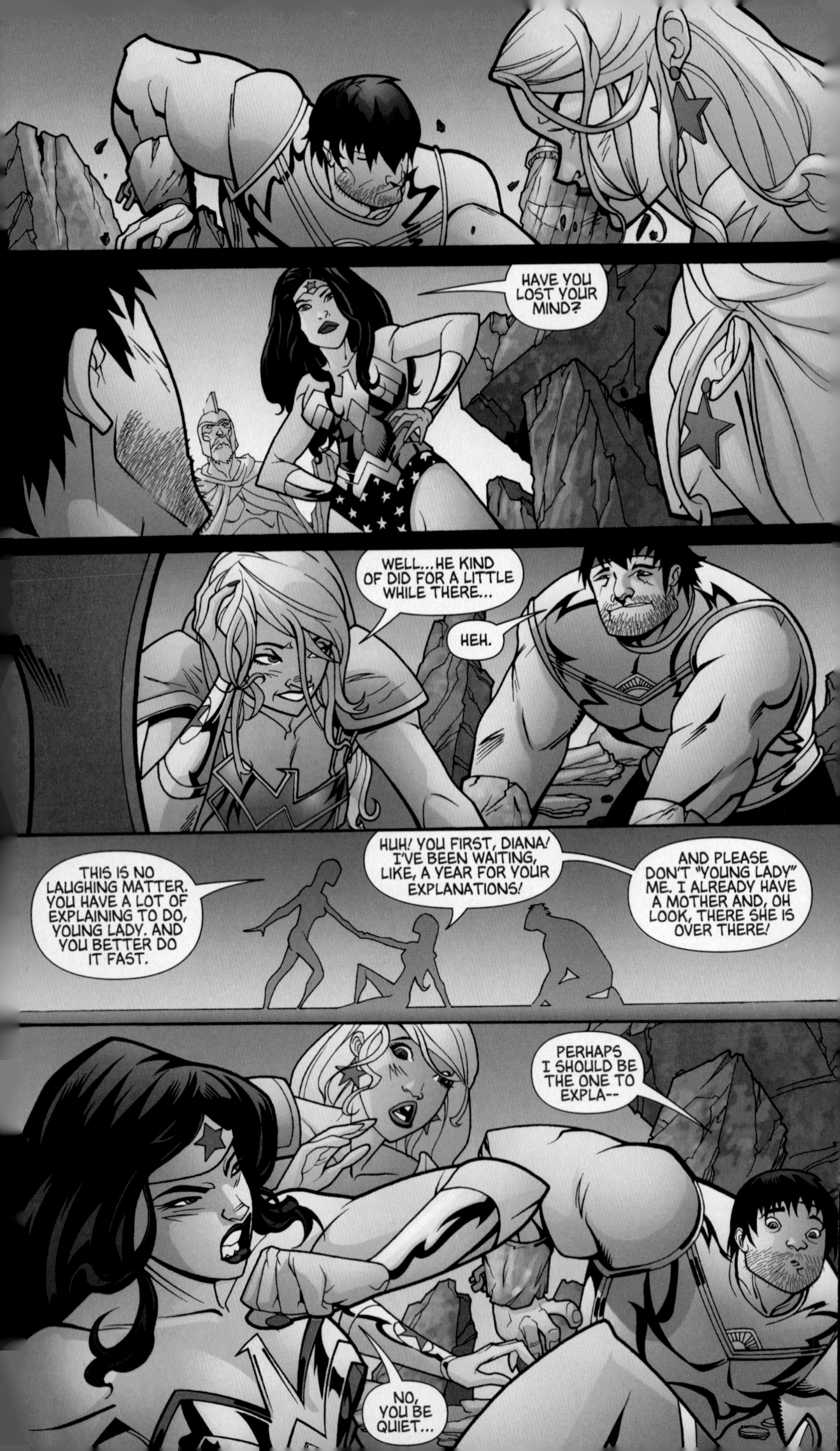
HAVE YOU LOST YOUR MIND?
WELL...HE KIND OF DID FOR A LITTLE WHILE THERE...
HEH.
THIS IS NO LAUGHING MATTER. YOU HAVE A LOT OF EXPLAINING TO DO, YOUNG LADY. AND YOU BETTER DO IT FAST.
HUH! YOU FIRST, DIANA! I'VE BEEN WAITING, LIKE, A YEAR FOR YOUR EXPLANATIONS!
AND PLEASE DON'T "YOUNG LADY" ME. I ALREADY HAVE A MOTHER AND, OH LOOK, THERE SHE IS OVER THERE!
PERHAPS I SHOULD BE THE ONE TO EXPLA--
NO, YOU BE QUIET...

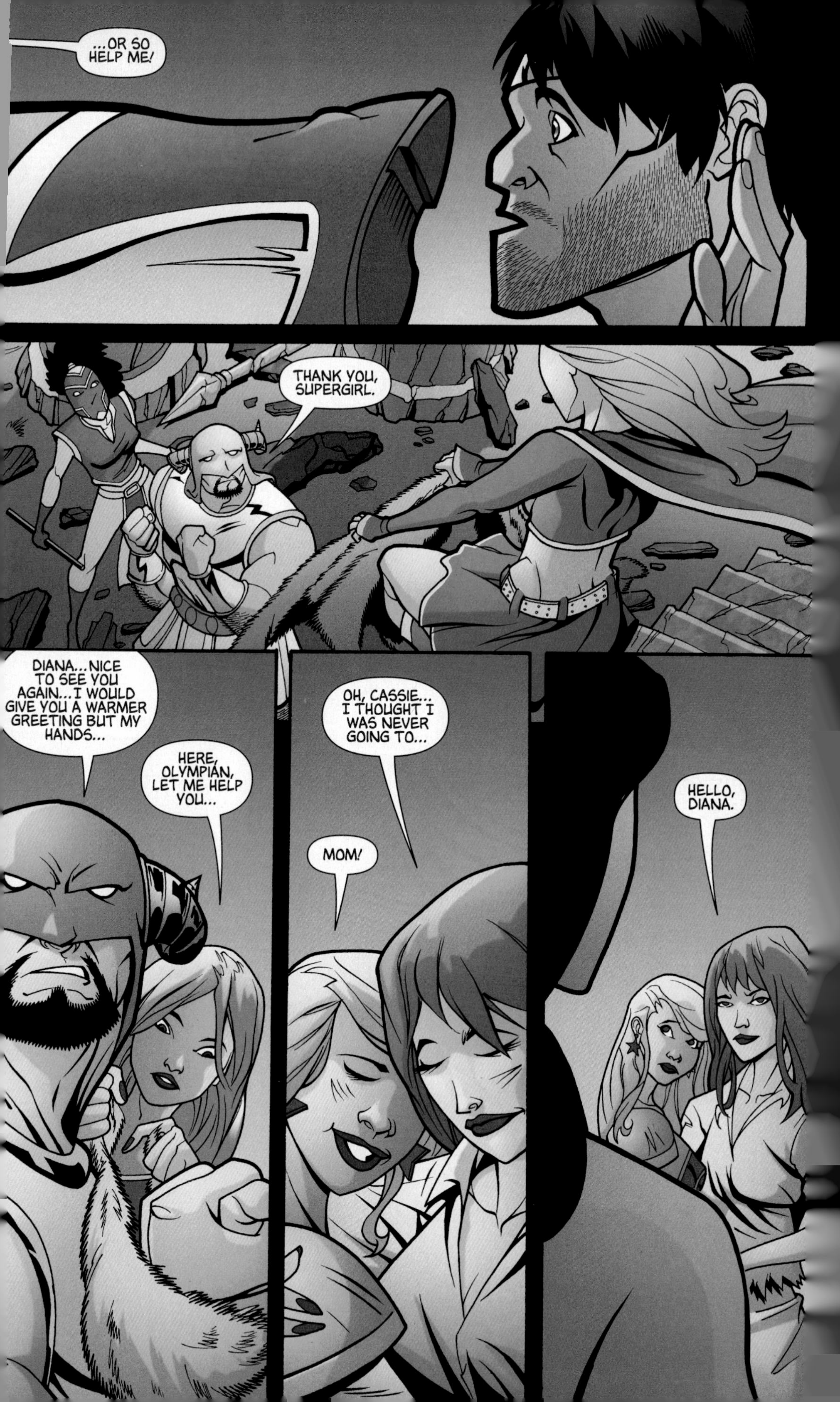
...OR SO HELP ME!
THANK YOU, SUPERGIRL.
DIANA...NICE TO SEE YOU AGAIN...I WOULD GIVE YOU A WARMER GREETING BUT MY HANDS...
HERE, OLYMPIAN, LET ME HELP YOU...
OH, CASSIE... I THOUGHT I WAS NEVER GOING TO...
MOM!
HELLO, DIANA.

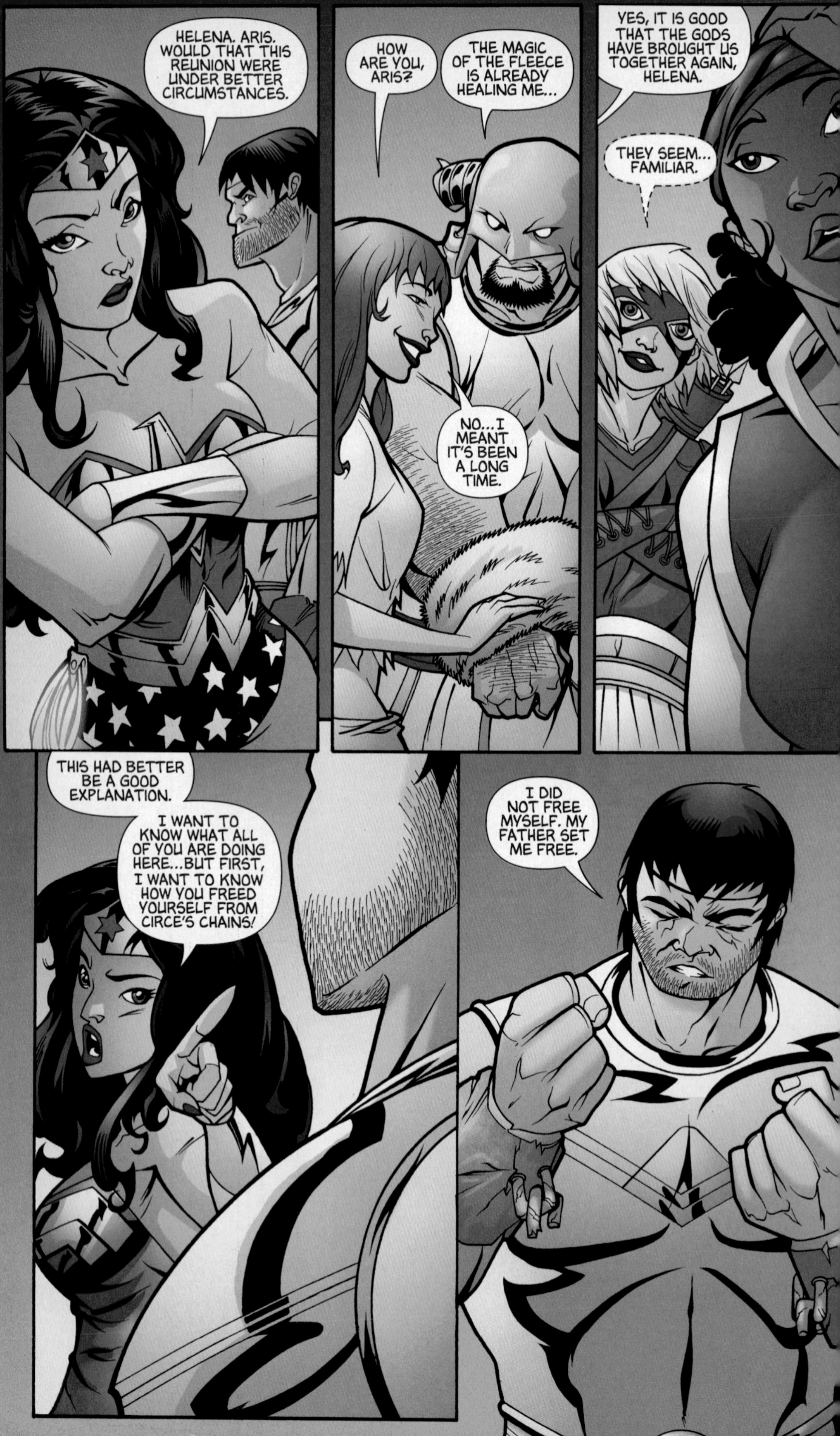
HELENA. ARIS. WOULD THAT THIS REUNION WERE UNDER BETTER CIRCUMSTANCES.
HOW ARE YOU, ARIS?
THE MAGIC OF THE FLEECE IS ALREADY HEALING ME...
NO...I MEANT IT'S BEEN A LONG TIME.
YES, IT IS GOOD THAT THE GODS HAVE BROUGHT US TOGETHER AGAIN, HELENA.
THEY SEEM... FAMILIAR.
THIS HAD BETTER BE A GOOD EXPLANATION.
I WANT TO KNOW WHAT ALL OF YOU ARE DOING HERE...BUT FIRST, I WANT TO KNOW HOW YOU FREED YOURSELF FROM CIRCE'S CHAINS!
I DID NOT FREE MYSELF. MY FATHER SET ME FREE.

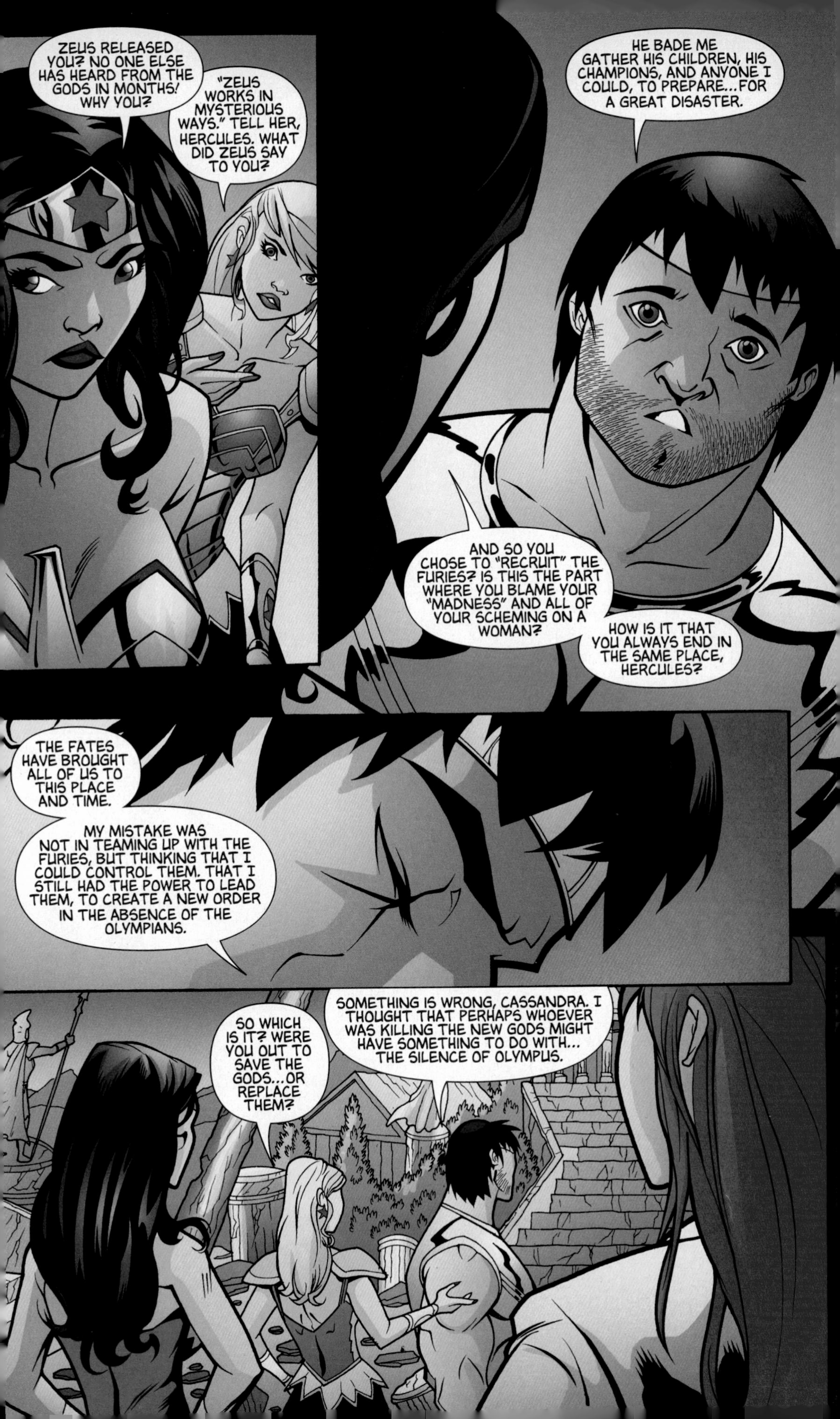
ZEUS RELEASED YOU? NO ONE ELSE HAS HEARD FROM THE GODS IN MONTHS! WHY YOU?
"ZEUS WORKS IN MYSTERIOUS WAYS." TELL HER, HERCULES. WHAT DID ZEUS SAY TO YOU?
HE BADE ME GATHER HIS CHILDREN, HIS CHAMPIONS, AND ANYONE I COULD, TO PREPARE...FOR A GREAT DISASTER.
AND SO YOU CHOSE TO "RECRUIT" THE FURIES? IS THIS THE PART WHERE YOU BLAME YOUR "MADNESS" AND ALL OF YOUR SCHEMING ON A WOMAN?
HOW IS IT THAT YOU ALWAYS END IN THE SAME PLACE, HERCULES?
THE FATES HAVE BROUGHT ALL OF US TO THIS PLACE AND TIME.
MY MISTAKE WAS NOT IN TEAMING UP WITH THE FURIES, BUT THINKING THAT I COULD CONTROL THEM. THAT I STILL HAD THE POWER TO LEAD THEM, TO CREATE A NEW ORDER IN THE ABSENCE OF THE OLYMPIANS.
SO WHICH IS IT? WERE YOU OUT TO SAVE THE GODS...OR REPLACE THEM?
SOMETHING IS WRONG, CASSANDRA. I THOUGHT THAT PERHAPS WHOEVER WAS KILLING THE NEW GODS MIGHT HAVE SOMETHING TO DO WITH... THE SILENCE OF OLYMPUS.

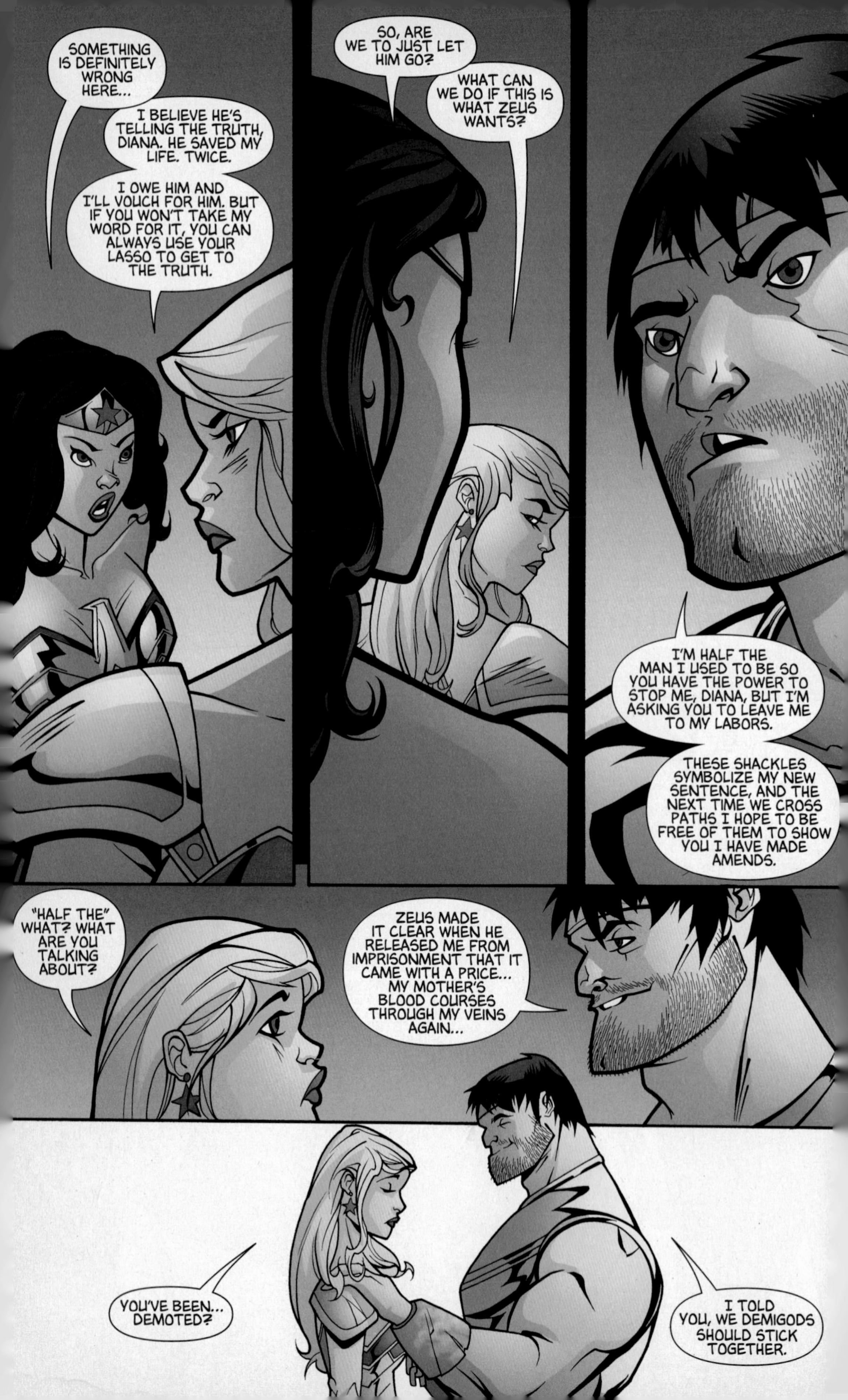

SOMETHING IS DEFINITELY WRONG HERE...
I BELIEVE HE'S TELLING THE TRUTH, DIANA. HE SAVED MY LIFE. TWICE.
I OWE HIM AND I'LL VOUCH FOR HIM. BUT IF YOU WON'T TAKE MY WORD FOR IT, YOU CAN ALWAYS USE YOUR LASSO TO GET TO THE TRUTH.
SO, ARE WE TO JUST LET HIM GO?
WHAT CAN WE DO IF THIS IS WHAT ZEUS WANTS?
I'M HALF THE MAN I USED TO BE SO YOU HAVE THE POWER TO STOP ME, DIANA, BUT I'M ASKING YOU TO LEAVE ME TO MY LABORS.
THESE SHACKLES SYMBOLIZE MY NEW SENTENCE, AND THE NEXT TIME WE CROSS PATHS I HOPE TO BE FREE OF THEM TO SHOW YOU I HAVE MADE AMENDS.
"HALF THE" WHAT? WHAT ARE YOU TALKING ABOUT?
ZEUS MADE IT CLEAR WHEN HE RELEASED ME FROM IMPRISONMENT THAT IT CAME WITH A PRICE... MY MOTHER'S BLOOD COURSES THROUGH MY VEINS AGAIN...
YOU'VE BEEN... DEMOTED?
I TOLD YOU, WE DEMIGODS SHOULD STICK TOGETHER.

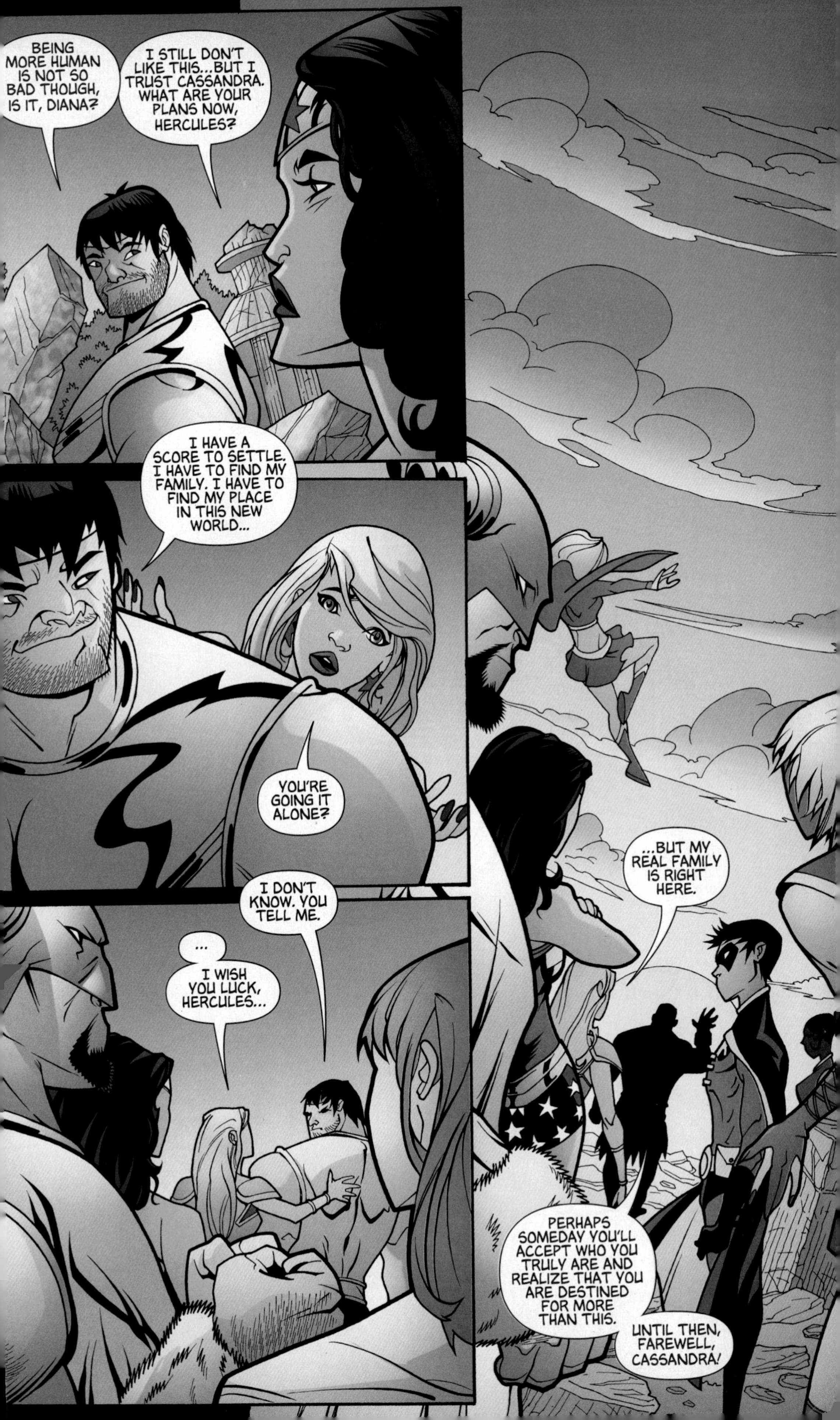
BEING MORE HUMAN IS NOT SO BAD THOUGH, IS IT, DIANA?
I STILL DON'T LIKE THIS... BUT I TRUST CASSANDRA. WHAT ARE YOUR PLANS NOW, HERCULES?
I HAVE A SCORE TO SETTLE. I HAVE TO FIND MY FAMILY. I HAVE TO FIND MY PLACE IN THIS NEW WORLD...
YOU'RE GOING IT ALONE?
I DON'T KNOW. YOU TELL ME.
...
I WISH YOU LUCK, HERCULES...
...BUT MY REAL FAMILY IS RIGHT HERE.
PERHAPS SOMEDAY YOU'LL ACCEPT WHO YOU TRULY ARE AND REALIZE THAT YOU ARE DESTINED FOR MORE THAN THIS.
UNTIL THEN, FAREWELL, CASSANDRA!

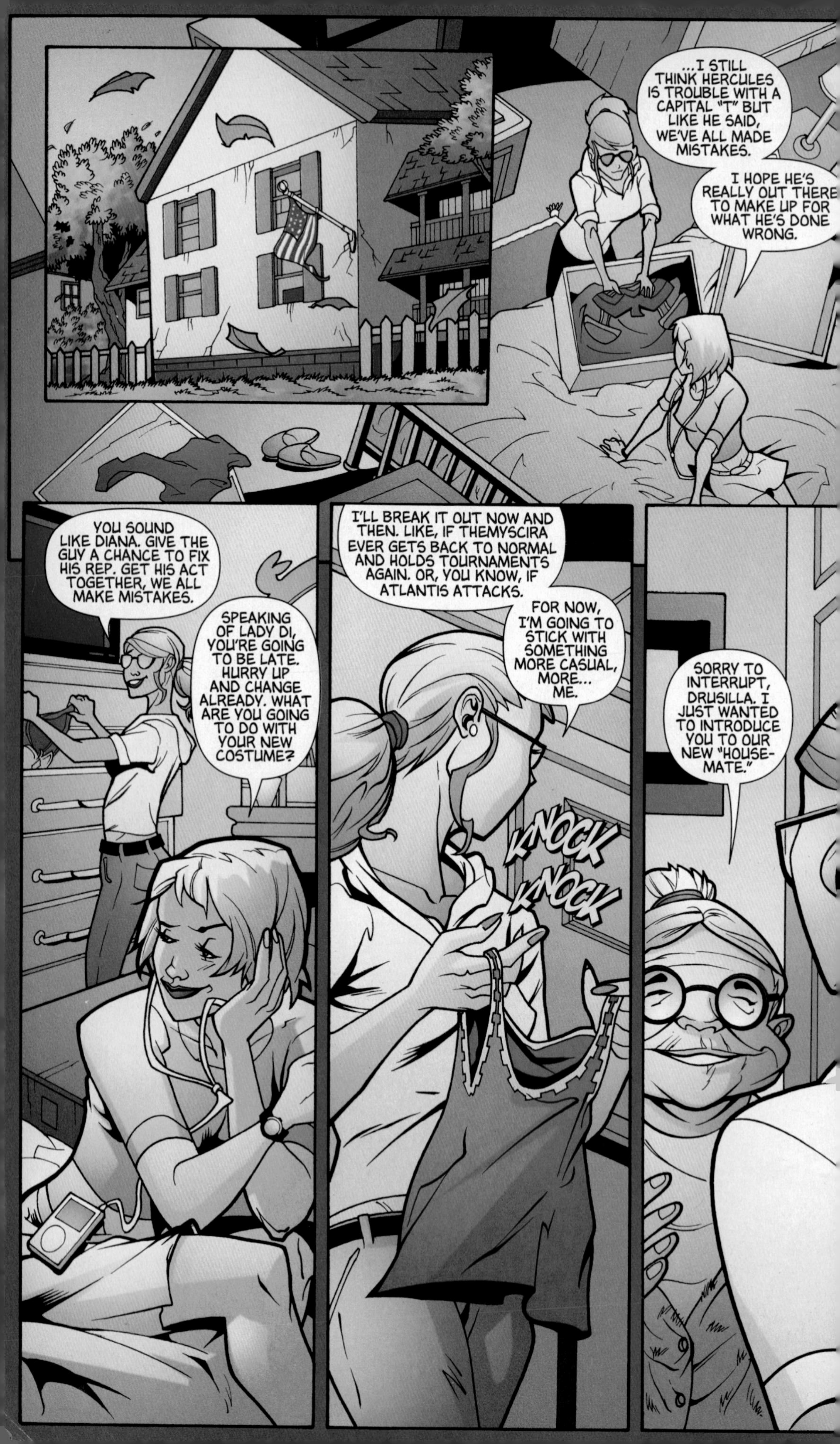
...I STILL THINK HERCULES IS TROUBLE WITH A CAPITAL "T" BUT LIKE HE SAID, WE'VE ALL MADE MISTAKES.
I HOPE HE'S REALLY OUT THERE TO MAKE UP FOR WHAT HE'S DONE WRONG.
YOU SOUND LIKE DIANA. GIVE THE GUY A CHANCE TO FIX HIS REP. GET HIS ACT TOGETHER, WE ALL MAKE MISTAKES.
SPEAKING OF LADY DI, YOU'RE GOING TO BE LATE. HURRY UP AND CHANGE ALREADY. WHAT ARE YOU GOING TO DO WITH YOUR NEW COSTUME?
I'LL BREAK IT OUT NOW AND THEN. LIKE, IF THEMYSCIRA EVER GETS BACK TO NORMAL AND HOLDS TOURNAMENTS AGAIN. OR, YOU KNOW, IF ATLANTIS ATTACKS.
FOR NOW, I'M GOING TO STICK WITH SOMETHING MORE CASUAL, MORE... ME.
KNOCK
KNOCK
SORRY TO INTERRUPT, DRUSILLA. I JUST WANTED TO INTRODUCE YOU TO OUR NEW "HOUSE-MATE."

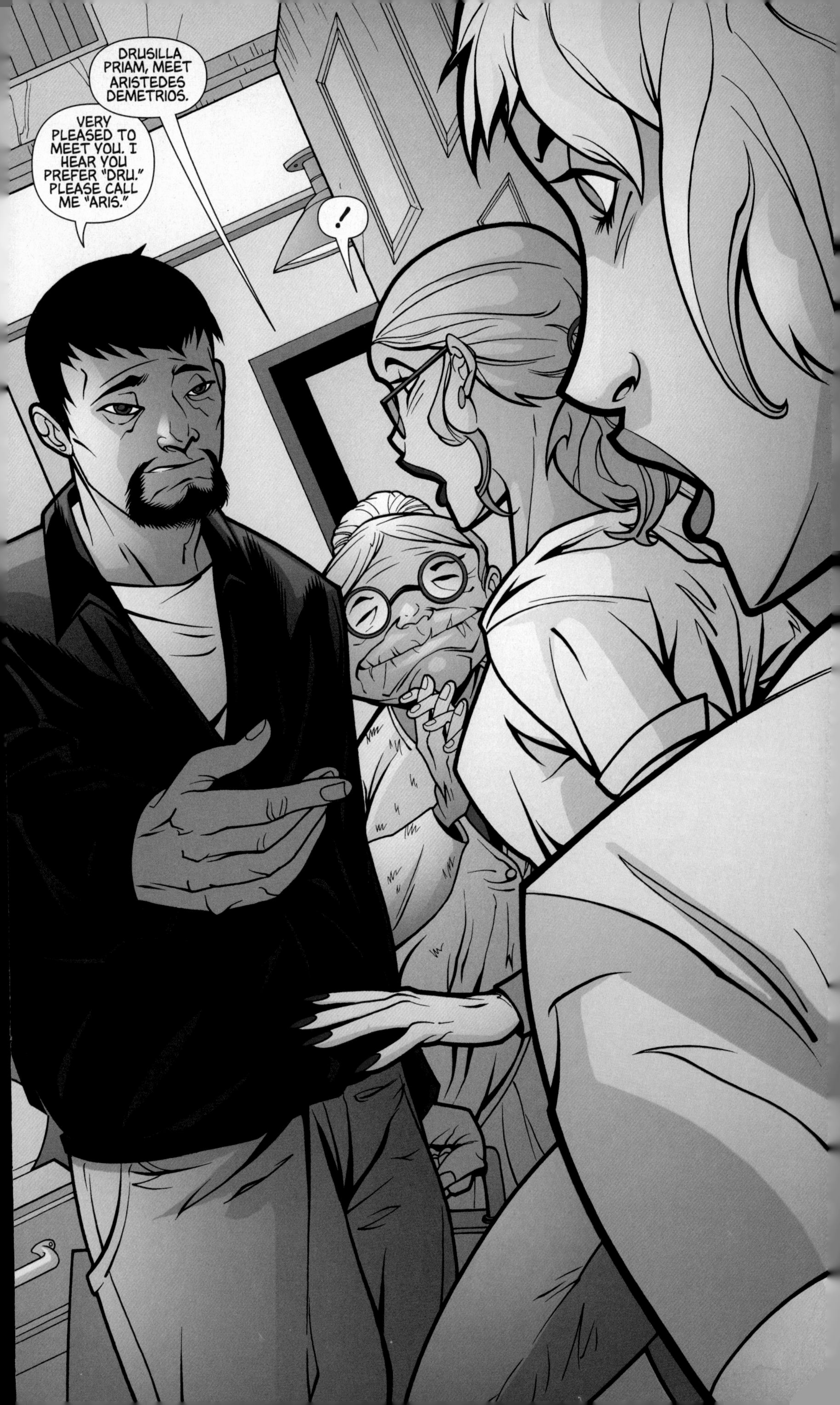
DRUSILLA PRIAM, MEET ARISTEDES DEMETRIOS.
VERY PLEASED TO MEET YOU. I HEAR YOU PREFER "DRU." PLEASE CALL ME "ARIS."
!

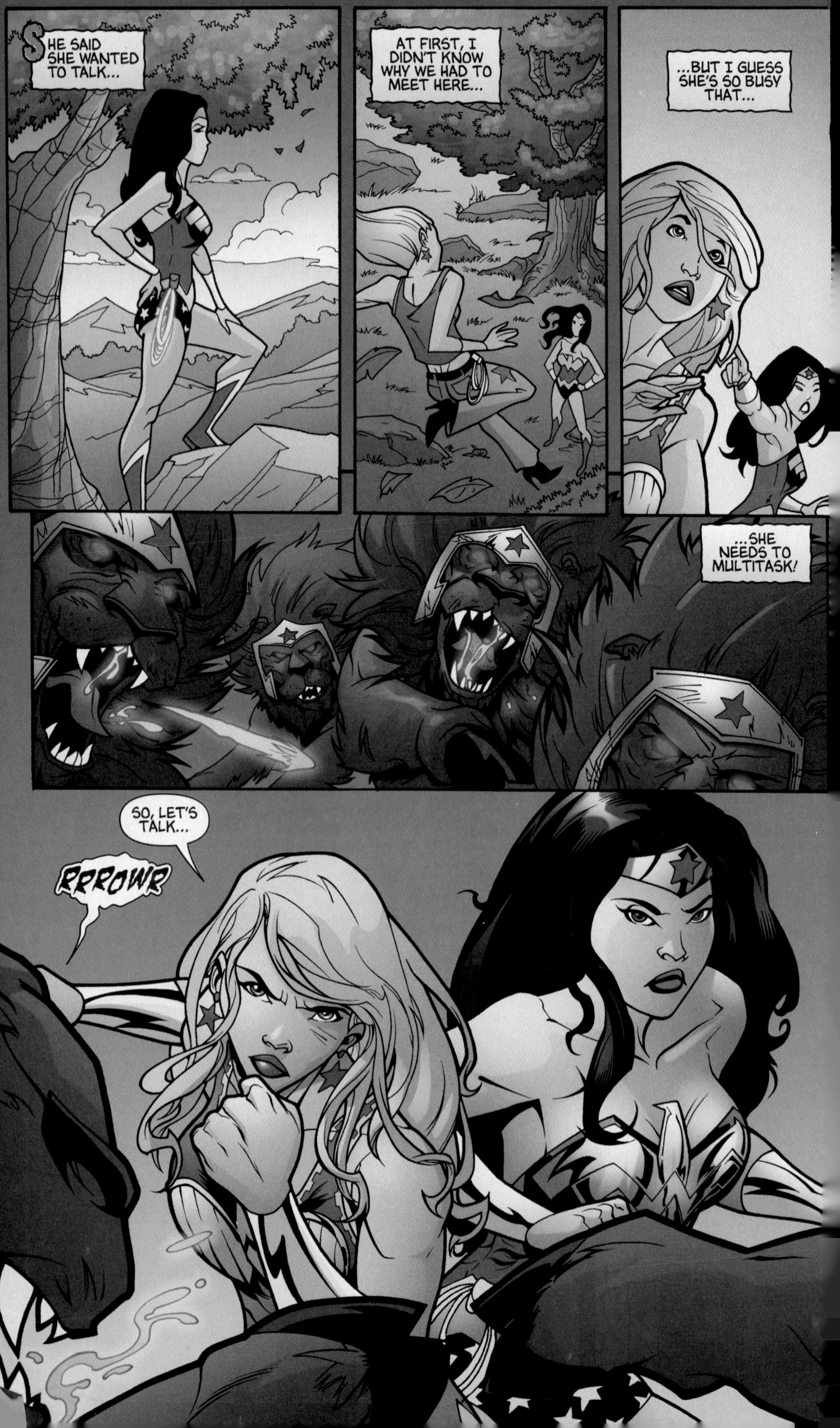
SHE SAID SHE WANTED TO TALK...
AT FIRST, I DIDN'T KNOW WHY WE HAD TO MEET HERE...
...BUT I GUESS SHE'S SO BUSY THAT...
...SHE NEEDS TO MULTITASK!
SO, LET'S TALK...
RRROWR

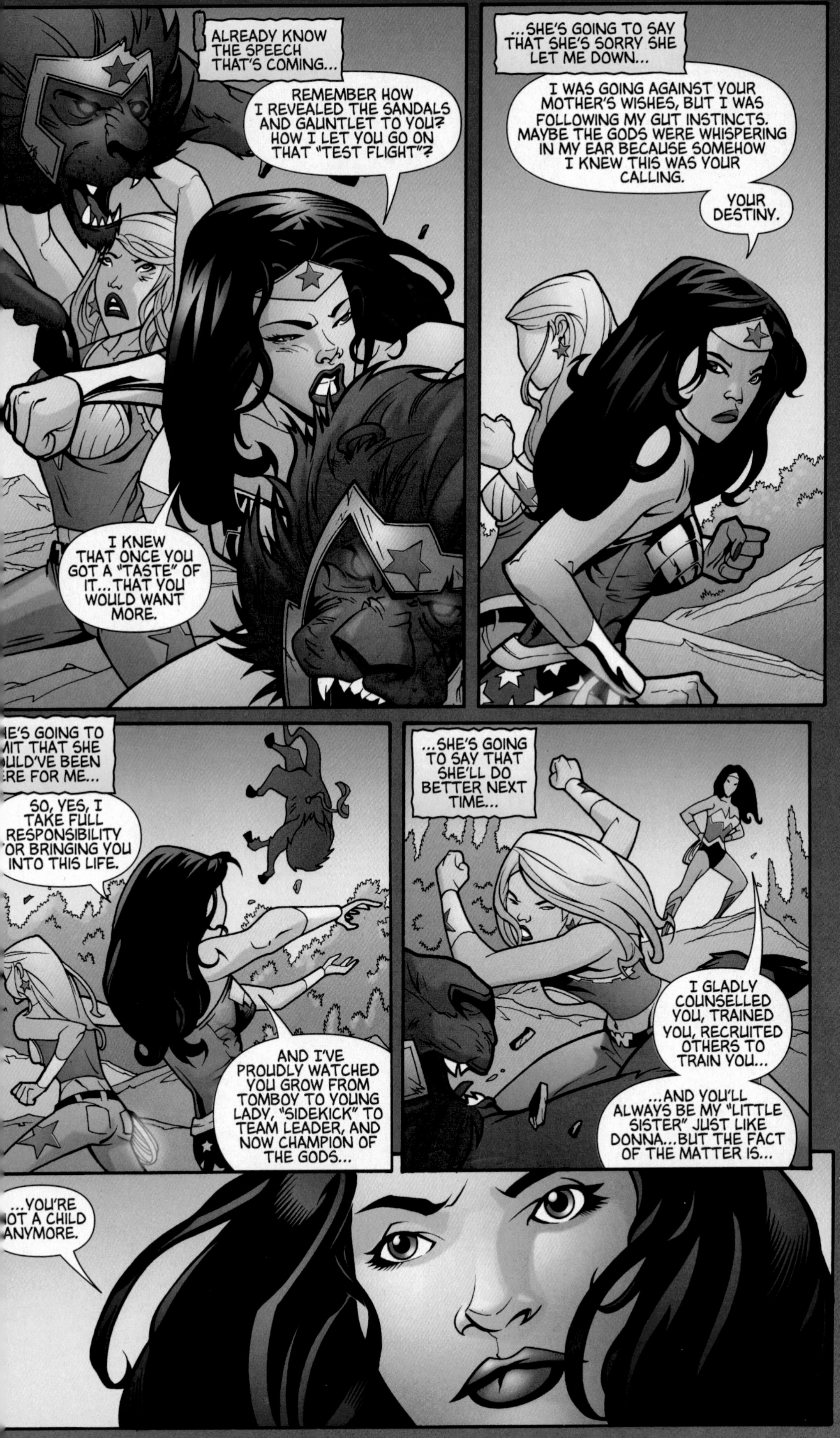
ALREADY KNOW THE SPEECH THAT'S COMING...
REMEMBER HOW I REVEALED THE SANDALS AND GAUNTLET TO YOU? HOW I LET YOU GO ON THAT "TEST FLIGHT"?
I KNEW THAT ONCE YOU GOT A "TASTE" OF IT... THAT YOU WOULD WANT MORE.
...SHE'S GOING TO SAY THAT SHE'S SORRY SHE LET ME DOWN...
I WAS GOING AGAINST YOUR MOTHER'S WISHES, BUT I WAS FOLLOWING MY GUT INSTINCTS. MAYBE THE GODS WERE WHISPERING IN MY EAR BECAUSE SOMEHOW I KNEW THIS WAS YOUR CALLING.
YOUR DESTINY.
HE'S GOING TO MIT THAT SHE ULD'VE BEEN ERE FOR ME...
SO, YES, I TAKE FULL RESPONSIBILITY OR BRINGING YOU INTO THIS LIFE.
AND I'VE PROUDLY WATCHED YOU GROW FROM TOMBOY TO YOUNG LADY, "SIDEKICK" TO TEAM LEADER, AND NOW CHAMPION OF THE GODS...
...SHE'S GOING TO SAY THAT SHE'LL DO BETTER NEXT TIME...
I GLADLY COUNSELLED YOU, TRAINED YOU, RECRUITED OTHERS TO TRAIN YOU...
...AND YOU'LL ALWAYS BE MY "LITTLE SISTER" JUST LIKE DONNA... BUT THE FACT OF THE MATTER IS...
...YOU'RE OT A CHILD ANYMORE.

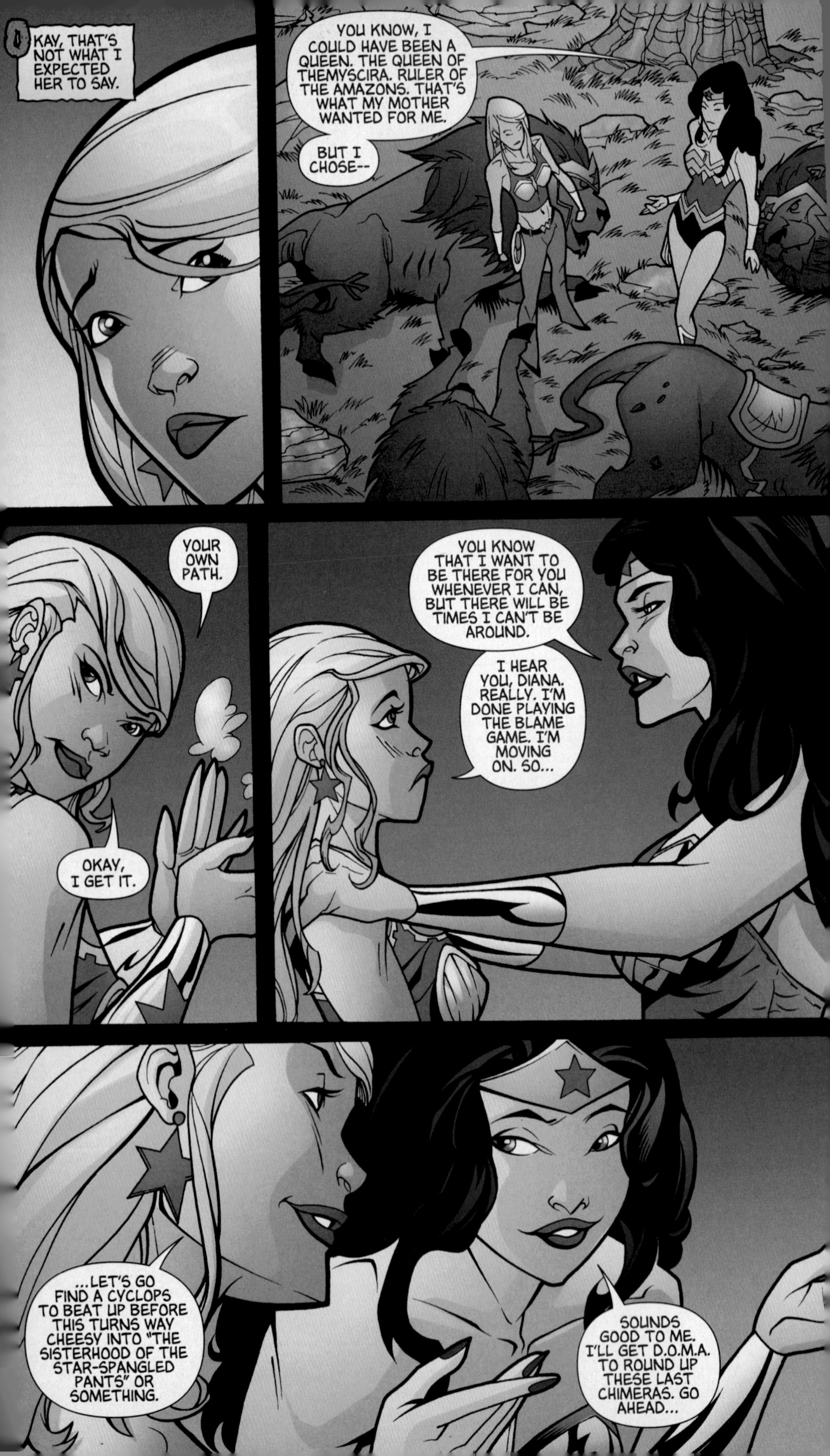
OKAY, THAT'S NOT WHAT I EXPECTED HER TO SAY.
YOU KNOW, I COULD HAVE BEEN A QUEEN. THE QUEEN OF THEMYSCIRA. RULER OF THE AMAZONS. THAT'S WHAT MY MOTHER WANTED FOR ME.
BUT I CHOSE--
YOUR OWN PATH.
OKAY, I GET IT.
YOU KNOW THAT I WANT TO BE THERE FOR YOU WHENEVER I CAN, BUT THERE WILL BE TIMES I CAN'T BE AROUND.
I HEAR YOU, DIANA. REALLY. I'M DONE PLAYING THE BLAME GAME. I'M MOVING ON. SO...
...LET'S GO FIND A CYCLOPS TO BEAT UP BEFORE THIS TURNS WAY CHEESY INTO "THE SISTERHOOD OF THE STAR-SPANGLED PANTS" OR SOMETHING.
SOUNDS GOOD TO ME. I'LL GET D.O.M.A. TO ROUND UP THESE LAST CHIMERAS. GO AHEAD...

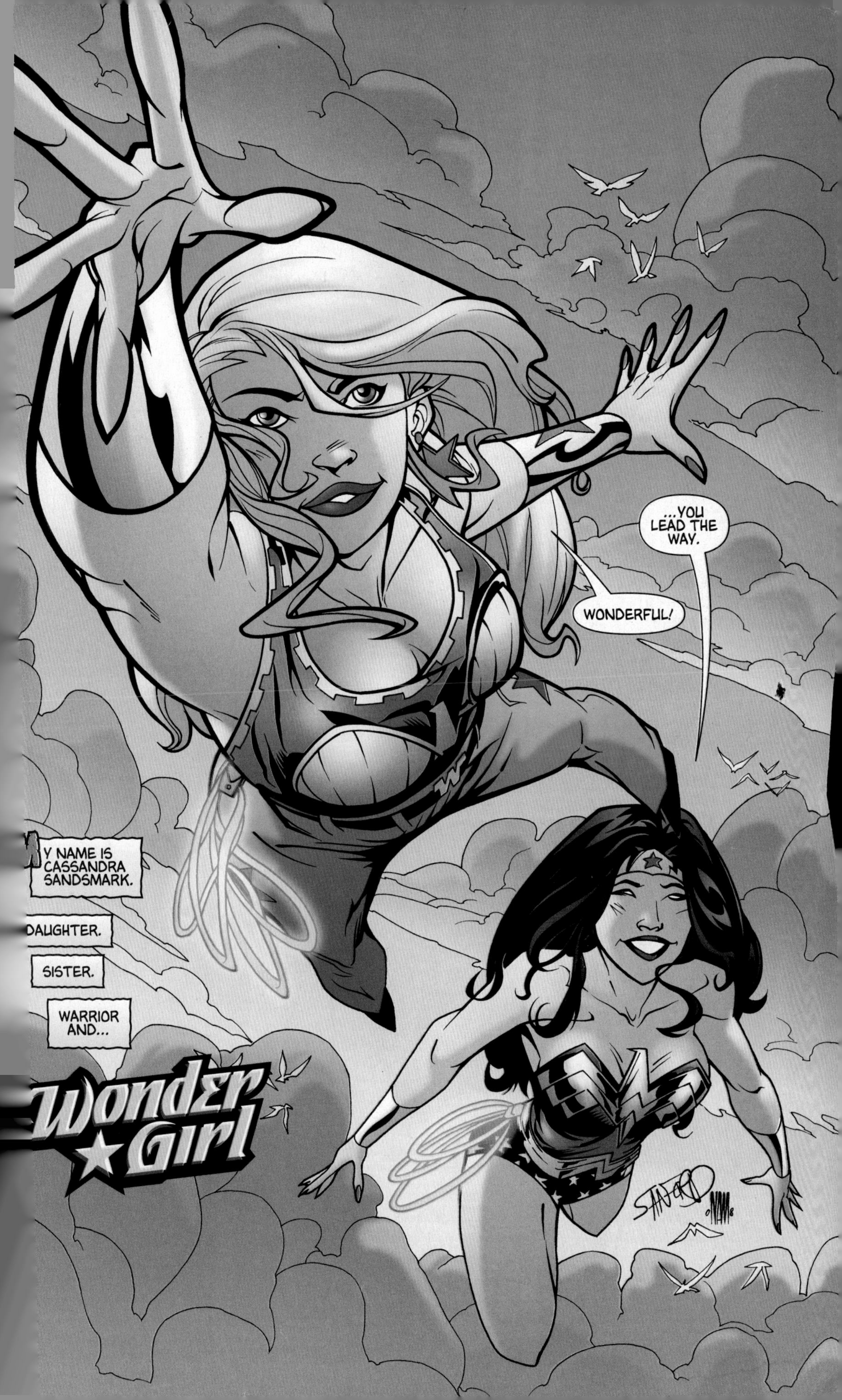
Y NAME IS CASSANDRA SANDSMARK.
DAUGHTER.
SISTER.
WARRIOR AND...
Wonder Girl
WONDERFUL!
...YOU LEAD THE WAY.

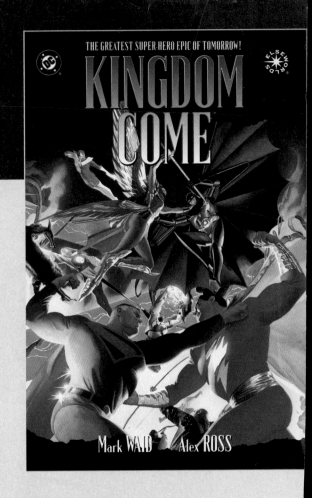
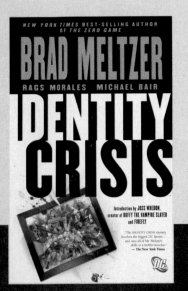